PARACHUTING F[...]
The Evolution of Freefall

by

Michael Horan

> *Darius was clearly of the opinion*
> *That the air is also man's dominion*
> *And that with paddle or fin or pinion*
> *We soon or late shall navigate*
> *The azure as now we sail the sea.*
>
> *J.T. Trowbridge*

PARACHUTING FOLKLORE

The Evolution of Freefall

By
MICHAEL HORAN

Editor
LINDA H. DRUSKIS

Published by

PARACHUTING PR RESOURCES

P.O. Box 1333
Richmond, IN. 47374, U.S.A.

All rights reserved. No part of this book may be reproduced or transmitted in any form or by any means, electronic or mechanical, including photocopying, recording or by any information storage and retrieval system without written permission from the author, except for the inclusion of brief quotations in a review.

Also By The Author

INDEX TO PARACHUTING, *1900-1975*
An Annotated Bibliography

Copyright © 1980 by Michael Horan

First Edition

Printed in the United States of America

Library of Congress Cataloging in Publication Data
Horan, Michael, 1943 -
    The Evolution of Freefall

    (Parachuting Folklore)
    Bibliography: p. Includes index
    1, Parachuting — History
    2, Parachuting — History
    GV770.H67 797.5'6 80-12378
    ISBN 0-933382-01-4 Softcover
    ISBN 0-933382-02-2 Hardcover

ABOUT THE AUTHOR

MICHAEL HORAN

MICHAEL HORAN began jumping out of airplanes in 1963 while a member of the U.S Marine Corps. Since then he has held positions in the parachute industry testing and developing a variety of systems. He is a contributing author to most of the major sport parachuting publications in the United States and is a member of the Aviation/Space Writers Association, the National Aeronautic Association, and the American Society for Aerospace Education. He is also a member of the United States Parachute Association (USPA) and holds a Class "D" license, Jumpmaster and Instructor Ratings, Diamond Wings, and Gold Freefall Badge. In addition, he is USPA's Archivist, a member of the USPA Board of Directors, and the USPA Mideastern Conference Director. He publishes *Freefall*, a conference newsletter, and has published *Index To Parachuting, 1900-1975*, an annotated bibliography, which has become a standard reference in the field of parachuting. Mike is a FAA Master Parachute Rigger with over 2500 parachute jumps and resides in Campbellstown, Ohio.

ACKNOWLEDGMENTS

A work of this scope would not be possible without the cooperation and help of many people. My gratitude and thanks go out to Jean Crane, Joyce Crane, Linda Druskis, Jack Fitzwater, David Gold, Doug Hartley, Bob Kiehfuss, Al King, Peter Krieg, Martha and Peggy Kutche, Sandy Lodge, The Montgomery County Historical Society of Dayton, Ohio, The Morrisson-Reeves Library of Richmond, In., Dan Poynter, Paul Proctor, Claude Shafer, U.S. Parachute Association, Patt Valley, Jim West, Shelby Wickham, A.F. "Woody" Woodall, The Graphic Press, especially Nancy Minor, Ruth Williams, Sharon Via, Valerie Hughes, Chuck Redman, and Bob Carver. A very special thanks and debt of gratitude go out to David Gardner, Chris Kappes, Linda Cummins and Rich Snelson of the Ball State University School of Journalism.

PHOTO CREDITS

JACK FITWATER — Cover Photo
Ken Alderman, Jeff Atteberry, Boeing Company, Bromo-Seltzer Co., Clarence and Lois Cornish, Laima Druskis, Linda Druskis, Don Dwiggins, Flying Magazine, Martin Folb, Jim Ginter, Arthur W. Hendricks, Peter Krieg, Life Magazine, Chip Maury, Parachutist Magazine, Skydiver Magazine, U.S. Army, and U.S. Parachute Association.

PARACHUTING FOLKLORE

Introduction

Making a parachute jump, whether from a balloon or an airplane, has always been an exciting adventure. This is as true now as when parachutes first came into usage in 1797. A jump by parachute explodes a full array of senses across our consciousness. The anticipation can cause a stirring in the stomach and bowels, which in turn heightens our psychological instincts for survival. The ride to jump altitude reverbrates with droning engines and wind whistling past our ears. Pungent smells of burning gasoline and oil, and the cold, fresh air, constantly reminds us of our ultimate journey. Bursting away from the aircraft into freefall, released from the rigid confines that held us safely, is a voyage of spectacular proportions.

Freefall parachuting is a totally unique experience. Nothing else in mankind's sporting repertoire of thrills comes close to matching this exhilerating experience. Falling at an average speed of 120 mph, and even to speeds in excess of 200 mph, freefall is the ultimate form of human flight. Each person is the master of their fate in freefall. No one can help by holding your hand or giving words of encouragement. It is a solitary endeavor; one person against the elements.

Each parachutist implicitly trusts his life to his own judgement and a few hundred square feet of nylon, to brake his freefall flight. The senses are constantly being bombarded with kinetic stimulation from the clouds, wind, horizon, ground, and other jumpers in freefall. The wide open, spacious sky is imposing and dwarfts each jumper; but gravity compels each person to travel unemcumbered on their way earthward. The "moment of truth" comes for a parachutist just before the parachute inflates. Waiting for a chute to open after the ripcord is pulled, is akin to wading into a cool lake; the water is never as bad as the anticipation. Sitting under an open canopy, the jumper is treated to an aerial panorama of the countryside. On a clear day it's possible to see ten miles and further. Landings can be tense, particularly for beginners. Normally the ride down results in a soft, oftentimes, tiptoe landing. It is a quiet and peaceful ending to a dramatic flight.

Parachuting is not for everybody; it just isn't that kind of activity. Nevertheless, estimates run that as high as 20 million people in the United States have made a parachute jump at one time or another. Other untold millions vicariously enjoy sport parachuting as a spectator. This pastime has gained wide acceptance in recent years. Many wish they could be a parachutist, but few accept the challenge. Perhaps because of this psychological barrier, most people tend to view jumpers as a colorful, but eccentric personality. This makes a parachutist a likely prospect as a folkhero. Contemporary psychology has taught us that sport parachutists are not consumed with a suicidal death wish. No one appreciates life anymore than those who leap from airplanes. If anything, their appreciation of living drives them to seek out the most stimulating aspects of their environment. The new term used to describe a parachute jumper is "stimulus addict," and it more realistically reflects the positive state of mind of this culture.

Discovering the folklore of this exciting aviation activity is much like putting the pieces of a gigantic puzzle together. Parachutist have never been the most prolific of people. They would rather jump and leave the writing to others. Of the 150 or so books written about parachuting, only a small number are written by jumpers. Consequently the task of discovering, analyzing, and piecing together the people and events that shaped the evolution of parachuting has been left to those who were least qualified to do it.

One of the problems associated with writing about this folklore is the disconnectedness of parachuting. Sections of the United States, and for that matter the world, evolved at different speeds and in different ways. Before the advent of television and the mass media, many places were islands unto themselves. This is particularly true of Russia and other foreign countries where the word travels slowly. Until the flow of information started circulating more freely, not many groups knew how the other groups were advancing. Therefore the difficulty in gaining access to the "pieces of the puzzle" was made very difficult. Attempts to learn the folklore of parachuting, down to the customs, traditions, and beliefs, has always been an "ex post facto" endeavor.

It would be logical to assume that the best sources for this sort of information would be derived from people who participated during a certain time period. Oftentimes, but not always, these sources are less than completely reliable. With parachute jumpers in particular, time has a way of distorting reality. Parachuting, like fishing, lends itself to exaggeration. Oftentimes the description of a jump becomes a little more dangerous and exciting each time the story is told. The perfume of heroic deeds can make for a "heady" recalling of experiences. In the course of time, jumpers go higher, pull lower, escape from the jaws of death later, and only barely survive by the slimmest of margins.

It is this sort of jump story telling, affectionately referred to as the "chortling propeller syndrome," that originated and continues to perpetuate a number of folkmyths about parachuting. For example, one folkmyth tells us that breathing in freefall is impossible. This one has been around for a long time. In the early going, before freefall jumps came into vogue, most considered that a person would be wretched into unconsciousness, unable to move or think, while making even the shortest of freefalls. Despite countless experiences to the contrary, this myth still persists to some degree today. The chapters about Dayton and batwing jumping recount some attempts to debunk this unfounded assumption.

Another folkmyth tells us that women are too weak, fraile, and not mentally together enough to make parachute jumps. "Stay on the ground where it's safer," is the usual advice women receive about parachuting. This absurd myth had it's beginnings with the male dominated military. Though male paratroopers do receive some of the most gruelling training for combat parachute jumps, this fact has been generalized to all aspects of parachuting, even to popular skydiving. The chapter on Women in Parachuting tells another story. One that discovers the true abilities and contributions of women jumpers.

No other folkmyth is set so strongly in the minds of non-jumpers as the image of the parachutist as a daredevil. The reckless, thrill seeking, anything for kicks, accident looking for a place to happen stereotype is well known to most people. The barnstorming days of the roaring twenties helped perpetuate this myth more than any other single period of time. Since parachutes were used mainly as an entertainment device until the early

1920's, most people came to view them as a foolhardy device suitable for use only by crackpot stuntmen. Crowds were always attracted by the spectre of danger or death. If there was a chance to watch some crazy fool "buy the farm," people wanted to see it.

Early jumpers and promoters always capitalized on the public's insatiable appetite for gore. By always playing up the most dangerous aspects of the jump in these shows, the public eventually came to believe totally, that parachutes were unsafe and jumpers were not playing with a full deck. Though times have changed significantly for the better in terms of equipment, attitudes, and training procedures, this daredevil image still persists.

One view of parachuting which is the philosophy of this book looks at jumping as a continual process of evolution. Over the 183 years since the first official human use of a parachute, people have been relentlessly searching for new and safer methods to jump by, as well as perfecting the ones in use. This unusual, dynamic, and sensational evolutionary process has been filled with countless untold stories of courage and adventure. Parachuting is a search for the ultimate form of flight. Since the middle 1950's when Skydiving, the Sport of the Space Age, was inaugurated, this process has been exploding at a faster and faster rate.

Ultimately, the story of parachuting has to evolve around the people who jumped for fun, profit, war, and competition. Parachutists are mortal beings, contrary to what some might say. It's the individual, alone with a parachute, that produced the color to this unusual activity. This book deals with a number of colorful persons who added immensely to the folklore of parachuting. The Lone Eagle, Charles A. Lindbergh, was a parachute jumper before he ever soloed an airplane. His pre-Atlantic crossing days were filled with many close encounters with death and enough unusual experiences to last a life time. But these times are usually downplayed or ignored by aviation enthusiasts. Joe Crane, the Father of American Parachuting, devoted a lifetime to jumping out of airplanes. His experiences and leadership abilities shaped the present skydiving community to a large extent. Smoke ballooning, the original form of parachuting, is almost an extinct folk art. But these hardy men entertained and won the hearts of millions who watched them at county fairs, carnivals, and airshows.

Like the story of mankind itself, the evolution of parachuting will never be completely told. All of mankind's endeavors are born into primitive shapes and progress to highly exotic states. The stories in this volume of Parachuting Folklore are meticulously researched for detail, analyzed, and written about. This is not the total knowledge about parachuting. One book would not scratch the surface. But Parachuting Folklore does reflect the "state of the art" for parachuting knowledge in certain areas. Hopefully these efforts will inspire others to explore this field. This material is a new piece of the total mosaic about parachuting. It is expected there will be future volumes using this concept as more information about aviation's most exciting form of flight is re-discovered.

TABLE OF CONTENTS

INTRODUCTION

Chapter		Page
1	EARNING ONE'S SMOKE The original method of parachuting that is almost an extinct folk art.	9
2	THE FATHER OF AMERICAN PARACHUTING The legend who dedicated his life to parachuting.	31
3	JUMPER MAKES GOOD The exciting five years before aviation's greatest folkhero became the first to solo the Atlantic.	53
4	PROGENY OF ICARUS The daring "Batmen" who attempted to perfect the ultimate form of flight.	75
5	WOMEN IN PARACHUTING The untold contributions to parachuting by the not-so-weaker sex.	93
6	DAYTON: CRADLE OF U.S. PARACHUTING Rich in aviation folklore, this Ohio city gave birth to the modern life-saving parachute, and more.	113
7	BUSTIN' NEW SKY The men who dared challenge the hostile environment high above the earth.	135

BIBLIOGRAPHY	156
WHERE TO SKYDIVE	157
PARACHUTING RESOURCES	161
INDEX	163

PETER KRIEG - 80'
"AERONAUT"

Chapter 1
Earning One's Smoke

There is a special fascination people have with balloons. They possess a quality difficult to define, but one which many swear borders on the mystical. Balloons attract admirers whenever one is being inflated. Perhaps the attraction is the immense size. Most modern balloons can range in size from 23 to 108 thousand cubic feet, and stand up to eight stories tall. Another quality is the quiet and serene manner in which its passengers are carried aloft to an aerial rendezvous with adventure. Ascending gracefully into the heavens with flames jutting into its underbelly, these aerial ships evoke a sense of majesty with those who would seek to vicariously travel with the gods. Any noble soul who has spent time aloft can only grope for ineffective words to describe a most delicious taste of thrilling adventure.

One of mankind's fondest and most vivid dreams has been to fly. It was the advent of balloon flight which finally made him an airborne creature. For quiet, peaceful, and unencumbered flight; ballooning has no equal. Every balloon ascension is a constant reminder of a heritage that began to unfold nearly two hundred years ago. With man taking to the skies, the dark ages began to crumble and an epic adventure of the grandest scale began to evolve. The age of manned flight was beginning. Fantasy evolved into reality; man could now see past the horizon. It helped open the minds of a new generation which hastened the pace of aviation progress. Since the early 1780's, balloons and the people who flew them, historically referred to as aeronauts, have been challenging the skies to both entertain and add to the scientific advancement of knowledge.

The Birth Of Flight

Tuesday, November 21, 1783 was an historic date in the annals of aviation. Pilatre de Rozier and the Marquis d'Arlandes became the world's first aeronauts by flying a straw burning hot air balloon, built and designed by the Montgolfier Brothers, for a distance of 9,000 yards over Paris during the twenty-five minute flight. This feat produced dramatic repercussions everywhere. Other would be aeronauts waiting on the sidelines were inspired to attempt the same feat. It did not take long until there were a host of other balloonmen taking to the skies. If the general public did not quite understand all this nonsense about flying they did not show it. It was exciting to watch and that was all that really mattered anyway. Balloon ascensions became in vogue throughout France and most of Europe during this time. Curious spectators traveled great distances just to watch and marvel at the aeronauts perform.

Drawing depicting Garnerin making the world's first parachute jump.

Then there was the matter of expenses; balloons were expensive, even back then. It was the wealthy who could afford to spend the time designing and building one of these lighter-than-air contraptions. Flying around the countryside was a costly and time-consuming affair. In order to afford such aviation activity one had to be rich, sponsored by someone who was, or find a way to make ballooning pay for itself. This is an important dividing point because it split the course of ballooning into two distinct directions.

On one side, aerostation, another term for ballooning, was an upper class endeavor. It was filled with all the pomp and grandeur that only those born with a silver spoon to their mouths could dream of. A balloon ascension wasn't worth going to unless the mayor, various landed officials, and a host of assorted dignitaries were in attendance. The fashionable aeronaut was attired in tailored uniforms complimented with various medals, decorations, and ornaments signifying their nobility or status. A bottle of wine or champagne helped wash away the dust and take the edge off a long flight.

Many balloons were elaborately decorated and handcrafted by artisans. The basket or car was usually built to the specific needs of its captain and passengers. The material was the finest available and the envelope was oftentimes decorated with expensive cloth. Some baskets were finished with gilding to produce that right touch. Not every balloon was an artistic creation, but many were. Most early balloon systems however, were designed and built with an eye to their practical use. Such things as weight, balance, and function were taken into consideration. Many balloons carried out scientific experiments using the most sophisticated measuring devices of the time. All in all it was still an expensive burden that few could afford.

Great strides were made in man's knowledge of his environment from the use of balloons. The birth of aeronautics led to scientific achievements which could not have been done otherwise. If the advancement of aviation was produced by those who could most afford it, then that was the way it should have been. Every history of ballooning alludes to this. Scientific ballooning deserves a well earned niche in aviation history. It was a dynamic part of an adventurous lifestyle, capped only by the resources of time and courage. However, there were other types of ballooning whose focus was all together different.

Carnivals, Fairs & Balloons

On the other side, for those remaining creative and adventurous souls who were not blessed with the timely opportunities provided by wealth, other measures had to be resorted to. And it is in this context that the class difference is important and the folklore of their efforts becomes an opportunity for knowledge. If not wealth, or scientific inquiry, then what? For legions of unheralded aeronauts, ballooning provided a timely way to make a living by entertaining the masses who would pay to watch them perform. And perform they did, and in ways totally different from their upperclass counterparts.

The task simply was to entertain. Balloons were a natural at bringing people together. Early aeronauts capitalized on this power to promote their flights. More times than not the promoters of traveling fairs and other outdoor shows were glad to see a foolhardy aeronaut who wanted to make an ascension during the show. This was an extra attraction that would bring in additional paying customers.

The arrival of a travelling show usually marked the beginning of festive times. The work stopped while peasants, laborers, and other working people came to the outskirts of neighboring towns to relax for a day or so. A light hearted mood usually prevailed. This made for dancing, drinking, and being entertained in ways that made one forget the everyday drudgy at least for a while.

There was always time for the folks to watch a madman climb into something called a balloon and fly it away. Strutting about prior to the flight and exhorting the dangers involved in risking his life, he helped pump up the crowd by playing on their ignorance. This was fine for them. If he wanted to earn a little money risking his neck that way it was alright with them. The spectators did not understand much but were ready to watch all the same. And if for a brief lapse of time one forgot his everyday hardships, well maybe life wasn't all that bad.

Though balloons were relative safe, spectators were led to believe that danger was always eminent. This was part of the promotion. The idea was to make them believe that something catastrophic was going to happen for certain. Crowds were attracted by the prospect of watching something exciting, dangerous, and out of the ordinary. Carnival owners and aeronauts became partners driven with mutual interest. Their common bond was a desire to relieve the peasantry of all their money. It did not take long until they were joined by yet another performer whose interest paralleled their own. As it turned out, these performers offered yet another facet of dangerous activity that could entice crowds to come out to watch.

Have Parachute — Will Jump

If somehow the minds of the spectators had trouble rationalizing the need for someone to fly, they were dumbfounded to justify why foolhardy men would want to jump with a parachute. It just did not make any sense. This attitude is part of a historical pattern. Parachute jumping has always been viewed as something of an unnatural activity; a danger fought with peril.

During aviation's primitive years, from the late 1700's until the advent of powered flight in the early 1900's, aeronauts and parachutists became inseparable partners. The prospect of watching a balloon ascension and a parachute drop during one show was an electrifying event that could draw people from great distances. The partnership of balloons and parachutes is one of aviation's least heralded but necessary friendships. This combination always proved a great attraction.

Balloons and parachutes evolved at the same time for all practical purposes. Technically speaking though, manned decents with a parachute preceded manned flight in balloons. Legend has it that Emperor Shih Huang Ti of China was said to have enjoyed leaping from the newly completed Great Wall of China holding a large parasol. There is also some evidence that Chinese actors of the early 14th century used crude umbrella like parachutes to make spectacular entrances onto theater stages. History further records that Leonardo de Vinci sketched the earliest design of a parachute which he called a "tent roof." Joseph and Etienne Montgolfier are known to have conducted parachute tests with animals nearly a decade prior to developing a man-carrying balloon. Some writers have stated that J.P. Blanchard made a jump with a parachute in 1777, before the invention of the balloon, but this is not confirmed. On December 26, 1783, Sebastien Lenormand, jumped from the tower of Montpellier Observatory to demonstrate the possibilities of the parachute as a means of escape from burning buildings. Realistically though, with the advent of balloons, man finally had a way to get high enough to need and use a parachute. As interest in balloons grew, so did the interest in parachutes.

The world's first bona fide parachute jumper was Andre-Jacques Garnerin. He earned his place in the history books by jumping from his hydrogen balloon with a thirty-two gore canvas parachute over London on October 22, 1797. Garnerin landed safely, but the trip down had been a precarious one. Unlike the calm ascent and descent of the Montgolfiers, Garnerin experienced violent oscillations due to the instability of the primitive canopy. After landing he was unconscious for a brief period of time. All in all, considering the state of the art in parachutes at that time, it was not such a bad day for parachuting.

Realistically, and to be historically correct, aerostation has to be considered the original form of aviation. But the history of aviation and parachuting is closely related. For the next hundred or so years this relationship would grow even closer.

Hydrogen quickly replaced wood and straw and other combustible materials as a source of energy to power these early balloons. Though hydrogen was very expensive to produce it provided early aeronauts the opportunity to fly to much greater altitudes and for much longer periods of time. Garnerin's balloon was heated with hydrogen. His unopened parachute, suspended beneath his balloon, was attached by cable to the basket he stood in. Upon reaching an altitude of 3,000 feet, Garnerin severed the cable and descended by parachute. This basic use of balloons and parachutes was to establish a trend that grew increasingly popular as the years went by.

There was a concern initially about the safety of balloons and it was automatically assumed that parachutes could and should be developed as a safety device to aid balloonmen in emergencies. This idea was short lived. Balloons were for the most part very safe. Their construction, operation, and common sense usage normally prevented the needless expenditure of life. So long as the aeronaut did not fire his balloon too hot, which might disintregrate the envelope, there was little danger involved in aerostation. Common sense dictated flight operations: balloons should not be flown in dangerous weather such as high winds or rain. Thus any possible safety use for parachutes was negated.

The Cult Of Danger

Early parachutes were primitive to put it mildly and many performers lost their lives or were crippled due to the poor quality of construction and design. But balloon design reached an acceptably safe level rather quickly compared to that of parachutes. The size of parachutes, their weight, basic construction techniques, material used, and deployment took much longer to figure out. Unfortunately the image of parachuting suffered while this lengthy trial and error process continued. Since very few persons were using parachutes other than "ignorant circus daredevils", there was little chance to refine this art. Scattered individuals probably worked out the particulars of safe construction and design, but the word travelled slowly in those days and most people were strictly on their own. The greatest value at this period of time for the combined use of parachutes and balloons was for entertainment. Since parachutes were not used for any scientific or safety purposes they were relegated to the status of an entertainment device.

The public did not understand or necessarily approve of the uses of parachutes, but they were willing to watch somebody risk their lives jumping one. Parachuting performers provided a vital missing element for hungry promoters wanting to entice more paid admissions through their gates. That element was genuine foolhardy, reckless abandon. Fairgoers could realistically expect something in return for their money and parachutists provided that entertainment expectation. Parachuting was dangerous and everybody knew it. It was common practice for parachutists to be paid only after the successful completion of the jump. No circus owner wanted to chance payment before the jump, it was just too risky. If the performer didn't make it back in one piece, the promoter was out nothing and the audience was entertained. It was a nice arrangement for everybody, except of course, the parachutist.

During the entire historical sequence of events, parachuting slowly began to evolve into a safer activity, but the folklore of danger and death continued. It was in the best interest of all parties concerned to do so. After decades of death defying mishaps and near misses, the themes had been firmly established in the minds of the public. Everybody knew parachuting was dangerous. It was automatically understood and taken for granted that parachutists were suicidal maniacs with a definite death wish.

Thus a folklore culture evolved from public conceptions about this activity. With this much bad press going for them, old time parachutists were elevated to the status of folk hero. In their own right, parachutists were little understood, but respected members of a small fraternity of people who were admired by the common people. Like combat warriors or gunfighters, they were both feared and respected. Held in awe by people, they could be detested one day and praised the next. If each of these mystifying humans could evoke such emotions as outrage and respect, pity and sympathy, then it was all part of the game. Each parachutist who made a living evoking such responses was very careful to give the public what they wanted.

Smoke Balloons

During the last half of the nineteenth century the popularity of balloons and parachutes increased significantly. The theme of the jumper being carried forth by a balloon in a similar fashion as was Garnerin, was refined to perfection. A cadre of performers evolved who did the balloon ascensions and parachute descents by themselves. These entertainers came to be known as "Smoke Balloonists." Their craft was a true folk art and science that has all but died out in the age of jet airplanes, modern hot air ballooning, and sophisticated freefall skydiving.

This bygone craft has never been written about in books and except for a few sketchy magazine and newspaper accounts is a story almost impossible to trace with complete accuracy. Smoke balloonists were not the most literate and chic of artisans, as were many of their aviation cousins. Their mission was to perform, earn a living, and move on to the next performance. Scant thought was ever given to preserving in writing their craft; it just wasn't that type of business.

Just when aeronaut and parachutist decided to part company is even more difficult to surmise, but economics probably had a good bit to do with this decision. Parachutists are a passionately individualistic lot, and it seems a good bet they didn't always get along with the aeronaut. One was necessarily dependent upon the other, and this alliance of mutual subjugation was bound to cause friction. The parachutist couldn't get up without a balloon; the aeronaut couldn't draw the crowds as well without a jumper. Crafty promoters played on this to their advantage. Since both had to be partners he could just as well pay them as one. Neither jumper nor aeronaut realized much money after the split and this had to create further tension.

With the ever increasing popularity of aviation acts at fairs and carnivals it seems a good bet both decided they could do without the other. The separation probably worked out to the advantage of the parachutist. Forced to rely on his own imaginative and creative skills, the parachutist was faced with the difficulty of incorporating everything into one act. This wasn't all that difficult, and it could not have taken many years before an adequate method was devised. The main problems were obvious; build a smaller balloon to carry one man, create a simple system to release the jumper from the balloon, and devise a way to deflate the balloon and return it to the ground quickly. One of the earliest descriptions of a smoke balloon is described in a book written in 1873 by John Wise. Titled *Through the Air* he described a sectional view of a rarified air balloon in the process of inflation. He writes:

"A Frenchman by the name of Vardalle made several ascensions with a balloon of this kind from the vicinity of Philadelphia in the fall of 1849. His machine was about forty by sixty feet in size, and was composed of black twilled muslin. When prepared for inflation, it was suspended from a rope which ran across from two poles erected for that purpose, so that just before starting he could loosen one end of it and draw it out of the ring at the top of the balloon."

This was obviously a resurrected version of a hot air balloon designed to carry one man. Probably shortly thereafter, a crude, but adequate system was invented and the parachute jumper was now capable of going into business as a one man show. He or she, as often was the case, was now in a much better bargaining position. The money was theirs to keep for themselves, and the act proved most appealing to spectators. Another by-product, occurring almost without planning, was safer parachutes. It was rare indeed for a smokeman to be injured during one of these performances. There was undoubtedly an occasional sprained ankle, and perhaps a broken leg, but it seemed clear; few if any ever lost their lives "smoke ballooning." Smoke balloonists were a tough lot, and most of them lived long and productive lives. Another surprising fact is that most of them accumulated a fantastic number of jumps. Many profess to have made a thousand or more parachute jumps during their career.

In every sense of the word, smokemen, as they were affectionately referred to, were astute entrepreneurs. They capitalized on the vicarious nature of the crowds that came to be entertained. Smokemen made no pretentions about their trade. They were in it to make money by entertaining people. Smoke ballooning is a craft unique to aviation, and one that has been largely ignored by historians of aeronautics.

This was also a vocation which was not learned in fancy universities from books and one that was not professionally taught for money. Smoke ballooning was a craft usually passed on from father to son, in much the same way as the crafts of blacksmithing, leathercraft, woodcarving, farming, and the like. Each individual smokeman passed down to his son or apprentice the particular way he designed, constructed, and used his equipment. And each wanted something different—there was no universal standard which governed these people, only their instincts based on years of experience.

When this unusual activity began is lost in the dustbins of history. As nearly as can be surmised by this author, early smoke balloonists came into being during the middle of the nineteenth century, probably after the Civil War. Travelling with their families from town to town in search of outdoor activities where large crowds gathered for various festive occasions, smokemen plied their trade with an enthusiasm that always made them welcome. Once their reputation as a performer was established, no carnival or fair was complete without one. The folklore of this activity is remembered by the older generations who were thrilled by their presence. Once witnessed, these spectacular ascensions are not likely to be forgotten.

Claude Shafer

One of the few remaining smokemen still alive today is Claude Shafer, who lives in Indianapolis, Indiana. He is able to relate the experiences and wisdom collected in a career which lasted over forty years. From the time of his first ascension in 1923 to his last in 1966, he is a missing link in a folklore activity that has all but died out.

Claude related to this author how he got started in this business and of a man named Oscar E. "Mile High" Ruth. Shafer lived next door to Ruth as he was growing up on the west side of Indianapolis. Ruth was himself a famous smokeman, and as a neighborhood kid, Claude often times spent his time hanging around this eccentric man. Many years later as a young man of twenty-seven, Shafer was talking with Ruth. Since Claude was unemployed at the time, Oscar invited the younger Shafer along as a helper on his next exhibition. Instinctively Claude responded with a positive yes, provided he could make the jump. Ruth grinned a little and said that would be fine with him. As a result of replacing Ruth in the ascension, Shafer got his start in smoke ballooning in 1923. Claude related how Ruth wanted to see what he was made of. Shafer's first baptism into the world of show business in aviation was a triple jump where he was required to cut away two smaller chutes before riding down the main one.

Evidently Oscar Ruth was looking for somebody to take over his long established business. For the next three or so years, Claude Shafer was the right hand man of "Mile High" Ruth, and accompanied him on most of his balloon jumps. Shafer learned from Ruth all the necessary skills he would need to survive in a very competitive business. The old man passed on all his skills to the younger man in an effort to keep the business and traditions alive. Claude learned quickly, acquiring the knowledge to build, maintain, and repair both the balloon and parachutes used in the act.

Oscar Ruth died in 1926 and left his smoke balloon business to Claude Shafer. From that point on, Shafer never engaged in any other type of business nor held another job of any kind. For the remainder of his life his sole income was from the art and science of smoke ballooning.

With the help of Oscar Ruth's widow, an ad was placed in *Billboard Magazine*. This was an advertising medium for people who worked county fairs, circuses, carnivals and the like. Mrs. Ruth advertised that Claude Shafer was taking over for her late husband and that all inquires should be directed to him. Ruth was such a well known and established performer that most of his regular customers transferred their allegiance and business to Shafer. After about three or four years of advertising in *Billboard Magazine*, Claude had established himself as a reliable and excellent performer. In a short time he acquired all the business he could handle. Once a contract was let, it was automatically assumed by both parties that there would be another the following year. Smokemen made it a point of being loyal and dependable to their customers, knowing full well their livelihood depended upon it.

For the next forty three years Claude Shafer made a good living flying the midsection of the United States. He was helped by his wife, and two nephews, Archie Potter and Duane Robertson. Between the three of them they covered most of the state fairs, carnivals, centennials, and circuses. Shafer estimates he made more than 5,000 jumps during this time.

Shafer worked a number of places on a regular basis. Some of the ones he remembers most vividly were Ft. Recovery, Ohio; Macungie, Pennsylvannia; Walkerton, and Richmond, Indiana; and Cullom, Illinois. In addition, his hometown of Indianapolis, the base of operations, was a scene of frequent ascensions. During the summer months he worked for the city parks department and performed at Longacre, Ravenswood, Broadripple, and Riverside recreation areas.

Long Hours & Hardwork

Smokemen developed great endurance and stamina due to the nature of their work. The regular season for this work was about mid-March to mid-October. The winter months were spent repairing and building equipment and just relaxing. But during the hectic season it was "balls to the walls" activity scrambling from one site to another. It was not at all uncommon for these crews to travel all night in order that they could arrive at their next location to begin setting up early in the morning for an afternoon ascension.

The contract Shafer and his crew wrote with each town usually stipulated they were responsible for digging the inflation trench, and erecting two sixty to eighty foot poles about fifty feet apart. The day before the ascension Claude would load up one of his many balloons and parachutes into the back of his Oldsmobile (he always drove the same make automobile), and headed for the site. Many times the distance was short, but many times there was a great distance to cover; perhaps to Michigan, Tennessee, or even Oklahoma. After driving all night, the crew reached their destination in the early hours, and at a frantic pace, began to prepare for the afternoon performance. Most always the performance marked a special occasion which gave the working folks time to witness the excitement of the total process from setting up to packing up. The evening hours just before sundown, during calmer winds, were usually the favorite time for liftoff. Once the balloon ascension and parachute drop was completed, the sooty smoke filled balloon had to be retrieved from a cornfield, woods, or the like. It would then be returned to the launch site, rolled up and packed into the Oldsmobile. And back into the trusty Oldsmobile they all climbed, and Claude and his crew, scurried off to another location. It was not unusual to repeat the same process on four or five consecutive days running. When they found time to sleep, get cleaned up, and gather their wits, is open to speculation. This was obviously hard work, but it must have been great fun and excitement.

With a few exceptions, most smokemen constructed their own balloons and parachutes. Claude Shafer was no exception. He worked in his backyard cutting and assemblying the material, and sewing it together with an old Singer sewing machine he bought for $15.00. If the weather was pleasant, the neighborhood kids usually collected around him, struck with curiosity,

Claude Shafer and crew discuss setting up for a flight. The inflation trench and chimney are on the left.

and begging to help in any way he would let them. Since he was a special personality around the neighborhood he usually obliged and let them help feed the material through the machine. If he required an errand to be run, or needed a misplaced tool inside the house, the kids raced each other to win his favor. It was a fun time for everybody.

Balloons were usually made out of unbleached "Black Rock" muslin, a fairly porous material about 80-90 thread count per inch. Claude didn't operate from any blueprints or written specifications. Things were done by feel and what plans he had were not too specific and were kept in his head. When he set about to build a balloon it usually required three or four days to complete. He built one of three sizes; a seventy-two foot tall balloon was the smallest, an eighty foot tall was his medium size, and a ninety foot high was his biggest. The latter had approximately forty-two gores and ten reinforcement bands. He estimates the eighty foot balloon weighed about 380 pounds. If his workmanship were judged by modern standards it would probably appear rather crude. In actuality, the balloons were sewn together quite well and were definitely strong enough for the purposes he had in mind.

Compared to the enormous size of the balloons he constructed, the parachutes were quite easy to build. Chutes were constructed from material called Shroud Cloth. The brand name was "Cloth of Gold", with a thread count of 120 per inch. "Cloth of Gold" was a much finer and less porous material than that used for the balloon. His main parachute, the one he landed with, was sewn with thirty gores and measured about 30 feet in diameter.

Both parachute and balloon were sewn with cotton thread. The parachute was supported by three or four reinforcement bands around the circumference. Everything was done by feel. Very little was actually measured, and if he didn't like the way it worked when he jumped, back to the sewing machine he went. A little bit was cut from here, a little bit was cut from there, until it was right, and he had it the way he wanted it. His methods weren't too scientific, but they worked.

Professor Claude Shafer, as he was known on the tour circuit, generally tried to wind up his hectic season by Labor Day. This wasn't always possible, but rarely did the season last longer than the end of October. With all the frantic running around to meet schedules it's a wonder anybody had the strength to make it through the season. Somehow he and his hearty crew always made it through. This kind of stressful activity comes with the territory, as they say, and after a few decades of this kind of work one gets used to it. Claude never thought it was a big deal at all.

With the advent of colder temperatures people would start to stay indoors, and the outdoor activity season would come to an abrupt halt. The winter was spent arranging the schedule for the next season, taking a well deserved rest, and of course, building and repairing the equipment.

Melting snows gradually gave way to dry ground and warmer days. The show season once again was upon him and Shafer and his crew were always ready to hit the circuit in early spring. They were always guided by the realities of their business. Smokemen needed food and clothing like other mortals, and if they didn't make it early in the season, there probably wasn't going to be any reason to hang around for the last part. Bills have a way of piling up in the winter and those collectors would only wait so long. So it was usually back on the road, this year to work harder than the last; but it was still a job, no matter how glamorous it all appeared.

Setting Up

Shafer usually carried one or two assistants with him. It was their job to unload all the equipment and miscellaneous material and to help with the inflation of the

The muslin smoke balloon is hoisted between two tall poles.

balloon. The inflation process couldn't be completed without at least one person. After the balloons and parachutes were crammed into the trunk of the faithful Oldsmobile, a variety of other tools filled the vacant spaces. Sledgehammers, stakes, rope, kerosene, and knives were required to inflate the balloon. The townsfolk were usually required to have the inflation trench all ready dug, provide an open ended fifty-five gallon drum, and erect two large poles in the ground. These reminded everyone of oversized telephone poles. With the initial work already completed, the crowds waited for the Professor and his crew to do their thing. The balloon ascension and parachute jump were spectacular to watch, but the inflation of the big black monster was an operation nobody wanted to miss.

Digging out the inflation trench was the first step. This was a narrow slit in the ground about eighteen feet long, two feet deep, and about two feet wide. Iron rods were placed across the top of the trench every few feet. Over the rods were placed corrigated metal sheets to seal the trench.

At one end of the trench the fifty-five gallon drum was set upright. The drum acted as a chimney and over it the mouth of the balloon was pulled and sandbagged. The other end of the trench was left open and filled with a variety of wooden scraps, straw, and other combustible material to start the fire. Positioning the balloon over the chimney was critical. After the large envelope was spread completely out, one of the assistants crawled inside, repositioned the envelope in the middle, and sandbagged it securely down from the inside.

Meanwhile, the other assistant shimmied the eighty foot pole and began to string a crown rope between the upright poles. The rope was strung from one pole, back down and through a crown ring on top of the balloon, and back up to the top of the pole. The crown of the balloon was then hoisted up about twenty-five to thirty feet to prepare for inflation. Once the balloon was suspended between the poles it looked very much like a tent. Now inflation could commense. Tension built in each spectator as the prospect of the impending ascension took final shape. Thus far the sequence of operation had taken about three to four hours. Most onlookers hadn't been able to fully comprehend what all this had to do with flying a balloon; but gradually they became aware of how each step was a necessity. Claude and his crew, like most smokemen, were a friendly group, and readily talked with spectators. This was usually a time of crowd participation. The talk was casual but informative. The professor explained what was going on, how everything worked, and what he was going to do. There were many skeptics in every audience. Some sneered catty remarks, others professed disbelief that this unlikely contraption could actually get off the ground. When he told everybody he would actually cut away from the balloon and descend by parachute, this usually evoked even more criticism. Shafer was used to this digging at his profession; it came with the territory. Smokemen had to have an unusually thick hide which shielded them against unkind remarks. But they also had to have compassion and understanding for the ignorant. Most people had never seen a demonstration of smoke ballooning, and many had never even seen an airplane up close. For the majority in most crowds, this was their first experience with lighter than air flight, and if they did not quite believe things at this stage of the preparations, in a half hour or so they would. Suspense, disbelief, and gawking curiosity were necessary ingredients in a successful show. If everyone stood idly by, uninterested and emotionless, there would not be much of a show would there? The professor figured the more skeptical and arrogant the crowd behaved the more likely they would be entertained.

Some of the more adventurous ones in the crowd got to help digging the trench. Others were privileged to assist with the inflation by holding onto the balloon. Later, after the ascension and drop were over, some would even help haul the smoke covered balloon from some almost inaccessible landing area

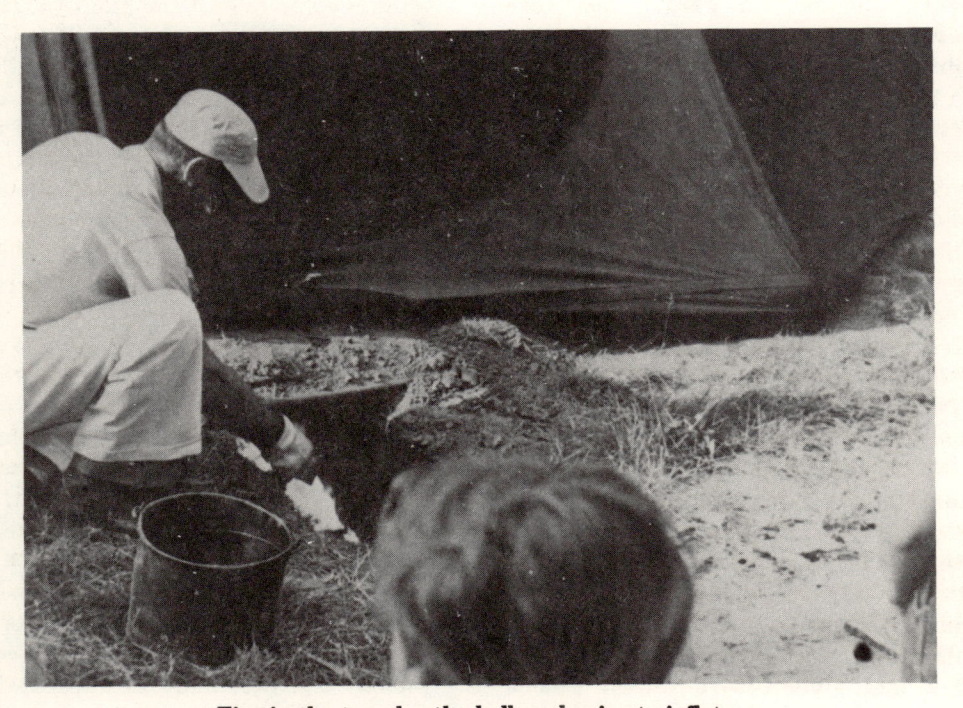

Fire in the trench — the balloon begins to inflate.

where it would usually come to rest.

"On Its Feet"

But at this point the time for talking was at an end. A small fire was ignited at the open end of the trench, while the crowd inched forward to get a better view. Whoosh! The fire exploded as a cup of kerosene was tossed on the red hot embers. A tremendous amount of heat was generated and the balloon began to fill with black smoke. The drum inside the balloon acted as a flue, forcing hot air into the underbelly. As the balloon slowly began to bulge outward the man inside continually had to reposition the sandbags to allow for expansion. Meanwhile, Claude or another assistant hoisted the crown higher between the poles giving more room for the enormous bag to expand. Smokemen never used a thermometer inside the balloon to tell how hot it was, such as the type used by modern hot air balloonists. The idea was not to fuel the fire so fast to cause damage to the material. Only with years of experience inflating balloons could one judge the right time to add more fuel, or when to lay back and let things cool down a bit. Normally the fuel was fired with kerosene every few mintues or so. Inflation mesmerized the crowd and made them into a cohesive unit. Every eye was pinpointed on the balloon as it grew larger and larger. It would grow so big people had to back off just a bit to take the whole thing in. Every now and then the poor assistant inside the balloon poked his head out to wipe his brow and breathe in some cool fresh air. And back inside he went to monitor the expansion.

When the massive envelope was able to begin supporting its own weight the guide ropes suspended between the two upright poles was pulled away. This allowed for total expansion of the balloon. Continual expansion constantly required repositioning of the sandbags. Eventually all the sandbags were removed and all that kept the balloon on the ground were numerous wooden stakes pounded into the ground circling the perimeter. As the cloth machine reached its full height from the heat, it was ready for takeoff, and is said to have been "on its feet." Confined only by the stakes, straining to break loose, the black muslin bag was an awesome and vivid monument to lighter-than-air equipment. Claude knew that when the balloon is "standing on its feet" the time was at hand for the aerial phase of the show to begin.

Nearly "on its feet"

He hooked on one or more of his parachutes to the balloon. The professor never used a reserve parachute, or for that matter, a traditional harness system used by regular parachutists. Instead he fitted himself into a padded sling. Shafer had also used a trapeze bar on many occasions, but he preferred the sling system because of the comfort. It was typical for practically all smoke balloonists to forego the use of a reserve parachute. This indicated the trust they placed in their systems. There were two types of parachute systems used by these performers. Probably the more common was the string out method. The apex of the canopy was attached by a cord and the balloonist simply attached a knife system to sever the cord and release himself. The parachute was strung out completely while the jumper dangled below the outstretched lines during ascension. The other method, which the Professor preferred, was the packed system. His parachute was enclosed, or packed, into a cloth container above his head. The apex was tied to the bottom of the balloon with a break cord. After disengaging himself, the weight of his falling body deployed the canopy and snapped the break cord, allowing inflation of the canopy. Shafer preferred this system because it allowed him the opportunity to do multiple cut-away jumps. The extra chutes were merely packed one on top of another, connected with the break cord. Claude did not like to be limited with one type of jump. The professor claims to have invented a rather unique cut-away system specifically for his purposes. Either the padded sling or a trapeze bar was attached to a wooden automobile steering wheel. Across the diameter of the wheel were crisscrossed some rope that supported the packed parachute. The butt sling, steering wheel, and the chute are connected by rope to a central point just underneath the mouth of the balloon. This system could easily be severed to release himself once the proper altitude was reached.

An Airborne Monster

With the bag inflated, parachutes attached, and the jumper snugly fit into the butt sling, all that remained was to release the balloon. This was the moment of truth. Takeoff was an electrifying event that boggled the minds of those who witnessed it. The Professor signalled for the release of the balloons from the circle of stakes.

An assistant wielded a heavy axe that slashed through the cinch rope restraining the balloon. Without hesitation, the massive muslin bag bolted into the air while the Professor hung on for dear life. Veering back

Liftoff!

Late evening liftoff using the string out method to deploy the parachute

and forth in an erratic flight path the balloon surged upward. Sometimes this ascent rate would exceed a thousand feet per minute. The gods were mostly in control now; the dangling parachutist was at the mercy of nature. Most of the control the smokeman had over the wildly oscillating balloon was left on the ground. It all depended on the experience of smokeman and how tight the bag was inflated. To a point, the hotter the inside the better. For the greater the temperature inside, the higher and faster the balloon would climb. Too little heat and the balloon might only carry its passengers several hundred feet. Too much heat and the balloon would catch fire or split open in flight ruining the act.

Higher and higher as the balloon climbed, higher and higher it drug its human cargo, and expended its heated energy. Gradually the heat began to abate and the upward surge became no more than a gentle push against the gravity. By 1500 feet or so the balloon had usually settled down considerably, allowing the jumper a brief time of relaxation to collect his thoughts and prepare for the return trip. When the right time approached and the smokeman estimated he was over a safe landing area, he readied himself for the cut-away.

The knife was stored in the sheath attached to a safety belt. The Professor severed the main rope which attached himself and the parachute with the balloon. Once the rope was cut, Claude and his parachute would go into a brief freefall. The apex of the canopy was attached to the bottom of the balloon and was drawn from the bag in which it was packed. His weight snapped the break cord—jumper and parachute were now free of the balloon. While still in freefall, the canopy began to inflate immediately, and the jumper swung under an open canopy in a very brief period of time. The entire cut-away sequence from the balloon usually took about three seconds to complete.

Sometimes the muslin bags failed to deflate immediately and continued upward until it became unbalanced. A popular method used by smokemen for turning the balloon over so it would deflate and fall to the ground, was to attach a long rope to the crown and weight the free end with a ten or fifteen pound sandbag. After the parachutist cut-away, the unbalancing effect of the sandbag pulled the balloon over upside down. All the black smoke inside spewed out of the mouth like a giant dragon in the sky puffing out fire. The muslin bag streamered to the ground in a final blaze of glory and dirt. Some smokemen returned their balloon with the aid of a small parachute, but they were the exception rather than the rule.

After the canopy had inflated, and the bag turned over, the jumper then gave his full attention to his landing area. The thirty-foot flat circular parachutes used by the Professor were all but unsteerable. He was at the mercy of whatever winds prevailed. The only control he could exercise over the parachute was to increase his rate of descent. He did this by grabbing a set of riser lines and slipping to the right or left, trying to avoid an obstacle or perhaps attempting to land in an open area. In extreme situations, where there was a chance of landing in water, power lines, trees, or a group of buildings, Claude grabbed both front risers and pulled them down to deflate the canopy. This caused him to lose altitude rapidly and helped him avoid these obstacles. He had to be careful not to do this maneuver too close to the ground. The increased rate of descent could mangle him were he to land like that. Claude claims in drastic situations he pulled the lines down so far he could actually grab the skirt of the canopy. Normally his landings were uneventful. Other than a few scrapes and bruises which could normally be expected in a forty year career, Claude Shafer claims never to have been seriously hurt as a result of any of this activity. However there were a few close calls he remembers.

Claude likes to relate a story about a job he had one time in Quincy, Illinois. He was contracted to do an ascension, but the townfolks were reluctant for him to make it because there was bad weather headed their way. Evidently Claude had traveled a great distance and had already collected the fee in advance and felt he had to live up to his end of the bargain. So up he went anyway! After releasing himself from the balloon, the winds picked up something fierce and began to carry him into a far away area where there were a number of large buildings.

Slipping had little effect, and collapsing the canopy didn't help much either. He was in the awkward position of heading right into the side of a very large grain elevator. The winds caused the chute to oscillate badly. Just before impact with the building, an oscillation threw him into the sixth floor through a glass window, scaring some secretaries half to death, not to mention himself. It was a harrowing experience but he emerged from this landing unhurt. From this episode he claims to be the only jumper in the world who went up in a smoke balloon and came down in an "elevator."

Cullom, Illinois

Of the many parts of the country which have featured Professor Claude Shafer and his famous balloon ascension and parachute jump, none is more famous than Cullom, Illinoise. This small rural farm community in northeastern Illinois, with a population of about five hundred people, is steeped in smoke ballooning tradition. While it may be small, its citizens are keenly aware of their history and proud of their contribution to aviation folklore.

This author became aware of Cullom through a close friend named Peter Krieg. Peter is a well known hot air balloonist himself and does many exhibition flights around the Indiana, Illinois, and Ohio regions. Krieg has known and been friends with Claude Shafer since the middle 1960's. He had the fortunate pleasure of watching the Professor perform a smoke balloon ascension at the Marion County Fair in 1965. In later years, when Claude was winding down his long career, he decided to let Krieg take over the Cullom balloon ascension. Since Peter used only modern hot air balloons a smoke balloon ascension and jump were out. Therefore he had need of a skydiver who would jump from his balloon. He asked me to do the jump one year, beginning in 1974 and I have had the distinct pleasure of doing it every since. During the long ride from Indianapolis to Cullon we would pass the time telling balloon and jump stories, generally relating our experiences, while his wife and kids and my wife listened on. As a result I became very familiar with the traditions of Cullom, and the career of Claude Shafer. Krieg is an astute historian on ballooning and aware of the significance that Cullom plays in its long history.

Smokemen have long performed in this quiet and scenic village since the late 1880's. It is perhaps the only town left in the United States that is still keeping alive the tradition of using balloonmen and parachute jumpers at its annual county fair. It is also believed that Cullom is the only town in the United States that has provided a continuous balloon act for close to eighty years. And while there have been a few times when smokemen did not perform, it was usually the result of bad weather. These times have generally been few and far between.

The Homecoming

Every year this agricultural community celebrates its "Homecoming." This festive occasion began in Cullom as a Roman Catholic holiday. The Feast of the Assumption of the Blessed Virgin Mary, celebrated on August 15, was a joyous and festive day. Many Cullom residents went to Church on that date, and since it was a holy day, it was also a holiday. People not working on holdays came to the town for picnics and to visit friends and relatives they had not seen for a time. The activities built up and pretty soon persons from surrounding communities and outlying areas made it a point of coming back to Cullom on that date. Relatives and former residents joined in and before long August 15th came to be known as the Homecoming.

The Skinner-Trost Post No. 122 of the American Legion was organized shortly after World War I in Cullom and began to sponsor the event in the early 1920's. This fine patriotic organization continues to sponsor the Homecoming. The Cullom Junior Fair began in 1947. It was founded by John Perring, a vocational and agricultural teacher at Cullom High School. Among the many activities featured are livestock judging, equipment displays, judging in domestic products, plus the usual tents, midways, and carnival type amusements. It is a combination county fair, carnival, church social, and town picnic rolled into one. But of course the trademark of the Homecoming was the balloon ascension and parachute jumping. No Homecoming could have ever been complete without one. It is as true today as when the first Homecoming was celebrated in 1889.

Despite the absence of a genuine smoke balloonist, the Cullom residents still come out in large numbers to watch the festivities start with the traditional balloon ascension. Peter Krieg, myself, and the rest of his crew start unloading the basket and envelope from the small trailer used to haul the equipment. This yearly outing is usually a family affair. Everybody likes to visit Cullom, not only for the balloon ascension, but to meet old friends and enjoy the carnival atmosphere. Pete's wife Ruth, and their two kids Lisa, and Christy, and my wife Linda, start spreading out the envelope across the street. This ascension will take place in just about the same area Claude Shafer used to use. A.F. "Woody" Woodall and Anita Harrell, two of Peter's trusty copilots, carry out the wicker basket, set the in-flight instruments, and hook the steel cables to the balloon. Somebody usually inflates a tiny toy balloon and releases it to check the wind direction. It is not like the old days exactly, but it still fascinates the crowd that begins to swell. Most of the old timers remember Claude Shafer very well. They come up to Peter or Woody and inquire about how he is doing, because they know they are all good friends with the Professor.

About this time, without fail, the local newspaper editor, Lewis Van Alstyne, known to his multitude of friends as Toby, shows up to take a few pictures for his newspaper, The *Chronicle-Headlight-Enquirer*, three newspapers that have combined over the years to service the area. Toby has worked on the paper since 1912 and has been editor since 1919. In February, 1979, Toby was honored by the Governor for his long and distinguished career in newspaper publishing, by proclaiming February 11th as "Toby Van Alstyne Day in Illinois." It is believed

Mike Horan [left] holds the balloon while Peter Krieg fires the "Indiana Banana."

that Toby is the oldest active editor in the United States, both in years and in terms of service. Toby always has a good word to say to us and wants to take a few pictures of everybody with his faithful Polaroid camera. He has witnessed more balloon ascensions than anybody in Cullom and can tell some great stories. After lining everybody up for a few quick shots, he lets us all get back to the business of entertaining the local folks.

The balloon ascension is almost always on a Thursday evening about six o'clock, just in time for most people to get in before everything starts. It always marks the official opening of the Homecoming. As launch time rolls around, Peter breaks out the fans used to blow the hot air from the gas burners, and prepares for inflation. The burners are lit, and a whoosh ignites the fire and jogs the fibers of interest in the crowd. Krieg's balloon, affectionately called the "Indiana Banana", because of its oblong shape and yellow color; is large compared to most hot air balloons. Called an AX-7 model, it holds about 80,000 cubic feet of hot air, and stands about seven stories high. It slowly begins to fill as Woody and Anita hold tether ropes to keep it under control.

Cleansing The Soul

In the meantime, I have been putting on my parachute gear and getting psyched up for my yearly cleansing of the soul. Balloon jumps for a skydiver are a rarity and I cherish each one with a fervor. Somebody usually asks me if I am scared to which I usually reply "No, only when I jump", or what happens if both parachutes do not work properly, and I say "I'll take it back for a new one." Everybody is in a lighthearted mood, some have been nipping a brew, and I wish I had one myself.

In a few minutes, everything is ready and Pete hops aboard, followed by myself, and maybe a lucky passenger from the town. Most of the time Woody or Anita act as co-pilot. The balloon is fired with more hot air until it "stands on its feet" and Peter checks the thermometer high inside the envelope. A few more blasts of hot air and away we go.

It is important to get a good fast takeoff in order to avoid smacking into adjacent trees or buildings. Once we are up about one or two hundred feet the danger is over and we settle into a rate of climb of about six to seven hundred feet per minute. More times than not we began drifting to the northeast. Since I will be freefalling for about ten seconds with a smoke flare so the crowds can see me better, I won't be jumping from 1500 or 2000 feet; that's for the old-timers.

"Say Pete, how about going up to four or five thousand feet this time?" I ask.

Pete always replies, "Well, we can't drift too far or the people won't be able to see you. Besides, a big hero like yourself doesn't need much altitude anyway."

"Well that is true", I counter, "but that's on the ground. Besides you are always trying to get me to jump too low. You know how those low jumps bother me."

A little haggling and we agree on about 3500 feet or so for the jump altitude. It is a ritual we go through every year. Part of our tradition you might say. Soon it's time for me to carry on the long tradition of jumping at the Cullom Homecoming. Sitting on the edge of the basket and looking down is a little strange. The burners are shut off and it is deathly quiet. It's like sitting on top of a very tall building, completely unlike a regular skydive from an airplane. The stillness is the attraction and we continue to slowly drift. Every year I wait for this moment, and the closer the time nears, the more rapid my heart pounds. Unlike jumping from a powered airplane, there will be a definite feeling of falling. It's going to be a real rush. I love it, and am perhaps addicted to the pleasure; but I'm nervous as hell. This is definitely a real thrill. My hand held smoke flare is ignited; now there is nowhere to go but straight down. Off I go and for a few brief seconds my adrenalin pushes me into an indescribable void. My body speed increases at an alarming rate! In eleven or twelve seconds I'm cruising along at 120 mph. My altimeter reads about 2000 feet and

"The Indiana Banana"

it's time to end this yearly dream. The rush is over all too quickly and already I am mentally preparing for next year. By the time I land, usually in some farmer's front yard, there are already some eager people ready to talk with me, share a brew or two, help me pack my parachute, and give me a ride back to town. In short order I'll be at the local tavern telling jump stories, eating some food, shooting some pool, and sipping a cold beer. Everybody wants to buy me a drink and I just can't refuse. This is all part of the tradition.

It takes the balloon crew longer to pack the balloon than I to pack my parachute, so by the time Pete, Woody, and the rest of his crew find me about an hour and a half later, I'm usually half in a bag from all the festivities. But it won't take long for Pete to catch up. After Pete arrives we both sit down with Merle Corbin, the legionnaire who is usually in charge of the Homecoming, settle some finances, and continue with the stories. Only this time my fabulous jump stories are cut short by Pete who has to interrupt with some wild balloon stories. He usually tells some good ones so it's not so bad. Tomorrow's workday will come early for all of us, so the merriment must come to an end shortly. It will be a long ride back but a most satisfying one. Cullom will be there next year and so will all of us. It's part of the tradition.

"Earning One's Smoke"

After being a part of the Cullom tradition, the smoke ballooning bug inspired Krieg to duplicate Claude Shafer's efforts. Peter is keenly aware of the tradition of these glorious smokemen, and is eager to follow closely in their footsteps, and hopefully keep alive their fading customs. He talked with the Professor on many occasions to learn all that he could about how to design and build his own smoke balloon. For several years he worked diligently in his basement with modern equipment duplicating the handicraft of the early smokemen.

An engineer by trade, Krieg was able to translate many of the ideas given to him by Shafer so he could come as close as possible to building an authentic smoke balloon. Learning a new skill is never easy, but after a couple of years of painstaking and time consuming work the balloon began to take shape. Finally, Pete was ready to test jump his own smoke balloon.

The first practice flight occurred in August 1976 at Peru, Indiana. Due to the fact that the balloon material was new and not completely sealed, he was unable to get sufficient altitude to use the parachute. He learned the material needed to be smoked up some more to capture and retain the heat. After returning home he took the balloon to a local park for a final installment to seal the material. A fire was built from old rubber tires and tennis shoes and used to inflate his cloth balloon. Once he was satisfied the sealing was complete he could get on with the business of making a genuine smoke balloon ascension and parachute jump.

With the help of Dave Thiel, Anita Harrell, and "Woody" Woodall acting as his ground crew, Peter was able to complete his first successful smoke jump on October 3, 1976 at Whitestown, Indiana. His story and reflections on this unique experience offer the best insight possible. Written and published in *"Ballooning Magazine"*, and reprinted here, is a personal account of the day Peter Krieg earned his smoke.

"Cut it, Woody! The axe falls and I hear the muffled click as the cinch relaxes around the stake and the balloon lifts. In an instant I am being accelerated upward. It is completely uncontrollable as it strives to satisfy its natural hunger for altitude. It is a monster, this muslin creation, and it seeks only what its primeval brain knows — to rise. I am still the master, but the

Peter Krieg "earning his smoke"

monster doesn't know this and I have no power to prove the point. It bucks, it sways, it tips and it seems that it is almost ready to turn on its side."

"Slowly it is tiring, its earlier display of strength and virility is diminished somewhat as its driving force of life, heated air and smoke, cools and leaks through millions of tiny pores. Gradually it comes to its senses and settles down to an easy undulating kind of pattern. It is still hungry for altitude, but its appetite is more easily satisfied now after the first 1000 feet. I think it is having stomach cramps from the ingestion of too much altitude too quickly."

"Completely spent, the beast is at rest at about 1,200 feet and it is my turn to play out the role of this great atmospheric stage and hurl myself into the fraternity of the balloonmen. Time has run out. The Indiana countryside is just starting to burst into a multicolored panorama and even now a myriad of shades of brown, beautiful from my vantage point, stretches below me. It beckons come return to me as you must, do not delay. My finger flicks the lever, releasing the pack and harness from the muslin monster. An eternity passes — I am falling. . . .falling. . . .falling, and then a flutter, a pop and a jerk, it has deployed. It is beautiful! I have earned my smoke."

Surely this is the type of experience Claude Shafer went through thousands of times. Peter Krieg had the daring fortitude to step into the aerial arena, in an effort to relive, and walk in the footsteps of an aviation heritage that carried mankind from balloons to rocket ships.

200 Years Of Tradition

The number of authentic smokemen in the United States has dwindled down to a small handfull. Claude Shafer is past eighty, as are the other remaining few, and they have retired, just like the Professor. Each passing day brings us closer to the end of an era whose story began to unfold close to two hundred years ago. For all practical purposes, these glorious smokemen, and their muslin balloons and parachutes, are extinct.

The legacy they leave behind is one that will be relived and kept alive within the historical annals of ballooning and parachuting in the United States. For this was very much an aviation activity of the people, and for the common man. The sole intent was to entertain the crowds that came out to watch their ascension. It is unlikely these folk heroes ever failed in this mission. Generations of balloonists and parachutists have come and gone, each bringing with them new and better improvements that refined their respective trades. For untold decades, aeronauts and parachutists were partners in aviation, and still are in many respects. However, modern technological advances have made a permanent and distinct separation of these two colorful aspects of aviation. Both fields of aviation share a common heritage. It is a bond that can never be forgotten.

The vicarious needs of these crowds are still being met, but in a different fashion. Sophisticated hot air ballooning of today, and the modern techniques of skydiving reach out to fill the void of these needs. Smoke ballooning is an antiquated source of activity to contemporary aeronauts and just not worth the trouble to keep the tradition alive. Smoke ballooning will shortly be but a remnant in the stretch of aviation imagination, but its folklore will long be remembered.

Chapter 2

The Father Of American Parachuting

In August 1957, Tivat, Yugoslavia, was the host city for the first running of the Adriatic Cup, an international parachuting meet that would attain great stature in later years. The gentle breezes blowing in from the Adriatic Sea, and the warm, balmy air made for ideal jumping conditions. So perfect were the conditions the chief judge feld an urge to make a jump during a lull in the competition. There was a scurry of activity when he announced his intentions, and a variety of people were set about borrowing the necessary gear. In short order the judge was properly outfitted with the latest parachute equipment. Many were concerned, not only about the man's intentions, but his ability as well. Their anxieties were futile. Though Joe Crane was 55 years old, and had not made a parachute jump in twenty years, he was no stranger to parachutes.

Amid the hopeless protests of many officials and spectators, this quietly smiling man boarded an airplane and made his way to an altitude of 500 meters. This was to be an easy fun type of jump for this 250 pound, 6'2" gentleman. No hard landings for him; this was to be a water jump. After making a steady climb to altitude, he exited and landed fairly close to a marked off target area near the beach. Anxious bystanders and admirers were amazed at the agility and confidence with which the shy man was able to steer the chute. After his successful landing, he was retrieved from the water and greeted with handshakes and congratulations. This was Joe Crane's 689th jump. It was also his last. The Grand Old Man of Parachuting had made his final exit from active parachuting.

Not many jumpers at the Adriatic Cup Meet knew of Joe Crane, but then, not many of them had been around parachuting for as

Joe Crane

long, or had been as involved as this gentleman. However, it didn't take long for the word to get around about him. Never wanting to toot his own horn, Joe usually remained in the background, content to be enjoying the company. That was the style of this international sage. Throughout the remainder of the meet, Joe would be making many new friends and reliving some fond memories.

At a time when most jumpers could measure their parachuting careers in terms of years, Joe could look back and recall his experiences in terms of decades. He spoke of his last jump, twenty years earlier, which had caused him to hang up his parachute in favor of less stressful activities. By then he had been jumping almost fifteen years, and had accumulated enough experiences and skills to last a lifetime.

It was in Cleveland, during the 1937 air races, that Joe broke an ankle and decided it was time to retire from active parachuting. With 688 jumps to his credit, he still maintained an active involvement with the sport he so dearly loved.

Already Crane's contributions to parachuting were significant. Under his determined leadership, he helped guide and mold a national organization of parachute jumpers so their voices could be heard. Almost single-handedly, Joe was responsible for the new respect and admiration parachutists were being accorded at a national level. Parachuting and parachutists were beginning to arrive in terms of status, and be accepted as equals in the brotherhood of the aviation community. But the struggle had been a long and difficult process, and there were still many other obstacles to hurdle. Joe knew from personal experience the problems that were involved.

Joe Crane's roots in parachuting extend back to March 5, 1923 the day of his first jump. During these early days of primitive parachutes, a successful jump was one which you could walk away from. His first parachute jump was in conjunction with a parachute riggers course he had volunteered for while in the U.S. Army Air Service. He had finished the rigging course in less than two months, and had even been an instructor during the last month. Joe was a quick and skillful student, and had learned in several months, what normally took a much longer time to absorb. He enlisted in the Army Air Service in search of excitement and adventure. In parachuting he saw an opportunity to satisfy these needs.

Born of mining parents in Carlinville, Illinois on February 23, 1902, it didn't take him long to see that the prospects for a happy and meaningful future were bleak at best. In this southwestern mining town survival was always a touch and go affair. Scraping out an existence meant rising before the sun and heading into an underground hell to mine low grade coal. More often than not, the miners would return to the surface after the sun had long since set. If the hours of backbreaking work didn't take their toll, then the ever present coal dust would. Small wonder then, at the age of eighteen, Joe rebelled and demanded a better life for himself. His alternatives were limited; hit the mines or hit the road. Fortunately for Joe, as well as for parachuting, he elected to hit the road.

Army Air Service

His rebellion guided him into a three year enlistment with the U.S. Army Air Service. Hoping to begin flying, he was initially happy to be assigned to Kelly Field as a member of the 94th Aero Squadron. This was the famous Rickenbacher Squadron. But instead of flying, Crane found himself behind a desk pounding a typewriter. This wasn't his idea of excitement. Shortly thereafter he was transferred to Ellington Field in Texas. But the only thing hot about this place, as he found out, was the bright Texas sun.

An argument with a loud-mouthed NCO had not settled well with young Joe. After the NCO had intimidated Joe with the fact that he was a parachute jumper, in order to settle the argument, Joe decided to make a jump out of spite. But as Joe was beginning to find out, things weren't that easy in the army.

Joe asked the Post Adjutant for permission to sign up for the parachute course, giving his meager reason that life was dull at the base, and his work didn't interest him at all. As a condition for being allowed to enter the parachute course, the Adjutant suggested Joe cound find excitement by painting the flagpole outside his office. Eager to get things rolling, Joe literally jumped at this opportunity.

Once outside the office building, Joe had second thoughts. He had been tricked; the flagpole was ninety feet tall! He wondered how he was supposed to climb to the top, let alone carry along a bucket of paint. The pole was too large to be gripped with the fingers, and too small to be held tightly with the arms. Joe was a persistant little cuss and he vowed to paint the pole or die trying. After two days of calculating and asking for advice he came up with the answer. Joe stole some rope and fashioned a slip knot that would grip the pole. Two stirrups were made for his feet, a small hangline to hold the bucket, and Joe was ready to start climbing. In less than two days the flagpole was painted and Joe was looking forward to some happy days at the parachute school.

Private Crane, though a young man, was a determined individual. You just about had to be in those days, especially if you were climbing from an open cockpit and about to make your first parachute jump. Joe was a long way from home and deeply emerged in a search for excitement. The military biplane that carried him aloft for his jump was his first airplane ride. It never occurred to him until now, but being a parachute jumper meant many takeoffs, but few landings. Training jumps were simple in those days. The jumper had to climb from the cockpit seat, wiggle through the wing struts and support wires, and walk to a small platform on the bottom of the wing. All the while bracing himself against the wind blasts of the propeller. After a signal from the pilot, he gave the ripcord a healthy yank and waited for the canopy to begin inflating. Joe was snatched from the wing of the airplane by the deploying canopy. There were no static line jumps made at this time; all military jumps were made by this pull-off method. Joe followed instructions perfectly; except for one detail. He forgot to let go! The quickness and force of the inflating canopy caught him mentally unprepared. He left some chunks of skin attached to the strut where he had been holding on; and his landing wasn't much better. With little or no control over the parachute, and no experience to use it even if he did, Joe drifted

Early military and civilian jumpers used the "pull off" method to make parachute jumps.

into an area filled with huge boulders and numerous construction vehicles. Luckily he managed to avoid these obstructions, but in the process sprained his right ankle. Not too bad for his first jump he figured, but he would do better the next time. Joe was able to limp away from his first aviation experience, and at the time, that was enough to ask for. At last Joe had found the excitement and adventure he dreamed of.

Shortly thereafter, Pvt. Crane was transferred to Selfridge Field, Michigan, and assigned to rigging duties in the base parachute loft. During this tour of duty he made fourteen more parachute jumps, one of which was from an altitude of 17,500 feet. This was the first altitude record in the history of parachuting. Whenever Joe had the opportunity you could always find him getting ready to make another jump. On February 25, 1924 Joe completed another high altitude parachute jump without special oxygen equipment. This one also was a world record from 20,300 feet.

The local newspaper carried an account of that sensational jump. Their story detailed how Crane had made his record leap from miles in the air in what was practically a blizzard with temperatures thirty degrees below zero. Even though he landed safely two miles southeast of Pontiac the army took a dim view of his activities. Crane was subsequently confined to the base and ordered to stand a court martial.

Pvt. Crane could never be accused of being a stickler in regard to military regulations. His was a free soul that didn't like the confining regimentation of military life; and this was an attitude that didn't win many friends. After his record altitude jump, several self-serving officers decided to make Joe an example for the other enlisted men on the base. He was charged with willfully running guard, and for jumping without permission. Neither charge was true, but still Joe had to suffer through a lengthy acquittal. Since no reliable witnesses could be found to testify against him, nothing could ever be proven, and the court martial was eventually dropped. Joe was glad but he really didn't care. His enlistment was nearing an end and it was his intention to become a free man once again.

Though he didn't like the military way of life, Joe realized he had learned some valuable skills while in the service. He was determined to put them to good use after his discharge. Much to the satisfaction and consent of all parties concerned, Joe Crane was honorably discharged from the U.S. Army Air Service in the summer of 1924. What he found on the outside world disappointed him. Making a living from parachuting was a long and difficult road to master.

Jumping Jack

Civilian parachutes were difficult if not impossible to buy during the post-World War I years. And without a parachute, making stunt and exhibition jumps for money was impossible. Throughout the summer of 1924, Joe took a job as a steeplejack. It sounded easy, but climbing around high buildings, flagpoles, and water towers was dangerous work. The work paid alright, but after nearly falling from several projects, Joe decided to look for other work. He was getting high, but not the way he loved best.

As luck would have it, a solution to his problem soon flew into town. The Burns Flying Circus included a motely assortment of pilots, crew, and eight stunt airplanes. Missing from the regular barnstorming act was a regular parachute jumper. Since Joe was one of the few civilians capable of making a free fall jump he applied, and was accepted for the job.

While drinking a few beers with his new partners, Joe came to find out why there was a missing parachute jumper from the troupe; he was recently killed while attempting one of his more difficult stunts. When Joe asked what the stunt involved he was told not to worry; everybody was sure he would learn to do it properly. Everybody had a good laugh on Joe and the beer poured freely during the rest of the evening. Joe was learning what it was like to be a barnstormer. This was their way of relaxing.

Joe was able to borrow one of the circus owned parachutes when it was his turn to jump during the show. Nobody expected Joe to be able to perform complicated stunts right away, but he would have to learn fast. He was back in the skies, which he loved, making his living as a parachute jumper. If this meant learning dangerous stunts, then that would be all right with him.

Crane was an official barnstormer now and he traveled throughout the Midwest & West with the Burns Flying Circus. As usual, he learned his craft with a quickness that earned the respect of his fellow tradesmen. Joe performed a variety of daredevil feats and stunts which helped attract large crowds wherever he appeared. In short order Joe was something of a star attraction. The crowd loved him because of his uncanny ability to entice them with his dangerous appearing act. According to the oldtimers, which Joe always listened to very attentively, the secret of being a successful and well paid performer, "was to make the crowd think you were going to get killed for sure. At about the time they're feeling guilty about wanting to watch you die, you yank open your chute and make them feel good." The crowds loved Joe's ability to do just that. These and other tricks he learned to make himself the star attraction.

Joe liked the excitement of an airshow, and he liked the crowds that shelled out their hard earned bucks to see him perform. Joe was usually billed as the "World's Marvel Parachute Jumper" or as "Jumping Jack Crane." In those days crowds were attracted to these barnstorming airshows for the pure excitement; the gutsier the better. Everybody wanted to see pilots push their planes to the breaking point, and stuntmen who would risk everything to please them. And seldom did Jumping Jack disappoint the crowds. Joe often bragged he could land his parachute anywhere. On one occasion he

Poster of the Gates Flying Circus which was typical of many barnstorming aerial shows.

just about had to eat those words. Crane's advance publicity men had contracted him to make a Santa Claus jump for a large department store in Port Huron, Michigan. Crane was expected to land on a rooftop some ninety by one hundred feet square. After landing, Joe was to be replaced by the regular Santa Claus, and then he could collect his money. It all sounded so simple, but it turned out to be a nightmare jump.

On the day of the exhibition jump, Joe and the pilot circled the shopping center to build up the drama. Bad weather was building up and moving in from the northwest. The ceiling was becoming lower and lower. Joe instructed the pilot to stay under the cloud layer. Lower and lower the pilot flew until the altitude was only 700 feet. That simple jump was now turning into a horror show for the pilot, and especially for Joe. No matter what the conditions were, Joe felt obligated to try and make the jump, even if he had to jump at an unbelievably low altitude. Joe knew this was the code of honor every barnstormer had to live with. As far as the paying customer was concerned, there was no such thing as too dangerous a jump.

As the plane circled below the safest of margins, Joe began noticing the jutting edges of the surrounding buildings. By this time it was too late! Both jumper and pilot were at the point of no return; neither could collect the fee unless the jump was made. Several thousand children and their parents wanted to see Santa make the parachute jump, and the decision weighed heavily on Crane's mind. Figuring he had no option, Joe exited the airplane at just under 700 feet and waited for his chute to open. In what seemed like an eternity, as any jump from that altitude would, his chute blossomed open and carried him to the unknown dangers waiting for him on the rooftop.

Skillfully slipping towards the white cross used as a target on the roof, Crane noticed a cluster of white spots below him. He didn't know at the time but he was shortly going to learn of their potential danger. The rooftop was scattered with steel reinforcing rods left sticking up after construction. So meanwhile, probably due more to luck than anything else, Jumping Jack managed to avoid becoming impaled on one of these spikes. He landed about two feet from the white cross. After landing, Crane stared in disbelief at the white cross he had been trying to aim for. The cross was not painted on the rooftop as he had been led to believe. But was built up about three feet high to be sure that he would see it. If he had managed to actually hit this yard high three dimensional cross, he probably would have spent some time in the local hospital. Barnstorming was a risky business.

In his usual nonchalant attitude, Joe shrugged his shoulders and figured that everything had turned out for the best. Besides he mused, what he didn't know couldn't possibly hurt him. So why worry about what might have been.

High Altitude Freefalls

From 1925 to 1929 Joe Crane made his living primarily as an exhibition jumper and stuntman for a variety of aerial circuses. He even found time to develop an interest in high altitude parachuting. His insatiable appetite to know all he could about his profession drove him to make several record free fall jumps. He developed a curiosity about how far men could safely free fall without losing consciousness. The folk myth shared by most pilots and jumpers at the time was that a man would lose his senses if subjected to even a short free fall. From his vast experiences Joe suspected these attitudes were based on myths.

On July 19, 1925, Crane made a delayed free fall of 2,250 feet. This was made at Southfield, Michigan, and was a world record. Joe was one of the first men to disprove the theory regarding free fall jumps. A short time later he made delayed jumps of 2,500 and 3,500 feet that attracted much interest from Army and Air Force officials. This bit of free fall parachuting brought Joe a good bit of national attention and respect. He was now rapidly becoming an established expert in the field of parachuting.

May 30, 1926, witnessed Joe making a Memorial Day exhibition jump at Hill Airport in Latrobe, Pennsylvania. He experienced one of the few malfunctions he had during his long and distinguished career. A few broken lines and some blown panels caused Joe to be hurled to the ground at a high rate of descent. Fortunately, the remainder of his parachute caught on the edges of a tree thereby breaking his fall and saving his life. Joe was to spend the next two months in the Latrobe County Hospital with a broken back and two broken ankles.

During the two months convalescence in the hospital Joe was frequently visited by one of the volunteer nurses named Genevieve Jones. Both became very close during this time and their relationship continued to develop after Joe was released from the hospital. Joe wanted to return to Latrobe next Memorial Day, not only to make another parachute jump, but to see this woman he was beginning to be quite fond of. It was during this return performance that Joe and Genevieve decided to become engaged. They were married November 24, 1927 and eventually had a daughter named Joyce, and a son by the name of Joseph, Jr.

Spot Landing Contests

During the middle 1920's spot landing contests had become in vogue, and whenever he had the time, Joe took part in these popular events. Joe almost always walked away with first prize. His skill with a parachute was uncanny and his consistent accuracy made him legendary. Jumping Jack possessed an uncanny relationship between his parachute and the ground. He unerringly sensed the right time to slip to the right or the left in order to land near the target. He did all this in the days when parachutes were considered unsteerable. At a time when most jumpers considered themselves lucky to land on the field, Joe consistently could land within twenty-five to fifty feet of the target. His reputation as a skilled artisan with a parachute put him in great demand throughout the United States.

Cleveland, Ohio, was the site of the 1929

Joe Crane, far right, with officials at the 1929 National Air Races, held in Cleveland, Ohio.

National Air Races. This ten day meet proved to be quite profitable for Jumping Jack. Not only did he win first prize of a large trophy and a merchandise certificate, but he collected $700 to line his pockets. During the pre-depression days Joe made a substantial amount of money from jumping. The combination of stunt jumping, exhibition parachutist, and spot landing champion, made Crane the foremost parachutist of his time. He was the man who could do anything with a parachute.

By the time 1930 rolled around, twenty-eight year old Joe Crane could look back upon a career in parachuting with a great deal of pride. He had risen from obscurity as a coal miner's son to become America's premier parachutist. He accumulated over 500 jumps — a staggering number in the days of early parachuting. He was practically a legend. Civilian aviation officials, military experts, and the public as well, all held Joe Crane in the highest esteem. His name and picture appeared in popular newspapers and magazines of the time. The World's Marvel Parachute Jumper made many newsreel jumps for Fox Movie Tone News, and was usually covered whenever he jumped. During the seven years since making his first jump, Crane had done everything; and he did it better than anybody else.

The story about most parachute jumpers could now come to an end. But Joe Crane was no ordinary parachutist, and his is no ordinary story. Even by contemporary standards, the tenure of most parachutists is usually brief. Modern jumpers often make four or five times the number of jumps Joe had already made at this time in life. And while their candle may burn brighter, it doesn't usually burn too long. By 1930 this legendary folk hero was just beginning to get into gear and his accomplishments just starting to unfold.

Like most mortals, time had a mellowing effect on Joe Crane. This dynamic parachutist matured, and in so doing, directed the course of his life in different and more challenging directions. His dedication and contributions to the field of parachuting would last over forty years. Joe was on intimate terms with parachuting and this relationship would become more intense over the years. He was in love with parachuting. This was a romance that could never be extinguished.

Joe was still a ruggedly independent sort of guy who never liked anybody telling him how to make parachute jumps. This basic characteristic made Crane a famous parachutist, and it was still intact. But over the years he gained some new perspectives about his role in parachuting. As he toured the country making jumps he came to know how most parachutists were treated by the public, and by the rest of the aviation community; all of which he thought was entirely too negative. He came to understand that parachuting was still in its infancy stage and continually needed to be developed, not only to make parachuting a safer and more reliable activity, but also to make individual parachutists more responsible for their actions. Joe's budding interest in promoting, developing, and advocating the sport of parachuting would demand more and more of his time as the years passed.

Roosevelt Field

Joe was a natural leader and a talented organizer. His voice and stature commanded respect from those who knew him. This asset, combined with his vast experience in parachuting, made him a natural to assume many leadership roles. In 1930 Joe had been offered a job as Chief Parachutist at Roosevelt Field on Long Island, New York. A good friend of his, Buddy Bushmeyer, Chief Parachutist on the field, had been killed making a demonstration jump. Joe was asked to take charge of operations on Roosevelt Field which had become a hub of aviation and parachuting activity on the east coast. Among other things, Roosevelt Field was the starting point for an epic

Joe Crane, Chief Parachutist at Roosevelt Field, preparing to make an exhibition cutaway jump.

journey made by another famous parachutist. On May 20, 1927, Charles A. Lindbergh departed from Roosevelt Field on his historic non-stop flight to Paris, France.

Roosevelt Field was a regular beat for many of the New York City reporters and newsmen of that time. He met and became personal friends with many of these famous media people. This already famous parachutist became the subject of even more publicity. As the result of his daily contacts with the news media, Crane became accutely aware that if parachuting was to progress, the public image had to be improved. He became convinced there should be more adequate rules and regulations to protect novice parachutists as well as help promote the safety aspects of parachuting.

While in charge of the parachuting activities at Roosevelt Field, Joe was responsible for having legislation passed that required the mandatory use of reserve parachutes. Although many jumpers at this time were wearing an extra parachute, many chose not to wear them — and many lives were lost needlessly. He also began advocating legislation to limit the wind velocity in which parachutists would be allowed to jump. From his own experience, Joe felt a 20 mph wind was the maximum velocity a jumper could safely land in.

National air races had become quite popular in aviation circles in the 1930's. The races attracted huge crowds, and the purses and prizes began to grow larger. Parachutists were usually invited to participate in spot landing contests. This feature helped attract even larger crowds. Joe attended the air races in 1929, 1931, and 1933.

The problem of the air races, at least from the parachutists standpoint, was the absence of supervision of the jumpers. The spot landing contests were usually hectic, poorly organized, and seldom run on schedule. Jumpers never knew when they were going to make a jump, and consequently had to be on call from early morning until sunset. This, of course, irritated most of the jumpers and made them feel like they were getting a bad deal.

In the fall of 1932, Roosevelt Field hosted a two day national air meet, and Joe was placed in charge of all parachuting activities. He made sure all parachutes were folded and packed by competent persons prior to making the jumps. For the first time all competitors had a spokesman who would stand up for their rights. The jumps were scheduled and made on time, and much of the rowdyism that was frequent at many of the air races was totally eliminated. Prior to this time, the National Aeronautics Association (NAA), which sanctioned all the large aviation events, could not see parachuting as an asset at these races. However, with the smooth running of the 1932 air races they became convinced that parachuting

Spud Manning [left], another well known parachutist with Joe Crane [New York 1933].

could be an excellent attraction and addition to the races. Crane's smooth running operation had helped alter their attitudes favorably.

National Parchute Jumpers Association

In the early days of parachuting, jumpers generally received little if any cooperation from, nor were they recognized, by the NAA or the Federation Aeronautique Internationale (FAI). The NAA issued sporting licenses to pilots, but jumpers were completely ignored. Until this time, however, there was not a national organization that could help jumpers bargain for status, nor was there a person considered a national spokesman. Early parachute jumpers had a wide streak of independence and this is still true today to some degree. Getting jumpers organized and agreeing to the same ideas is still a frustrating process. But when it comes to money, just about everybody will listen to ways to save it or make it.

Later in 1932, the Cleveland Air Races held a special parachute competition in conjunction with their air show. Each contestant was required to put up an entry fee. And if by chance the jumper was either late in registering, usually fifteen days prior to the meet, or if he did not appear for the meet, the fee would be forfeited. When and if he took part in the competition, and providing he was not late for registration, the fee was normally refunded.

At this particular air race, however, the organizers planned to keep all the entry fees. This caused quite a stir among the pilots and parachutists alike. They banded together and demanded the return of their fees. With attendance over 100,000 expected on each day of the races, jumpers and pilots could not see why their entry fee should not be returned. There was a substantial admission fee for the spectators, and the entry fees were really a small part of the total money received. For the first time parachutists banded together, and with the help and support of the pilots, demanded their entry fee be returned—or else there would be no air races! With their backs against the wall, race officials relented and returned all entry fees. This was the start of the first grass roots parachuting organization in the United States. The man in the middle, urging everybody to stick together for their own benefit, was none other than Joe Crane. As a result of this direct confrontation with race officials many parachutists came to realize the necessity of establishing a national organization for parachute jumpers. Shortly thereafter, Joe called a meeting and invited all professional jumpers he knew. There weren't many, probably less than ten, but together they formed the National Parachute Jumpers Association (NPJA), and Joe was elected secretary-treasurer of this new group. This early organization was mainly social and the dues were only $1.00 per year. NPJA did send out a monthly bulletin on jumping news.

An elementary beginning organization for jumpers had started. But as the years progressed and the membership increased, the influence of this organization was to become more substantial. NPJA was now the official spokesman for its member jumpers and was of benefit to anyone who made enough jumps to enter the field professionally. Although the membership in the early stages was only about 100, it was essentially a one man operation, and Joe Crane was the man running the show.

About this same time Joe was accorded a very special and significant honor. The NAA invited him to become part of a special committee on parachuting. It would be Joe's responsibility to formulate rules and regulations for the issuing of NAA licenses to parachutists. He had long been recognized as an expert in parachuting, and NAA was impressed not only with his credentials as a competitor, but the attention he paid to organizing meets, and especially his attitude about enforcing existing regulations. This new division set up by the NAA was called, "The Board of Parachute Experts." Joe was honored with the title of President of the Board.

It was obvious that parachuting was beginning to move in a positive direction. And with the help of NPJA, Joe Crane began to focus his energy into more public areas. Even though parachutes were accepted as scientifically reliable devices to save lives in the military, civilian parachuting was usually portrayed as a dangerous activity by the newspapers of the time. Over the years parachutists had developed much bad press, primarily because the more dangerous aspects of the sport were always highlighted in the barnstorming performances and exhibition jumps. Public attitudes, which of course initially could not tolerate or understand men wanting to fly in the air on a mechanical device, later began to accept airplanes as a safe and reliable mode of transportation. And while the public could generally understand that flying was somehow natural, and in man's best interest, they never could understand what motivated a man to jump out of an airplane when he didn't have to. In

Joe Crane and daughter Joyce, Mascot of the National Parachute Jumpers Association.

the years to come it would be the goal and responsibility of NPJA, largely spearheaded by the iron-willed dedication of Joe Crane, to educate the public and the media as well, that parachutists were professional and respectable members of the aviation community.

Los Angeles was the host of one of the national air races in 1933. Since Joe had won first and second place the previous four years, he was planning to attend the event to be held on July 1-4. Unfortunately, Crane did not receive the application until June 20, five days after the closing time for entries on June 15. Since he could not make the deadline for the Los Angeles meet, he decided to participate in an unsanctioned meet in Chicago. Two major air races had been scheduled for the same date, and the NAA was getting hot under the collar about it. The Chicago meet was labeled as a wildcat affair by the NAA. And though the Chicago race attracted many of the better jumpers and pilots, the NAA suspended the FAI licenses of all contestants in the wildcat Chicago meet. Later that year, over the Labor Day holiday, Chicago was once again the site of a major air event, the National Balloon Races. Crane's application for the jump contest was rejected because he earlier attended the unsanctioned meet. Joe was furious! He sent off a stinging letter to the NAA and asked them how they could suspend a license when none had ever been issued to a parachutist. He rationalized quite persuasively that since parachutists had never been required to have FAI licenses, the NAA had no jurisdication to penalize parachute jumpers.

He suggested that if the NAA wished to control parachute jumping, as they now did for pilots, perhaps issuing licenses to parachutists might not be a bad idea. He formally proposed the issuance of such licenses. But Joe concluded, until such action was taken by the NAA, they would have no legal basis to impose sanctions on jumpers. And until they did, the field would be wide open. With the backing of the NPJA, the NAA realized there was little they could do to stop Joe from entering the jump contest. He was advised to resubmit his application, which he did. As a result, he was the only person to attend the meet who had previously participated in the wildcat Chicago meet; except for another jumper who used an assumed name. Although affilation with the FAI and subsequent issuance of licenses would not become a reality until 1947, the NPJA had enough clout to prevent unnecessary harrassment from other aviation officials and organizations. The NAA began issuing annual sporting licenses in 1933 and thereby created respect for parachute jumpers.

Joe had it figured this way; unless jumpers got together to organize themselves and put their own house in order, no one was about to do it for them. If jumpers wanted status and respect in aviation circles, which all said they did, then it was imperative to organize and be counted. Because Joe had the guts to confront the NAA over his invalid suspension, he not only gained their respect, but started to develop a relationship that continues to the present time. Over the years, the NAA has become one of the closest allies and friends of the United States Parachute Association. During the 1930's, there were many problems that came to the attention of the newly formed NPJA. Working closely with the NAA and other aviation officials, Crane was instrumental in pushing through a variety of changes which had a direct impact on the jumping conditions of his fellow parachutists. Jumpers were put in charge of all parachuting activities at sanctioned meets. A wind limit of 20 mph at sanctioned meets was also established. In later years,

Joe Crane, first Secretary/Treasurer of the National Parachute Jumpers Association.

Watch JOE CRANE, stunt jumper, getting relief from a HEADACHE!

I ALWAYS GET MORE ALL-ROUND RELIEF WITH BROMO-SELTZER. IT EASES PAIN, STEADIES NERVES, SETTLES MY STOMACH, TOO

Bromo-Seltzer does more than simple pain relievers for ordinary headaches. It does all this for you:
1. RELIEVES PAIN—works quickly and pleasantly
2. STEADIES NERVES—eases the nervous strain
3. SETTLES STOMACH—relieves the "sick" feeling

For frequent or persistent headaches, see your doctor. For simple headaches, take Bromo-Seltzer, relied on by millions for over 50 years. Follow directions on label. At drugstores, soda fountains. Keep it at home.

this wind limit was reduced to 15 mph to lower the risk of injury to jumpers. Simple rules were established to govern the conduct of jumpers at these meets. And over the years parachute meets began to run more smoothly and the jumpers began conducting themselves in a more professional manner. All in all, the overall effect of such measures has been a definite asset in promoting parachuting as a safe and respected activity.

NPJA was the national spokesman for its member jumpers, and Joe Crane was its number one advocate. No matter what the situation, whether it was securing prize money, from dishonest or bankrupt promoters, or securing legal help for its members, Crane was always in the midst of negotations and discussions. On numerous occasions, NPJA had refused to perform, and often times struck, until their demands for safe and monetarily acceptable conditions were met.

At the 1937 Cleveland Air Races, the prize money for parachutists was considerably less than what was offered in previous years. With the advise and guidance of Joe Crane, NPJA parachutists formed a boycott until the purse money was raised to the previous level. It was evident to most member jumpers that in numbers there was indeed strength. And where one voice was lost in the shuffle, the voices of many commanded attention. It had taken many years of hard work, but finally, parachute jumpers had begun to settle comfortably into their own protected niche in aviation.

National Parachute Jumpers and Riggers, Inc.

With the advent of World War II appearing on the horizon, and the spectre of U.S. involvement in global warfare, parachuting activity in the United States increased dramatically. World War II was the first time U.S. Paratroopers were to be used to wage combat against enemy forces. And with the creation of the Army Parachute Troops, many men and women were indoctinated into paratrooper and rigger training. By this time Joe was no longer working at Roosevelt Field, but was maintaining a small parachute company at Mineola, New York. During the War, Joe Crane and Company came under substitute management while Joe participated in the war effort. During the course of the war, he became chief inspector for the Atlantic Parachute Company located in Lowell, Massachusetts. He later focused his energies as assistant to the vice president of Pioneer Parachute Company in Manchester, Connecticut, helping to manufacture and inspect parachutes for the war effort.

As part of his wartime efforts, Crane helped author a book on parachutes. With the help of Major General James E. Fechet, and Glenn H. Smith, a book titled, "Parachutes", was published by the National Aeronautics Council in New York City in 1942. The book, primarily an instruction manual for military and civilian riggers, was largely the work of Crane, who provided the technical background and experience for the book.

After World War II began winding down, Crane returned to Long Island to

During World War II, Crane served as Chief Inspector at the Atlantic Parachute Company.

resume management of Joe Crane and Company. However there was another problem which demanded the time of Crane. After the war, many of the newly trained paratroopers and riggers left the service, much as Crane had done in earlier years, with the desire to continue actively in their new field of learning and interest. The membership roles of NPJA increased to over 500 jumpers. Because many prospective members were military riggers who had usually made but one jump, the NPJA changed its organizational structure in 1947 to include these people. Riggers could now affiliate with a national organization and have their interests represented. The National Parachute Jumpers-Riggers, Inc. (NPJR) as it was now called, would help sponsor legislation in regard to the certification of riggers as well as the types of approved canopies they could pack.

1947 was also a landmark year for Joe and

his NPJR members. One of his long sought after goals was finally realized when NPJR was affiliated with the NAA; the official representative to the international body governing parachuting, the Federation Aeronautique Internationale (FAI). Shortly after this affiliation, the FAI issued the first U.S. parachute jumping license. Utilizing a system based on the number of jumps as a criteria, the FAI issued an "A" license for 10 jumps, "B" license for 20 jumps and a "C" license for 100 jumps. In an honorary tribute to his years of dedicated work for parachuting, Joe Crane was issued "C" license number one — the most prestigious license in parachuting.

Starting in 1948, the Leo Stevens Award was given to the individual or group, "who had made the most distinguished contribution to the saving of life in aerial navigation by perfecting the parachute or other means of bringing individuals or disabled aircraft in safety to the ground." This award also includes the training and developing the art and use of such means to save lives. The first recipient of this highly respected and prestigious aviation award was Joe Crane.

With NAA affiliation, NPJR began to achieve international status. Not merely content to sit back and rest on his laurels for his achievements on a local and national level, Crane continued his hectic involvement in parachuting at the international level. Having been named as the U.S. delegate to the FAI commission meeting formed in 1948, Crane worked closely with this organization to help work out the rules by which parachute records could be sponsored and established. Later on Crane would be instrumental in helping to establish rules for the first international competition. Thanks to the involvement of this statuesque gentleman, it was now possible to establish national and international world records, and in a wide variety of categories. This system continues to the present day with the United States holding the majority of the records.

After spending considerable time at the international level, Crane returned to the U.S. to focus his energies on a growing problem. After World War II wound down, there was an influx of ex-military jumpers making long free falls without proper body control. Most of these ex-paratroopers were making their first free fall jump a long one,

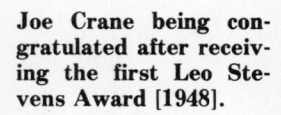

Joe Crane being congratulated after receiving the first Leo Stevens Award [1948].

and with surplus parachutes. There were a number of fatalities due to a lack of proper instruction and safe equipment. Most paratroopers had been trained to jump with a harness equipped only with a ripcord on the reserve pack. On many occasions they would deploy their reserve parachute instead of the main. In too many senseless incidents, the reserve chute broke loose from the harness and the jumper was subsequently killed without pulling the ripcord on his main parachute. Some negative publicity was being directed toward U.S. jumpers, and the Civil Aeronautics Administration (CAA) began issuing regulations banning free fall delays at any air meet. As you might expect, Crane became more than just a little upset. Joe felt that the CAA, later renamed the Federal Aviation Administration (FAA), was blowing hot and cold in regard to their regulation of parachuting. Years before he had worked successfully with the CAA's assistance, setting up basic safety regulations and guidelines that could have prevented most of these needless fatalities. Prior to this, the CAA had issued regulations making it mandatory that all parachutes be opened at 1500 feet, and further required the use of a floatation device if jumping over water. There was also a necessary requirement that parachutists wear two parachutes — so in the event that one failed, the reserve chute could be deployed independently of the main. However, many of these basic regulations Crane and NPJR had worked tirelessly to achieve were tossed out the window. When NPJA was incorporated in 1947, the CAA rewrote many of its parachuting regulations and deleted most of the basic rules. This was an obvious step backwards and one which Joe knew was detrimental to parachuting.

Crane contended all along it was the responsibility of the CAA to safeguard aviation interests. Since parachuting was now a full partner in aviation, Joe reasoned, it too should be properly regulated.

It seemed ironic to Crane that so much progress in regards to safety and regulation was being taken so seriously on an international level, only to return home to find attitudes of indifference on behalf of federal officials. In his usual quiet and dignified manner, Crane met with CAA officials and managed to persuade them that banning free fall jumps was not the solution to the problem; and certainly not in the best interests of parachuting. He frequently reminisced about his dealings with government regulatory bodies, and often commented how it felt like taking one step backward to go two steps forwards. But true to his nature, he seldom let minor setbacks deter him or lessen his determination to proceed with his life's work.

By 1950 the membership roles of NPJR

NATIONAL PARACHUTE JUMPERS-RIGGERS, INC.
MINEOLA, L. I., NEW YORK

THIS IS TO CERTIFY THAT

George Bosworth

IS A MEMBER OF
NATIONAL PARACHUTE JUMPERS-RIGGERS, INC.

1950

Joe Crane
PRESIDENT

SECRETARY-TREASURER

Joe Crane was also a charter member of this prestigious aviation club.

had dropped slightly, but parachuting in the United States was beginning to come of age. Thanks to the organizational efforts of Joe Crane, the U.S. was well represented at international levels, and voiced its concern through its affiliation with NAA. In 1951, the First World Parachuting Championships was held in Bled, Yugoslavia. Six countries competed, and although the U.S. did not participate, the international framework for competition and the establishment of basic safety regulations was in place.

After 1951, the NPJR began to receive invitations to participate at subsequent world championships. The Second World Championships was held in 1954 at St. Yans, France, with eight countries competing. Thus began the traditional precedent of conducting world championships on every even numbered year. Fred Mason, a Sergeant stationed with the Army in Europe, paid his own way and became the first U.S. entry in international competition. Mason, as the sole U.S. entry, finished a respectable twenty-first. United States parachuting made a small, but significant, advance in the field of international competition.

The Second World Championship was won by the Russians and they extended an invitation to other nations to attend the following championships to be held in August 1956 in Moscow. The FAI Commission on Parachuting held a meeting in Vienna that would start planning the details of the 1956 world meet. Due to a previous commitment, Crane was unable to attend this meeting. He sent as his representative a French-American named Raymond Young to vote and discuss on all important issues. Ray Young's report concerning U.S. participation at the international meeting brought concern to the members of NPJR. Many voiced their concern the U.S. did not have the personnel, nor the expenses, to field a team to the previous world meet; and all agreed the same thing should not be repeated. The NPJR voted to help select, train, and finance a complete U.S. parachute team to the world meet in 1956. In early 1956, tryouts for the U.S. Team were held at the Trenton-Robbins Airport, New Jersey, and a group of seven men were selected to represent the United States.

A young jumper on the 1956 team named Jacques Istel had been showing considerable enthusiasm for this budding sport. And through his own expense, and at the invitation of Joe Crane, paid his own way to the Second World Championships at St. Yans. During the course of the championships, Istel noticed many of the European countries were far better trained and equipped than anything he imagined. After leaving the competition, he vowed to do all he could to create interest in sport parachuting in the United States.

Istel later returned to France and arranged for a parachuting instructor at one of the local centers to educate him in free fall parachuting with body control. The French were leaders in this respect at that time; although as yet, no one in the U.S. or practically anywhere else in the world, had advanced to an appreciable degree. Though he made only eight to ten jumps of this nature while in France, Istel returned to the United States to begin training a group of competitors to enter the Moscow competition.

With Joe Crane attending to the details on the international scene, it was to be Istel who provided the spark for the formation and training of the 1956 U.S. Parachute Team. Istel would later figure prominently in the development of sport parachuting in the United States. One of his several major accomplishemnts in U.S. Sport Parachuting was the establishment of the first fulltime commercial parachuting center. Istel was also responsible for introducing the American parachutist to the design and use of steerable canopies.

Parachute Club Of America

Due to the combined efforts of Crane, Istel, and NPJR, the United States was not only able to train and equip the 1956 U.S. Parachute Team, but would be able to make them competitive enough to place sixth overall. All in all, it was a great showing for such a young and inexperienced team. The 1956 World Meet would provide an enormous boost for membership in NPJR. By now, Joe was President of NPJR and with the influx of new members, began to realize the necessity of restructuring the organization. In 1957, NPJR was reorganized into the Parachute Club of America (PCA). Once again Joe was at the leadership helm and was unanimously elected President of this new organization. He continued his willing and unselfish efforts on behalf of parachuting. Joe had as his priority the establishment of basic safety regulations and the implementation of an Area Safety Officer Program. All of which was carried through and contributed greatly to the growth and development of the new American aviation activity called Skydiving — Sport of the Space Age.

Joe Crane wearing his famous umbrella hat at the 1962 World Parachute Meet at Orange, Massachusetts.

Joe Crane remained President of the Parachute Club of America until 1963, when after forty years of involvement in parachuting, he finally retired. Though he formally retired from active organizational duties, he still remained the symbolic head of parachuting in the United States. He was accorded a tremendous honor by his fellow parachutists who loved and respected him, and was elected as Honorary Chairman of the Board for life. Though officially retired, Joe still maintained his own parachute loft in Long Island, New York. He continued a full time love of parachuting, coupled with a semi-active involvement in the business. On February 24, 1968, Joe Crane died of cancer. The long and distinguished career of parachuting's premier jumper had come to a peaceful end.

The Grand Old Gentleman of Parachuting was dead, but the legacy of his achievements will live as long as there are parachutes in our world. This dignified and quiet gentleman, who for over forty-five years skillfully guided the course of events in parachuting, left an indelible impression on everyone who knew him. Parachuting will probably never have another statuesque gentleman who so proudly contributed to the folklore of this exciting field. His accomplishments were legendary, and they began at the infancy of modern parachuting. Because of his vast involvement in parachuting, spanning over four decades, he is a folklorist's dream. The events he witnessed and participated in, and the tremendous changes he helped bring about, would probably fill a very large book.

During the 1920's, Crane was "Jumping Jack", the barnstorming stunt and exhibition jumper. During the 1930's, he was an expert competitive jumper as well as a national organizer and spokesman for all parachutists. During the 1940's, Joe directed his activities toward achieving national recognition and respect for all parachutists and for the field of parachuting. And during the 1950's, Joe Crane was an instrumental force in the new sport of Skydiving; helping it to achieve international stature and respect. Finally during the 60's, he continued to be actively involved in the administrative details of the Parachute Club of America. Joe Crane was a man who did it all during his lifetime.

The April 1968 issue of Parachutist Magazine, the official publication of the United States Parachute Association (USPA) and successor to PCA, NPJR, and NPJA, printed a brief story about the life and times of Joe Crane. The title of that article reflects probably the best summation of this number one legend in parachuting: "Record Maker, Steeplejack, and Renowned Parachutist." His memory lives on in those words.

On June 27, 1971, the Board of Directors of the United States Parachute Association established an annual award to recognize selfless and continuing contributions to the sport of parachuting; the USPA Achievement Award. It is the highest noncompetitive award any USPA member can receive. It was only fitting that Joe Crane be selected as the first recipient of this prestigious award. A letter to his wife, Jean, from the U.S. Board of Directors reads as follows:

"This award has just been established....and thus, Joe's selection as the first sport parachutist to be honored is of special significance — as a particular expression of affection and esteem for your husband's memory."
"We hope you are as proud of this recognition of Joe Crane's notable accomplishments as we, the Board of Directors are proud to make this award — for the first time in the history of our young sport — to honor Joe's conspicuous contributions to its development and growth."

During parachuting's formative years, circumstances dictated the need for a person with experience and vision to advocate its cause. It would be hard to imagine what direction parachuting could have taken and how our rights to free fall might have been restricted without his efforts. It is unlikely that parachuting will ever produce another giant of a man who so profoundly affected the course of events as did Joe Crane. His legacy is our right to skydive. If ever a man had earned a niche in the Parachuting Hall of Fame, there could be no doubt it would have to be Joe Crane, The Father of American Parachuting.

How Parachutes Are Packed or Stowed While Plane Is in Flight in Order Not to Hamper Movements of Flyers. The Lap Pack Is Used by Gunners and Observers, the Seat Pack Is Favored by Pilots. Note Design of Light and Strong Harness by Which Body Is Supported When Parachute Is Used.

Chapter 3

Parachutist Makes Good

All the world loves a hero. Born out of the need to glorify and immortalize their own kind, the whims of public sentiment often times loosely bestows this title on persons for actions great or trival. Frequently regarded as ideal models and worshipped as perfect persons, many heroes in fact, are burnished by Madison Avenue types, who promote the veneer and not the person. Small wonder a capricious public craves a constant replenishing of its fallen gods. Nothing causes the downfall of a hero faster than trodding back across the invisible line separating them from mortal humans.

Those crazy mixed-up years after the Great War, nostalgically remembered as the Roaring Twenties, was likely to enthrone the most unlikely of persons as a hero. Those who could dance longer, eat more goldfish, or run more bootleg liquor, were likely to win public favor. Transitory as public sentiment often was, it never-the-less helped provide pleasure and purpose in a world rebounding from the after effects of World War I.

If goldfish gulpers and gangsters captured the frantic imagination of a beguiled nation, then why couldn't an armada of parachutists and gypsy fliers do the same? The answer, of course, was they could! After World War I, thousands of ex-servicemen bought surplus Jennys and Standards to begin trying to win the hearts and pocketbooks of the American public. And without question they succeeded. No town was too small or any cow pasture too short for these roaming adventurers. If there was civilization, they reasoned, there must be a few loose bucks looking for a new home. And the barnstormers would risk all in an effort to win the favor of a public awe struck by their antics. The competition was keen and economic success depended on being able to out fly, out jump, and out hustle other touring daredevil aerial shows. Parachutists figured prominently in these rural aviation shows, adding that extra attraction by jumping squarely into the jaws of death. Because so many hayseeds and rednecks were terrified at the thought of jumping, it was the ultimate stunt any air show could offer.

The travelling air shows, complete with parachutists who regularly pulled low, performed multiple cutaway jumps, jumped for accuracy and altitude records, helped to build an image of daring and wrecklessness that endures to this date. Most parachutists are heros, if not by public acclamation, then by their own volition. While jumpers didn't particularly view their craft as any more dangerous than other forms of aviation, they capitalized on public ignorance to help build a reputation based on foolhardy carelessness. Public misunderstandings about parachuting helped contribute to the stories of jumpers as a folk hero. After all, most everybody figured, anyone crazy enough to leap from a perfectly good airplane must either be stupid or insane. Both of which are not precluded as heroic qualifications. It was the reputation, or the image, that attracted crowds to witness a daring parachute jump. The barnstorming air shows contributed greatly to preserving the daredevil image of parachutists.

From the ranks of these farm-hopping aerial performers arose aviation's foremost hero. He was a clean-cut, clean living teetotler, with more than an average puritanical upbringing. He had a basic simplicity that won the hearts of millions who were unconsciously searching for a genuine hero. Possessed with an engaging smile, keen mind, excellent athletic prowess and a distinct ability to remain cool in tight situations, Charles Augustus Lindbergh cut a swath through the skies that lasted over fifty years. As an aviation folk hero, Lindbergh had no equal. He was by far the most influential pilot of his time, and the effect he had upon civilian and military aviation was profound.

Lindbergh's epic solo crossing of the Atlantic Ocean in 1927 vaulted him into worldwide prominence. By this time he already had five years experience as a parachute jumper and gypsy pilot. During this wandering period, in search of himself and adventure, Lindbergh gained valuable experience in dealing with the harsh realities of the sky. But he also found other things that helped him mature and prepare for his role as the leading spokesman for a variety of causes. He found within himself a love of the lands he flew over and respect for those who came to watch him perform. He also found confidence in his abilities and learned to trust his feelings. In the sky, he learned how to make fast decisions; on the ground, he learned to take his time. For Charles Lindbergh, the future was in the skies, and he came to believe the future of mankind was also to be found there. His early parachuting and barnstorming days was a prelude, and perhaps a stepping stone that propelled him into the future. It was also a time of peaceful enjoyment, interspaced between exciting adventures and close encounters with death.

A Boy Named Slim

Slim was a natural nickname for a Minnesota farmboy who stood six foot three inches tall. A restless college student determined to avoid graduating into a job behind a desk, Lindbergh decided to parlay his long held interest in aviation into something tangible. Much to the dismay of his mother Evangeline, and the rest of his family as well, Charles broke tradition and headed West. It was a wise, but difficult decision for Slim to make. He travelled to Lincoln, Nebraska, where he enrolled in pilot training at a Nebraska aircraft factory. Arriving on the first of April, 1922, Lindbergh was looking forward to spending many happy hours as an apprentice mechanic and pilot. It was his intention to learn all he could about aeronautical theory, aircraft design, and airplane manufacturing and repairing.

During his stay at Lincoln, Lindbergh got tagged with his first nickname of Slim. Under the pensive eyes of Ray Page, president of the Lincoln Standard Aircraft Corporation, Slim became a favorite, if not a sometimes irritating work hand. His inquisitive nature sometimes got him into trouble while constantly nosing around every facet of the operation. Slim was full of rash ideas which often replused his senior and wiser workers. One time he suggested that he be allowed to ride his motorcycle underneath a low flying airplane while it towed a rope. His idea was to grab the rope and proceed to climb into the airplane cockpit. This crazy idea was vetoed. When asked what would happen to his motorcycle, Slim didn't have an answer.

Slim had given Ray Page $500 in advance to begin pilot instruction. For the money he was guaranteed a certain number of instruction hours with a qualified pilot. This was Slim's principle reason for travelling to Lincoln. As it turned out, the flight school was all but non-existent. The school consisted of himself as the lone student, one airplane, and one disgruntled instructor named Ira Biffle. Biff, as he was known, was always reluctant to take to the sky, students be damned. Several years before Biff had seen a good friend of his killed in a tragic plane crash. Since then his enthusiasm dwindled, and he didn't care much for flying. Slim was, of course, disappointed but still determined to get something for his money.

One of his first experiences after arriving in Lincoln, was an airplane ride by Otto Timm. Accompanied by a sixteen year old boy named Harlen "Bud" Gurney, both took to the skies for their first airplane ride. From this casual beginning, Bud and Slim would cement a friendship that lasted for some time. In between trying to squeeze out a few minutes of flight time with Biffle, Lindbergh kept himself busy by learning to become a mechanic. Working with Gurney, Slim learned how to lockstitch fabric, lap propeller hubs onto their shafts, pull maintenance on airplane engines, mend broken skids, and a thousand and one little things necessary to keep the Lincoln Standard Biplanes from meeting an early grave. Despite the contempt Ira Biffle had for flying, not much of it seemed to have worn off on Slim. He liked being in the air and enjoyed the thrills he associated with flying. He had a natural feel for flying and it didn't take long for him to develop an intimate relationship with an airplane.

But in May, after receiving only eight hours of dual instruction, Lindbergh unhappily learned the flying school was going to be closing down. Erold Bahl was a business minded pilot who was buying the school's only instruction plane to begin barnstorming throughout Nebraska. Very disappointed, and feeling he had not been given a fair shake for his money, Slim pondered his situation. And when Ira Biffle announced he was leaving the company as flight instructor for more saner activities Slim became more determined than ever to solo. But unless the current owner, Ray Page, agreed to allow him to solo before he sold the airplane to Bahl, it was unlikely he would ever get the chance to get off the ground. Everybody liked Lindbergh and had confidence in his ability to fly. But nobody was willing to chance letting him solo their airplane. Page agreed to let Slim solo his airplane, provided he could put up $500 as deposit against possible damage. Slim had as much chance of raising $500 as Biffle did regaining his confidence in flying. Slim was foiled every direction he tried to turn. All his savings had already been given to Page, and there wasn't any way he could dig up another chunk. Slim wasn't a pilot yet, and it was unlikely he would be so in the future.

Reluctantly, Slim began to accept the situation which kept him on the ground. But he was still determined to stay in aviation and began to look around for other ways to gain experience that might lead to flying. Erold Bahl was his answer. Bahl liked Slim and even felt a little guilty about his predicament, and after talking things over, agreed to take him on as a mechanic and helper on his forthcoming barnstorming trip.

Barnstorming Daredevil

Barnstorming was a term loosely applied to the most creative free enterprise activities in aviation. Any way that could be used to make money flying was often referred to as barnstorming. And often times this meant flying from town to town in search of a safe landing strip in some farmer's field, or in some back woods out-of-the-way place to set up a show. The basic service offered was hauling passengers for hire — usually five bucks a head. The low flying stunting, performed with wreckless abandon was great for attracting people out to where the show was located, but it didn't pay the bills. And the same was true for parachute jumps, but it was jumping and flying that helped keep the local yokels staying on the field. Without the income from flying passengers, there was little hope any barnstormer could earn his keep. Barnstorming wasn't the greatest business, but it was flying, and Lindbergh was fascinated with his part in it.

To help earn his way, enhance his aviation experiences, and gain the confidence of Bahl, Slim volunteered to become part of the stunting activities. He had already proved his usefulness on the tour by helping maintain the power plant and airframe of Bahl's airplane. Slim also carried fuel and promoted the show by canvassing the curious crowds for prospective passengers. Slim's enthusiasm didn't go unnoticed and Bahl realized what an asset he was. Not too much time passed before Slim began to get paid for his help and this made him an accepted member of the troupe. Lindbergh later volunteered to do some wing walking as they flew over the towns. Bahl accepted this idea, and although Slim had never wing walked before, was evidently good at it, because it became a regular part of the performance.

While on this barnstorming trip with Bahl, Lindbergh got tagged with another nickname. His new promotional name was "Daredevil" and it reflected the idea that he had no apprehension when it came to risking his life. Without serious thoughts as to the dangers involved, Lindbergh would gingerly climb from the cockpit of Bahl's biplane, stoop between the guidewires and wing struts, and make his way to an open area. There, Lindbergh would dangle by various means and perform a variety of chilling stunts. Daredevil Lindbergh, as he was soon billed on all the posters and tearsheets distributed for the shows, appeared calm and at ease during these performances. It almost seemed the chilling, dangerous activities were second nature to Daredevil. Later with more practice, Lindbergh perfected his wing walking act by standing on the mid-portion of the top wing, and braced for extra support, would thrill crowds as the airplane performed an inside loop. Daredevil took great pains to perfect his stunting activities and it made him a crowd favorite.

The Man Who Jumped

Lindbergh's daredevil inclinations drove him to seek out parachutes. After returning from his two week barnstorming tour with Erold Bahl, he proceeded to take a handyman's job at the airplane factory. This was in June, 1922, and he was aching for more aerial adventures. Charles W. Hardin and his wife, Kathryn, came to Lincoln on Sunday afternoon, June 18, for an aerial show. Hardin was a manufacturer of parachutes and was travelling from town to town demonstrating their uses. Hardin and his wife treated the local crowds to a display of their parachuting skills. Watching from the sidelines, Lindbergh took careful note of how the chutes were packed and how the parachute jumps were made. He was fascinated by parachute jumpers. Years later Lindbergh wrote,

"I watched him strap on his harness and helmet, climb into the cockpit and, minutes later, a black dot, fell off the wing 2,000 feet above our field. At almost the same instant, a white streak behind him flowered out into the delicate, wavering muslin of a parachute — a few gossamer yards grasping onto air and suspending below them, with invisible threads, a human life, a man who by stitches, cloth, and cord, had made himself a god of the sky for those immortal moments."

To make a parachute jump was a monumental task for Charles, and one that presented some psychological implications. Throughout his early childhood, Lindbergh had been plagued by nightmares of falling. And the thought of actually making a parachute jump was terrifying to him. In spite of such fears, Lindbergh was determined to meet this challenge. This trait of meeting an adversary head on was one that would serve him quite well in future years. Lindbergh recalls:

"A day or two later, when I decided that I too must pass through the experience of a parachute jump, life rose to a higher level, to a sort of exhilerated calmness. The thought of crawling out onto the wing, through a hurricane of winds, clinging onto struts and wires hundreds of feet above the earth, and then giving up even that tenuous hold of safety and of substance, left in me a feeling of anticipation mixed with dread, of confidence restrained by caution, of courage salted through with fear. How tightly should one hold onto life? How loosely give it reign? What gain was there for such a risk? I would have to pay in money for hurling my body into space. There would be no crowd to watch and applaud my landing. Nor was there any scientific objective to be gained. No, there was a deeper reason for wanting to jump, a desire I could not explain. It was the quality that lead me into aviation in the first place — it was a love of the air and sky and flying, the lure of adventure, the appreciation of beauty. It lay beyond the descriptive words of men — where immortality is touched through danger, where life meets death on equal plain; where man is more than man, an existance both supreme and valueless at the same instant."

Daredevil approached Harlin to make a jump — but it was no ordinary adventure! Hardin was flabbergasted when Lindbergh indicated he wanted to make a double jump!

"A double jump for your first parachute drop!" Hardin exclaimed. Showing a shy country grin, Lindbergh replied in the affirmitive. Slim slyly indicated he wanted the experience, and this just might be a good opportunity for him to buy one of Hardin's parachutes. Hardin didn't really take Lindbergh too seriously; how could he? But on the other hand he figured Slim just might end up buying a parachute, so Hardin gave in and decided to help this country boy make his first parachute jump. As things turned out, it almost proved to be his last!

Lindbergh grinned sheepishly trying to explain why he wanted to jump. Hardin was a veteran with over one hundred jumps and understood what Charles was at a loss to explain. As a balloon commander during World War I, and later a stunt flyer and aerial acrobat, he had been in many terrifying situations during his life. Hardin grinned back at Lindbergh in an understanding manner, and set about to pack and prepare the chutes for his first jump. After the parachute gear was assembled and attached to the lower wing of the biplane, Lindbergh climbed aboard to make his first jump.

The date was June 21 (the date is approx-

The Irving back and chest training parachute assemblies were used by many barnstormers.

proximate and is not officially recorded), and Lindbergh was filled with a cautious fear; a knot in his stomach belied his anticipation. Flying at 2,000 feet, the pilot slowly turned in on jump run over the field and motioned for Charles to climb out to where the parachutes were located. Slowly and methodically Lindbergh eased out to the end of the lower wing and began to snap on the parachutes. Shortly he was hanging beneath the biplane, preparing himself for the moment when his hand would yank him free. Grabbing the loose end of the bow knot, Lindbergh gave a hard yank, and dropped free of the airplane. His first chute blossomed quickly and arrested his fall. His fear was over now and Slim exalted in his performance. But once again, he prepared to face the same ordeal by parachute.

A quick slash from his knife cut the rope attaching the first chute to the second; speeding Charles back into freefall. This time the parachute failed to open smoothly and began to trail behind him. Unaware that his chute is not deploying as it should, Charles basked in the thrill of falling. Lindbergh innocently assumed that things were normal, although his chute had streamered! In time, at about 250 feet, the second chute cracked open, and he felt the reassuring tug on his leg straps and the crisp opening shock from the inflating canopy. A euphoric but dazed Lindbergh landed on the ground and immediately became mobbed by well wishers.

A double jump the first time, referred to as a cut-away, is a rare occurance in parachuting. Even the most famous and proficient of parachutists cannot claim such an honor. Lindbergh is one of the few to have successfully completed such a daring stunt. Ignorance is bliss might apply to Lindbergh in this instance, but there can be no doubt as to the impact his jump had on himself, and on others.

After landing, still unaware of how close he came to death, Lindbergh was rebuffed by Hardin. The culprit had been some lightweight breakcord used as a substitute for stronger but unavailable cord. The breakcord serves to hold the canopy and deployment bag until the lines play out, thereby allowing the silk canopy to inflate in an orderly sequence. The weaker cord broke prematurely and both lines and canopy fell from the bag in a clump fouling the deployment.

Slim didn't pay all that much attention to this close call. He made the jump, lived to tell about it, and felt good about himself. That night Lindbergh slept as solid a sleep as any in his life. He had overcome his gnawing fear of high places and of falling. For young Charles Lindbergh his first jump was filled with meaning. In the same manner a man often regards his first sexual experience, or love affair with great significance, Slim came to feel as though he had passed into manhood. Like the ancient traditions of "Rites de Passage", he later commented that he had "Obtained a level of daring which even few pilots could attain."

Slim performed the ultimate feat and daring by making a parachute jump. He passed quickly and confidently into manhood.

His double parachute jump also had a profound impact on his fellow workers at the factory. No longer was Lindbergh regarded as an apprentice, but had earned their respect, and was now regarded as a bonafide member of the barnstormers.

A parachute jump in those days was usually a solitary experience, and for Lindbergh, it provided an opportunity to loosen up a little. He began to feel a freedom and a relief from the confinement of his nerves. Intoxicated by his new confidence and freedom, his mental psyche allowed him to begin performing routinely what had normally been done with a good deal of apprehension. His early experiences with a parachute helped to develop an inner solitude. Thus Lindbergh found comfort and peace in the air, and it enabled him to hear more than his inner fears. For Slim, the sky was now a friend, and no longer an adversary.

Hardin was a man of considerable experience and Slim sought him as a mentor. He listened attentively, taking careful notes of his wisdom. Slim learned never to trust a parachute that is less than twenty two feet in diameter. Its too small for a big man like himself, and would land him with a jolt. Never use a parachute made of Pongee silk, Hardin warned. This type of silk was prone to generate an excess of static electricity which can stick the panels together during inflation. Slim learned other tricks of the trade from Hardin about landing: face into the wind, relax, and feet together. Steering the parachute was accomplished by pulling down one of the two front sets of shroud lines; right set, makes a right turn, left set, makes a left turn. If the wind was strong, Hardin showed Lindbergh how to undo the chest and leg straps, so he could land without being dragged. These and countless other tips about parachuting was passed on to the eager student. Lindbergh was a true daredevil professional now. Not only had he performed aviation's most hazardous and prestigious of stunts, but he now had the working knowledge of parachutes to give him added confidence.

One of the myths widely circulated in aviation is that Charles Lindbergh was a pilot first and a parachutist second. This is simply not true. Little attention is usually paid to his pre-Atlantic crossing activities, and this usually helps perpetuate this myth. Certainly his crossing the Atlantic overshadows what else he may have done up to that time. But history clearly records that Lindbergh was indeed a parachute jumper a year before becoming a pilot. It is the act of soloing an airplane which makes one a pilot. Slim had but eight hours of dual instruction before making his first jump. A person becomes a parachutist on the first jump. No one can help with the actual jump, nor with the landing, and this makes each parachutist the master of his own destiny. Little wonder most persons have feared parachuting over the years; it must be done alone, without assistance.

A Golden Opportunity

One of Lindbergh's foremost goals was to buy an airplane and start a career in flying, and he looked for ways to make this dream a reality. But due to finances being the way they were, it would be more than a year before Slim owned his first plane. In the meantime, an opportunity arose which he felt would contribute to the realization of his dreams.

Shortly after completing his first jump, Lindbergh teamed up with a man named H. J. "Cupid" Lynch. Lynch and another man named Rogers were planning a barnstorming trip. Slim asked to join them as a mechanic, stuntman, and gofer. Rogers was the owner and Lynch was the pilot. Both were glad to have young Lindbergh join forces and a strong bond of friendship developed between them. All three knew there wasn't a great deal of money to be made in barnstorming, probably enough to pay expenses, with a little left over for a few extras. Slim figured he might save some of the extra money to help pay for a plane at a later date. Besides, money wasn't the big factor that tempted men to barnstorming in those days. The prospect of some hot flying, a few thrills, and being your own boss meant much to these aviation nomads. Most looked forward to visiting strange places, having some fun, and gaining experience that might lead to a legitimate flying position. Lindbergh was no exception and he eagerly awaited the commencement of his next aviation adventure.

Just before leaving, Slim skillfully traded Page his unused hours of flight instruction and unpaid hours as a factory hand, for one of Hardin's parachutes and twenty five dollars cash. He left the following day to join Lynch and Rogers at Bird City, Nebraska. His heart was filled with an unspoken promise that things would turn out for the best.

During the hot summer months Lindbergh travelled with Lynch and Rogers. Those long, humid days were ideally suited to ply their trade in rural America. Weekends were the best time to set up a show, but even during the weekdays townfolk could be enticed to drop their work and come out to the nearest field to witness some barnstorming. The term is appropriate, because oftentimes a gypsy pilot would trade the local farmer and family a free ride for the use of his field, and an overnight stay in the barn. Attracting the paying customer, though not always easy, usually wasn't all that hard either. Many farmers, like most rural types weren't all that familiar with the advancements made in airplanes. A noisy, smoke belching airplane flying over their small town was a cause of excitement and wonder, and many would run out to see just what in the name of all thats good and holy was going on. Imagine a low flying Standard buzzing main street, scaring hell out of just about everybody, and there perched on the wing just like he knew what he was doing was usually one of the stunt men promoting the act by heaving out handbills and tearsheets. A few more passes over the town to wake up those still sleeping and the pilot would set the plane down in the most appealing pasture and wait to see if his aerial announcements had been successful. Usually the town folks hustled as fast as they could manage out to see what the excitment was all about. It was usually a race to see who could get first in line. Somehow the kids and dogs always managed to be the first on the scene; and the first ones to be captivated by the quick talking performers.

A quick deal was made with the farmer to use his field. Another deal got him a free meal and many pilots promised a free ride for the kid who wanted to lug five gallon buckets of fuel to feed the thirsty airplane. If the crowd was shy and unwilling to take rides, the barnstomers loosened them up a little with some precision flying, and of course, with some parachute jumping. An airplane ride was a big thrill and many gladly shelled out five bucks for the honor of a five to ten minute flight over their house. Some even paid extra if the pilot would loop the plane or do some other risky stunt. It was all part of the business and the barnstormers never quite knew what to expect until the crowds arrived. Sometimes, though not often, the local folks resented having the hell scared out of them and would run the barnstomers off. Normally the arrival of the barnstormers signaled the end of the day and the beginning of some good times. Daring pilots, reckless parachutists, and crazy stuntmen were a welcome relief from the drugery of farm routine.

Lindbergh was usually the nut riding the wings and heaving the handbills. Everywhere he traveled the handouts proclaimed that "Daredevil Lindbergh," wingwalker, parachute jumper, and daring stuntman would be thrilling the crowds. All the hullabaloo made about the show and his part in it was good experience for Slim, and he loved every minute of it. Sometimes, when flying between towns, Lynch let him man the controls of the standard. These times were few and far between; Lindbergh didn't seem to mind though. He was preoccupied with his "daring stuff" and other responsibilities he was given.

The typical barnstormer, clad in tightfitting breeches, leather flying jacket, and goggles cocked on the forehead of his oilstained face, cut a smart figure with the females who came out to watch them perform. Jumpers and pilots alike always kept a keen eye open for available women. Many a pretty head was turned by a flashing smile and pencil thin waxed mustache, and many a romance ignited, only to be left smouldering when the men left for another town.

There was another side to Charles Lindbergh, and one that was a marked contrast from the typical barnstormer image. Back then, barnstormers had quite a reputation for fast flying, dangerous stunts, hard drinking, and chronic womanizing. Slim may have appreciated fast flying, and dangerous stunts, but he had no use for booze or for women. He was a loner and not much of a social mixer. After the days activities were completed he would just as soon sleep under the wing of the plane, rather than go out carousing around with his fellow performers. Besides, what would he talk to a woman about, when all he knew was aviation and parachute jumping? Not many women in those days knew much of either. The puritanical attitudes he was raised by in rural Minnesota, and the undying love and affection he had for his mother Evangeline, often brought him into conflict. Any potental female he considered would result in a comparison with his mother. So deep were his maternal instincts no woman could be the equal of Evangeline for quite some time.

Despite his unusual tendency against partying, Lindbergh found time for other things. Among these was an appreciation of the land he flew over, and the people who lived and worked on it. He came to develop an abiding love the the American open spaces. Flying gave him new opportunities to see the golden wheat fields of Kansas, the lofty Rockies of Colorado, and the stark plateau beauty of Montana. This was an adventurous time as well as a time of personal searching for Lindbergh. The open spaces confined no one and it was just as well. His was an unsettled mind, unsure of just what the future held in store for him, but convinced that things would turn out well. Just like the hardworking dirt farmers who came to watch him, Lindbergh put his heart and soul into what he was doing because he believed he was doing something worthwhile.

When the flying season ended in October the trio found themselves in Billings, Montana. The cold and snow usually kept them on the ground more times than not, and when flying was indicated, few if any came to watch them. The frustrated Lindbergh had little choice but to sit and daydream for warmer weather. He was broke, groundbound, and restless; a wretched combination. Slim decided to wait the winter out in Minnesota.

The winter of 1922-23, the time of his 21st birthday, was spent in Minneapolis with his father, and occasionally, at his parents farm in Little Falls. Slim's father was a politican who felt flying was too dangerous an occupation for his son to be associated with. Attempts to interest his son in various business projects the two might enter as partners fell on deaf ears. Slim was dedicated to making flying his business and his father could little change that decision. Realizing the futility of his arguments, and the sincerity of his son's committment to aviation, Charles Sr. relented and backed off. He agreed his son should be his own boss: just as he was his own.

Just as Slim's committment to aviation was real; so was his fathers committment to help. Charles Sr. signed a note for nine hundred dollars so his son could borrow money from the Shakopee Bank. The winter rest was peaceful and profitable. Slim had the money to buy an airplane and this opened up still yet another new horizon.

Into The Wild Blue Yonder

From his experiences on the barnstorming circuit Charles knew he could purchase an airplane for a good price at Souther Field near Americus, Georgia. Many surplus Army training planes had been auctioned off in previous years for as little as fifty dollars. The surplus planes, called "Jenny's", were powered with a Curtis OX-5 engine that developed ninety horse power capacity. These underpowered lightweight planes were able to lift its passengers at a speed of sixty miles to an altitude of about 1,700 feet. A stiff headwind could cause serious problems. These JN-4D's were notorious for being barely able to clear the treetops with such problems, and on some occasions they didn't quite make it. In spite of these inherent difficulties, many post World War I pilots got their start flying these loveable little airplanes.

Slim wasn't at all detered by the shortcomings of the Jenny. With money in hand he travelled to Souther Field in April 1923, prepared to spend the whole chunk if necessary to realize his goal. He expected to pay about $250.00 for a surplus airplane. This was a disappointment because he had to spent $500.00. It was a sellers market, and surplus planes were starting to bring more on the open market. None-the-less, Slim was still pleased he was able to obtain an airplane that met his satisfaction. His surplus aircraft came equipped with a new engine, fresh coat of paint, an extra fuel tank and propellers. The extra tank was a benefit because it doubled his range of flight; but it also decreased his margin of safety.

To the folks at Souther Field, Slim appeared to be just another bush pilot. Little did they know he had never soloed an airplane. He neglected to inform these people of this fact, perhaps fearing that they would not sell to him. It probably wouldn't have mattered to anybody at Souther Field anyway, but by this time Lindbergh was so

"Lucky" Lindbergh with Walter Innes [center], and J.E. Schaefer in Wichita, Kansas.

confident of his ability to fly he was positive he would have no trouble learning. He soon found out the controls of the Jenny were sensitive to the touch. On his first attempt at a take off, Slim noticed the controls were very different from the Lincoln Standard he had flown before. As he taxied down the runway the sensitive Jenny flew itself into the air much to the surprise of Slim. And just as though the airplane had a mind of its own and had abruptly taken to the air, it also had its own idea about landing. The landing was frightening and occurred in a series of bumps and hops. It hardly resembeled a normal landing and Slim came within an eyelash of completely totalling his brand new companion. Lindbergh was embarressed and keenly aware his lack of pilot skills was obvious to the scrutiny of many onlookers at the field.

Sheepishly he taxied back to the hanger and was fortunate to be introduced to a man named Henderson who offered to help him become better aquainted with his airplane. This good samaritan accompanied Slim on several takeoffs and landings, and encouraged Lindbergh to continue flying to gain more practice. Henderson suggested that the best time to solo was in the evening hours when the air is thick and calm.

Later that same evening Charles Lindbergh became a genuine pilot. With the field deserted, except for an old black man who watched him takeoff, Lindbergh soloed his airplane uneventfully. After landing he was complimented by the old black gentleman who commented his flying was beautiful and praised him for his skills as a pilot. Charles grinned at the absurd compliment, but was still gratified to have gotten the task behind him. Slim now felt he was a complete barnstormer. As a pilot, parachute jumper, stuntman, mechanic, and entrepreneuer skilled in coaxing money from hayseed farmers, he was ready for adventure and anxious to get on with his dreams. Opportunities were waiting just the next cornfield over and he was itching to make some money. And into the wild blue yonder he flew.

Barnstorming's newest flyer was a restless birdman who didn't figure to nest in any one place too long. With less than five hours of solo time Lindbergh left on his first tour. Slim was entering a new phase of his life and one that was fraught with more danger and close escapes than he would ever imagine. His first stop was Meridian, Mississippi, and his very first paying passenger almost proved to be a disaster. Lindbergh clearly had no understanding of how to estimate the performance capability of his biplane because he hopped a passenger who was grossly overweight. Using the entire length of the runway the plane was barely able to break ground, and just narrowly escaped crashing into a fence, some trees, and a hilltop. During the brief flight he could only manage to gain 200 feet of altitude. The fat passenger wasn't bothered, and probably wasn't aware of the precarious situation. After returning the passenger to the ground, Lindbergh was complimented for his expert low flying ability.

Slim was lucky his inexperience carried him through, but this was the least of his dramatic experiences. During the next two months Lindbergh earned another nickname which reflected an acurate description of the experiences he was undergoing. His name was "Lucky", earned by surviving five separate airplane crashes while on his first solitary barnstorming tour.

The day following his harrowing passenger ride at Meridian, Lindbergh set out for a small town about a hundred and twenty five miles due west. His plane wasn't equipped with navagation instruments and Lucky got lost and ended up in a northly direction. An approaching storm caught him off guard and Lucky was forced to sit down in the nearest field he could find. Landing on a soft, lush green field, the wheels caught the edge of a hidden ditch nosing the plane over, shattering the propeller. He was fortunate the airplane wasn't severely damaged and the engine destroyed. Lucky wired Souther Field for one of his spare propellers and took off again several days after it had arrived.

Flying into the flat lands of Kansas, Lindbergh headed for the small town of Alma. Upon landing the left wing of his Jenny snagged a huge boulder hidden by the tall grass, causing the plane to ground loop, and rip a huge gash in the fabric. After a few repairs his plane was once again airworthy.

Several weeks later, while heading into Minnesota, he was unable to make a landing at the Shakopee Airfield near his hometown. Bad weather forced him around Shakopee so he flew toward the town of Savage. A heavy rain storm caused three engine cylinders to stop firing and again he was forced to land in a sloppy, raincovered field. His wheels caught in the soft mud causing the plane to flip completely over. Lindbergh was left hanging upside down suspended by his seatbelt. He had the common sense to carefully loosen his seatbelt which prevented him from falling to the ground on his head. He was grateful to be in one piece considering this crash could have been much worse. The only real damage encountered this time was a splintered prop and a broken spreader bar, both easily repaired. Once again he wired Americus, Georgia for the second of the two propellers which he purchased for the plane.

A new prop arrived in a few days and was fitted on the engine shaft. The spreader bar was mended and Lucky was ready to push into the sky. This time he reached his hometown and volunteered to fly his Dad around on a political campaign prior to election day. The tour with his father didn't last long. Within twenty four hours the engine failed and both crashed at Glencoe. Charles Sr. suffered a broken nose and shattered his eye glasses when his head struck the instrument panel on landing. Lucky escaped unscathed from his fourth mishap. Wisely his father continued to stump the campaign trail by automobile, while Lucky hopped passengers in his plane at the political rallies. After the crash, Charles Sr. insisted his son's plane had been tampered with. But such politicizing was to no avail since he lost the election.

The run of bad luck was not yet over for "Lucky" Lindbergh; he had one more notable crash. An emergency landing in a small pasture near Campwood, Texas, forced him to attempt a takeoff from the main street in this town. His Jenny measured forty feet from wingtip to wingtip. His task was to fly between two long rows of telephone poles which were only forty-six feet apart. This was a tricky situation that would tax even the most accomplished pilot. Lucky was almost up to the occasion. About midway of the takeoff one wingtip snagged a pole and the plane ground looped. Plane and pilot came to its final resting place after crashing through the wall of the local hardware store. Lindbergh offered to pay the owner for his damage but the proprieter said no, insisting the publicity was good for business.

The name "Lucky" bestowed upon him by everybody, was an appropiate name, not only because he was never seriously injured, but because somehow the Jenny was always able to fly again with but minor repairs. Most gypsy pilots were not as fortunate as Lindbergh. He had survived his own incompetence, ineptitude, and inexperience. But it was an invaluable experience, and in later years his training as a barnstormer would come in very handy. This was true of many famous avaitors who gained their early training with experiences similar to Lindbergh. Flying the rural, less populated, outlands taught men how to survive by their wits and to fly by feel. Gypsy flying was probably the best training ground of its time for young plane struck pilots. It helped Lindbergh mature and become a seasoned pilot.

Charles Lindbergh and fellow barnstormer Al Williams.

A Chance Encounter

On an impulse, Lucky flew to Lambert Field, St. Louis, in October 1923, to visit the site of the International Air Races. While attending the air races he came into contact with a variety of modern airplanes and met many sophisticated looking pilots. Compared to the rest of the "Aces", Lindbergh looked like a hayseed. He suffered many rebuffs from his fellow pilots, but this was insignificant and trifling compared to the new knowledge he was gaining. He saw new types of airplanes on display at Lambert Field as he walked around for hours upon hours examining every one in detail. Everything was so new and different from anything he had ever imagined; he regretted not having visited the Air Races sooner. Lucky was absorbed with what he saw and heard, and tried to commit as much as possible to memory.

Bud Gurney, an old friend of his during his early days at the Lincoln Aircraft Factory, was also in attendence at the airshow. Gurney was now an itinerant parachute jumper who worked county fairs hoping to save enough money to buy an airplane. The reunion of this friendship had a particular significance for Lindbergh.

Through this acquaintance with Gurney, Slim was introduced to a man named Marvin Northrop. Marvin owned a small manufacturing plant near St. Louis and immediately took a liking for young Lindbergh. There was something about Slim that made him stand out among the sophisticated and fancy dressed pilots at this aviation gathering. Slim's Jenny was dust covered and patched so much it looked out of place next to the clean, sleek airplanes on display. The entire plane gave the appearance of having fought its way through World War I. Lindbergh didn't look much better. His rumpled clothes, dusty breeches, and disheveled appearance presented anything but a polished appearance. Small wonder he stood out among the smartly dressed and fashionly attired airmen. Lindbergh played the part of the carefree gypsy pilot who was generally frowned upon by many who viewed this part of aviation with distaste. This didn't bother Slim though, for he was used to the division that existed between the so called professionals and the bastards of the airways. He was more interested in the planes and looking for ways to make a few bucks.

Marvin Northrop didn't seem to mind Slim's appearance, nor was he repulsed by his lack of professionalism. He struck up a conversation with Lindbergh because he looked so lonely. Slim was evidently eager for companionship because he took a liking for Northrop and immediately began relating all of his barnstorming experiences to him. He told of his plans to become a professional airline pilot, and his need to find that right flying job. Northrop listened closely and their friendship, though brief, was filled with mutual respect. Northrop recommended that Slim should sign up as an Army Air Cadet.

Having gone through the rigorous training as a cadet, Northrop realized Lindbergh could benefit from the regimented discipline offered by the Army Air Service. His experience in barnstorming would be an obvious asset, but he could expand his abilities much more with proper guidance. Northrop reminded Lindbergh he didn't have to make a career of the army but could use that time for extensive training that was generally unavailable to most aspiring pilots. The flying Army was filled with great adventures and he would have opportunities later he would not regret. Northrop noticed Slim was a loner and felt he could also benefit from the companionship he would have to live with in the service. It was an astute observation and a wise suggestion. Solo barnstorming was not a financially rewarding occupation and was also one that held few rewards. It was a time for Charles Lindbergh to come in from the sticks and rejoin the human race.

Slim was sold on the idea and quickly realized the obvious benefits. That same night he wrote to Washington, D.C. for application papers. He became enthused about the first class training he would receive. No longer would he have to be flying underpowered and junky planes like the Jennys and Standards. Northrop filled him with visions of manning controls of modern Army aircraft like De Havilands that were rated at 400 horsepower. During their talks, Northrop convinced Lindbergh aviation was going to be big business in the future, though several years off. Anyone who wanted to get on the ground floor could use the technical experience the Army was offering. Lucky realized he could learn more in several months of cadet training than he could in years of gypsy flying.

Several weeks later the application papers arrived which he quickly filled out and returned. He was subsequently authorized to report in January, 1924, to Chanute Field, Rantoul, Illinois for testing. After reporting to the examination board, and having passed his entrance exams, he was told to report to Brooks Field, Texas on March 15, 1924 to commence cadet training.

Charles wanted to have one last fling before reporting to the army in March. His was still a restless soul, and though he was eager for induction, he realized the change would mark a major shift in his carefree lifestyle. He wanted to feel the freedom he treasured one more time. In the early winter months of 1924 Slim headed south for warmer climate, accompanied by a St. Louis automobile salesman named Leon Klink. It was on this tour through Mississippi, Kentucky, Tennessee, Alabama, Louisiana and Texas that he flew for the last time as a free and unrestrained spirit. It was also the period of time when he crashed his plane for the fourth and fifth times. After his fifth smashup, near Pumpville, Texas, time was running out. It was close to March, and shortly he must report to Brooks Field. He and Klink parted company and three days later he landed his battered Canuck biplane at Brooks Field. Lindbergh was right when he figured the Army would have a profound effect on him as well as altering the course of his life.

Resigned that his rural oddesey was over, Charles Lindbergh reluctantly turned in his freedom as a gypsy pilot for the smartly tailored uniform of the Air Cadet. During the year or so after leaving Americus, Georgia, Lindbergh lived the impossible dream. He had many great adventures while barnstorming rural America, as well as many dangerous close calls. But he was a better man for it. His years as a barnstormer was fun, but hardly profitable. The $900.00 borrowed from his dad would remain outstanding for several more years. The meager profits made on tour during this time enabled him to repay only $50.00 of this debt. He never earned enough money from flying, parachute jumping, or wing walking to do anything other than meet expenses. Barnstorming was mostly a glorious adventure that paid little.

Cadet Lindbergh

Slim responded eagerly to the discipline and regimentation of army life. By the time he arrived at Brooks Field he had logged over 300 hours of flying time. On his first day as an army cadet he was allowed to solo the familiar JN-4D's which he knew so well. The 90 horsepower OX-5 engine had been replaced with a more powerful 150 horsepower Hispano-Suizas engine. The added horsepower only served to compliment his skill as he breezed through the basic maneuvers with ease. His instructors had little doubt he would be able to pass the flying end of his training as a cadet.

Lindbergh's considerable experience and expertise gained while he was a gypsy flyer was to prove an invaluable asset during his course at Brooks Field. He advanced to more complicated maneuvers. He learned to do all sorts of new flying he never thought about while barnstorming. Slim became proficient in formation flying, high altitude maneuvers, straffing, bombing, and of course gunnery. When it came time to learn about precision landings and takeoffs he had no trouble what-so-ever. His gypsy flying days taught him how to set down an airplane practically anywhere, and to fly from places thought impossible.

But flying was only part of the indoctrination he was expected to learn. Studying was not one of his greatest loves, but he wisely decided to make an exception in his own best interest. If he wanted to be a proficient military pilot it would be necessary for him to have a complete understanding of aeronautical theory. And this meant keeping his nose in the books at every opportunity. Methodically he attended all the classes and lectures, and read all the materials he could find to make him a better cadet. Property accounting, field service regulations, radio theory, and military law, were all new subjects for Lindbergh; but he proved adept at learning these ground school courses. He passed his written and oral tests with flying colors. Of the 104 cadets reporting for training at Brooks Field on March 1924, only 18 graduated to receive their wings in March 1925. Lindbergh graduated at the top of his class, due in no small part to his vast flying skill, and in his determination to succeed.

King Of The Caterpillars

Just nine days before graduating from cadet training at Kelly Field, Texas, Slim had occasion to write himself into the aviation history books. It was also a step toward yet another interesting nickname. In a period of just under two years he would be making four emergency parachute jumps from disabled airplanes. And so doing would qualify as a four time member of the

COLONEL CHARLES A.
LINDBERGH buckling on
his Parachute Harness
(Courtesy Irving Air Chute Company)

[INSET] LINDBERGH as a graduate flying cadet

prestigious Caterpillar Club; aviations most exclusive fraternity. There was only one way to earn membership into this elite club and that was by escaping from a disabled airplane and saving your life by the use of a parachute.

The first of his record setting emergency jumps happened on March 6, 1925. Lindbergh was flying in a nine ship formation of SE-5s at an altitude of 5,000 feet. During a practice strafing run, he began attacking a DH-4B pursuit, flown by Lieutenant C.D. McAllister. The ships collided and locked together in an approximate parallel position. The right wing on Lindbergh's plane was damaged and started folding back slightly. The seriousness of the situation was apparent to Slim and he wasted little time unfastening his seat belt preparing to jump. With little hesitation, he jumped backwards as far as he could from the ship, freefell several hundred feet, and yanked the ripcord. His parachute functioned perfectly, and while gliding back to earth, saw Lieutenant McAllister following his lead. Both landed unhurt in a plowed field below.

Thus Lindbergh became a "Caterpillar" after receiving his baptism in an emergency situation. Men and women who have saved their lives from emergency parachute jumps receive a small gold pin in the shape of a caterpillar. The eyes of the caterpillar were made of rubies. This club derived its name "Caterpillar" from the fact that early parachutes were made of silk. The caterpillar represented the silk spun by the small insects which produced the lifesaving silk used in the manufacturing of parachutes. Upon confirmation of his emergency bailout, Lindbergh was awarded caterpillar number 17 (McAllister was awarded number 16). Lindbergh's jump was historic because he and McAllister were the first persons ever to escape alive from a mid-air collision of airplanes. His experiences as a barnstorming parachute jumper undoubtedly contributed to his faith in parachutes. After graduating from Army Cadet School on March 15, 1925, Lindbergh joined the Robertson Aircraft Corporation in St. Louis as chief pilot. This was an interim job for Charles while he waited the results of some

The crash of cadets, Lindbergh and McAllister, both flying SE-5's, at Kelly Field, Texas, on March 6, 1925. Lindbergh became caterpillar #17, McAllister #16.

bids he submitted to carry the U.S. mail. Pending that decision he was induced to test a new commercial airplane.

While putting the newly designed plane through its paces on June 2, 1925, the aircraft stalled during tailspin maneuvers. Raging out of control, the ship dived toward the ground at a hellish speed. According to witnesses on the field at the time, pilot and plane parted company at about 250 feet; barely enough time for the chute to open. It did, and Lindbergh survived another emergency escape. He was now a two time member of the Caterpillar Club.

The Robertson Aircraft Corporation won a contract to start the early mail run deliveries from St. Louis to Chicago in 1926. This service was inaugurated on April 15, and two shifts were put into service to handle the deliveries. Lindbergh was in charge of these shifts.

Later that year, on September 16, Slim had occasion to crack open his chute in another emergency situation. Leaving Peoria about 6:00 p.m. he soon flew into darkness. Fog rolled in a short time later forcing him to fly a few miles northeast of Marseilles over the Illinois river. The black fog permeated the entire region and when he attempted to return home he was unable to see the ground lights of the airfield; even after dropping a bright signal flare. He continued to fly for several hours in an effort to drain the petrol from his fuel tanks. With tanks running dry he switched to his reserve tank and reckoned he had about 20 minutes of flying time left. He had been flying for over 2 hours in the dark murky fog and hadn't once spotted any openings he could descend through. Climbing to about 5,000 feet Slim knew he was running out of time, and patiently waited for the engine to start sputtering and croak: which it did. Once again, for the third time, he stepped out the right side of his ship, fell a short distance in total darkness, and opened his parachute. Minutes later Lindbergh landed safely in a cornfield and became a "Caterpillar of the third degree."

Flying north from St. Louis on November 3, that same year, Charles earned his fourth degree rating in the Caterpillar Club. Circumstances were similar in many respects to his third emergency bailout. Flying alone at night was treacherous in itself, but the added complications of ground haze and a thick fog were a combination of factors difficult for Slim to overcome. At 8:10 p.m. his reserve tank ran dry at 14,000 feet. Waiting until he lost some altitude, Lindbergh again hopped over the right side and fell into pitch blackness. This time he landed directly on top of a barbed wire fence but was protected from injury by the heavy flying suit he was wearing. He landed near the small town of Covell, Illinois, and subsequently called St. Louis to inform his bosses of his latest mishap. Within the space of two years, Charles Lindbergh made four emergency descents by parachute. This earned him the distinctive name of "King Of The Caterpillars," which at the time was a record. Several had earned their pins with two emergency drops, and one had recorded three bailouts; but none had ever used a parachute for emergency purposes four times. Whenever he was in company with other caterpillars it was not unusual for him to be referred to as the "Caterpillar Ace" or "Boss Caterpillar." It would not be until World War II, when an obscure English pilot reportedly escaped from seven wrecked airplanes, that Lindbergh's record would be broken.

During his jumping and flying career, which by now had been close to five years, Charles A. Lindbergh was known by a variety of nicknames. Each moniker was a story in itself, and helped reflect many of the experiences and adventures of which he was a part. His most enduring and practical nickname was Slim which he carried with him for most of his life. Known as Daredevil Lindbergh, attributed to his parachute jumping and wing walking skills, the name didn't last long, but he seemed to enjoy it. On his solo barnstorming tours he survived six mishaps and earned the rightful name "Lucky." Lucky might have also been a good choice for a nickname to describe his four emergency parachute jumps, but the title "King of The Caterpillars" is more appropriate and telling.

The Lone Eagle

But for all his activity while jumping and flying during his five year aviation career, Lindbergh was still a relatively unknown pilot and personality. Not that he tried to be anything more than he was already. Slim was by nature a shy, quiet type of guy who generally shunned publicity, and wasn't keen on mingling and on rubbing elbows with his fellow pilots. All this was abruptly to change on May 20-21, 1927, when he became the first person to fly solo across the Atlantic Ocean. This feat also earned him the most prestigious and famous of all his nicknames he would carry with him throughout his life — "The Lone Eagle."

His solo flight had its simple beginnings on September 16, 1926. This was the day of his third emergency jump when he decided to take a short break by going to watch a movie. The movie entitled "What Price Glory", wasn't that great, but one of the newsreels shown before the main attraction got him all fired up. One of the news clips relayed a story that detailed a three engine biplane being built on Long Island, N.Y. by an aviation manufacturer named Igor Sikorsky. The plane was being built with the intended purpose of carrying a crew of four over the Atlantic Ocean to Europe. As Lindbergh soon found out, the airship would be piloted by the famous French ace, Captain Rene Fonck. This tiny mannequin of a pilot stood no more than 5'2" tall: but he was recognized world wide as an excellent and capable aviator. He and Sikorsky had collaborated on the design and construction together which would compete for the famous Orteig Prize.

Raymond Orteig, a wealthy Frenchman, had offered $25,000 to any flier or group of fliers who would be the first to cross the Atlantic Ocean by airplane. The offer was originally made in 1919, but as of this date there had been plenty of persons who attempted the flight; but none came close to succeeding. Interest was revived when the original five year deadline was extended. Some eight years later there was a scurry of activity by various pilots and manufacturers to collect the huge fee and assume the prestigious title that went with it. Airplane technology had made great strides in recent years and Lindbergh speculated there was no reason it couldn't be done. After leaving the movie, Lindbergh had visions of making the crossing himself. From that point onward he was obsessed with the idea of being the first person to cross the Atlantic via airplane.

This project assumed an immediate priority and Lindbergh set out to realize his goal. He talked to a group of friends in St. Louis and persuaded them to be the financial backers for his flight. Normally not a gregarious person, Slim made a point of always being available to talk with persons who might help him with his project. He stressed the urgency of the project, explaining they were involved in a race for time, and many others were trying to accomplish the same goal. With the help of his St. Louis backers, he contracted with the Ryan Aeronautical Corporation in San Diego to build a single engine monoplane capable of carrying him across one of the world's biggest ponds.

Plans were designed according to Lindbergh's specific requirements, and built with exacting worksmanship. The airship was completed on schedule and Slim flew it from San Diego on May 10, 1927 to Lambert Field. Christened "The Spirit of St. Louis," the sleek silver monoplane was the envy of all who came to look it over. Most speculated Lindbergh had rocks in his head for wanting to attempt such a flight, but their negative comments fell on deaf ears. Several days

Charles A. Lindbergh, The Lone Eagle, with the Spirit of St. Louis.

later Lindbergh left St. Louis and after a seven hour flight arrived at Curtis Field, Mineola, Long Island, New York. Scurrying to beat the competition, Slim broke ground from Roosevelt Field, Long Island at 7:54 Eastern Daylight Time on May 20, 1927. The dreams and hopes of America flew with The Lone Eagle and the Spirit of St. Louis. His flight across the Atlantic took 31 hours and was a classic epic of one man fighting the elements. He was determined to succeed and the closer he flew the more dedicated he became to achieving the impossible. At 10:24 p.m. European Time, The Lone Eagle landed at Le Bourget Airport in Paris, France. The modest hometown kid from Little Falls, Minnesota, had caught the world's attention with his record making flight. He immediately became an international hero of spectacular proportions. He was to become the most celebrated hero ever to grace a ticker tape parade. After his perilous journey he immediately was thrust into the limelight and was the toast of all the nations he traveled to.

No longer was Slim Lindbergh ever to worry about publicity, or for that matter finances. Upon returning home from his triumphant flight he was flooded with over five million dollars in promotional offers. Later, the U.S. Congress voted him the Medal Of Honor to be presented by President Calvin Coolidge. This was the first time that medal had ever been awarded for a feat unconnected with war.

The nation finally had a genuine hero. Clean cut, quiet, conservative, Lindbergh represented the American dream of rags to riches. The American Press had a field day reporting his every activity while the American public was high on the perfume of heroic worship. It would be hard to imagine a more common household name than that of Charles Lindbergh and his famous nickname, "The Lone Eagle." He was immortalized by the world who felt sure he was capable of walking on water; so great was his impact on the lives of everyone. As far as the American public was concerned Lindbergh stepped out of nowhere to make his famous transatlantic crossing. But they were soon to find out this was no ordinary hayseed who just hopped off the pumpkin wagon from Minnesota. Lindbergh was the number one media event for 1927, and in subsequent years would remain on the front page of the newspapers. Everyone demanded to see their hero for every occasion and celebration, great and small.

The purpose of this chapter is meant to chronicle the events leading up to his crossing the Atlantic. His early training as a parachute jumper and gypsy pilot prepared him to step from the backwoods to the front pages. His popularity would fluctuate over the years and on many occasions he participated in sensational news events that rivaled his Atlantic crossing. His first son, Charles Jr. was kidnapped in March 1932. The sensationalism surrounding this event, and the investigation and subsequent capture of Bruno Richard Hauppman, followed by his eventual execution, continued to plague Slim and his family for many years.

The World War II years witnessed Lindbergh stepping into the political arena and on numerous occasions saw him clash with the administration of Franklin Delano Roosevelt. His pro-Nazi stance of World War II eventually made him quite unpopular as he tried desperately to prevent the United States from joining in a war he considered both immoral and unnecessary. While his non-involvement preachings went against public opinion, it didn't lessen his popularity as America's number one aviation folk hero. However, he was forced to resign his officers commission as a pilot because of his dissagreements with the FDR Administration.

The recollections of those who knew him before his pre-Atlantic crossing days tell us there could be little doubt they felt something was very different about him. Charles had a distinct personality pattern, quiet and pure, as if he was waiting for greatness to beckon him. His tall thinly stature, unassuming, mature, as well as his propensity to avoid crowds and socialize, all left a memorable impression with those who recalled him in later years. His skill as a daredevil stuntman, parachute jumper, and gypsy pilot are all recalled with fond memories during the time he was maturing and preparing himself for his public role as aviation's number one spokesman.

Few, if any, parachute jumpers, and few pilots for that matter, have ever attained the success and fame that was Lindbergh's. From his humble beginnings as a barnstorming parachute jumper, to the worlds number one aviation folk hero seems like a long trip. But for Slim it was a matter of five years. But most feel, as did Lindbergh himself, that his early training and experiences as a parachute jumper paid great rewards. Bred into him was an instinct for survival and the capacity to handle himself in situations that demanded cool and icy nerves. Within the community of men and women who parachute for fun and profit, Lindbergh is the number one folk hero. All jumpers can look back upon his career as the parachutist who made good.

Commemorative medallion struck to honor the voyage of "The Lone Eagle."

LE TOUR DE BELGIQUE EN AÉROPLANE

Organisé du 6 au 15 Août 1911
PAR L'AÉRO CLUB DE BELGIQUE
SOUS LE HAUT PATRONAGE DE S.M. LE ROI

Chapter 4

Progeny Of Icarus

According to Greek mythology, Daedalus, father of Icarus, spoke to his son, "Is it possible? Can we do this?"

Icarus replied, "Birds have them, therefore they have been made."

"But is it really possible, can man fly?" Daedalus questioned.

Icarus goaded his father, "You have made many things in your life that you have never seen before. And anything you have seen, you can duplicate."

Daedalus was convinced of his son's reasoning. "I will start immediately", he replied.

A gull was captured and then very carefully its wings were copied. Daedalus was a master craftsman and he studied the shape of the wings, the hollow bone struts, and the delicate feathers with their wind catching overlaps and hollow stems. Gradually he fashioned two sets of wings with real feathers.

Fitting the wings with wax to the powerful shoulders of his son, Daedalus and Icarus soon prepared to say goodbye to the island of Crete where they were held captive in the labyrinth. With a single swoop from a rocky promontory, Icarus and his father were free from the dank tunnels which confined them. Daedalus warned his son, "Don't fly too close to the hot sun or your wings will melt."

But the over confident Icarus forgot the foreboding advice of his father. He flew much too close to the sun, causing the wax on his wings to melt. The homemade wings disintegrated and the foolhardy boy crashed into the sea.

History has added an epilogue to the myth of Icarus in the form of a warning. Persons who reach for something beyond their grasp and attempt projects way beyond their capacity, are said to be cast in the mold of Icarus. Doubtless this admonition attempts to curtail the activities of those who would court disaster. Nevertheless, many believe every myth is based on some fact or living experience. Because of this human assumption, myths have the tendency to strikes one's imagination, fire the soul, and ignite the passions from which great deeds are made.

Down through the ages, man has never relinquished ownership of this unique trait. He is an incessant daydreamer and impetuous adventurer who demands his dreams be turned into reality. The oldest of all mankind's dreams just might have been flying; true flight like the birds. Fantasy became reality on the windswept plains of Kitty Hawk in 1907 when the Wright brothers pushed their way into the skies. From the start of that historic epic adventure in aviation, man's grasp seldom exceeded his reach. In short order, pilots began flying higher, faster, and farther: their appetite for flight knew no limits.

A few began to envision different forms of flight and their daydreams delved into different realms of dominion. They reasoned the sky no longer belonged to man, but to the machine. They questioned if man was truly in control of himself. Some felt he was a passive and constrained passenger in these powerful complex machines. These men imagined returning to a simpler and more authentic form of flight. Their goal was to place man, the individual, in the sky without aid of machine. Mankind has never been satisfied with the status quo, and as a result, aviation began evolving in a different direction in the 1930's. Sown with the seeds of ancient mythology, the progeny of Icarus began doing their own thing.

Roy "Red" Grant

In many ways the world was ready for something to take their minds away from the regrettable circumstances of the post-depression years. Those were difficult times to exist; more difficult still if you were a parachutist looking for ways to attract more crowds. People would pay to watch something different and daring especially if some guy was going to see how closely he could imitate the birds. With spreading wings attached to their arms, and webbing sewed between their trouser legs, these parachutists turned birdmen created a novel dimension in man's relationship with the sky.

Their homemade wings, popularly called batwings, were usually made of airplane cloth fastened to a frame attached to the jumpers body and arms. The ribs were frequently made from broomstick handles which allowed the birdman to pull taut the material stretched between his legs and arms. This made it possible for the birdman to have more control over his descent by slowing him down. Used properly, these wings helped these early batmen extend their time in free fall, and made human gliding possible. It was this intriguing capacity for gliding that attracted many to build their own set of wings.

These parachuting performers plied their skills at a variety of aerial circuses, fairs, and airshows. Birdmen, or batmen, as they became known, were the most unusual of all performers whose habitat was the sky. During the 1930's and the post World War II period, no airshow was complete without at least one of these colorful and eccentric performers. With wings extended, flapping in the air, performing a series of gliding loops, turns, and spirals, birdmen reminded crowds of a gigantic flying mantaray.

There were never large numbers of birdmen. Roy "Red" Grant, self proclaimed as the last of the birdmen, estimates there were never more than seventy-five of these characters. He figures three quit the business, he is alive, and the rest of the batmen made a big hole in the ground. Being a batman was a dangerous way to make a living, and most careers resulted in a spectacular death in front of a large audience.

Grant made his last gliding batman demonstration for CBS TV's Sunday Sports Spectacular of February 19, 1961. Filmed the previous year at an airshow in Doylestown, Pennsylvania, the program was shown during the winter months during a lull in sporting activity. With the help of TV cameras catching the trailing smoke behind him, Grant offered definite proof he could control his body in a horizontal glide. This demonstration was also Grant's 1,007th parachute jump, and probably the last batman jump made in the United States as well.

Red's career as an aerial performer had already eclipsed close to fifteen years. Grant was always a crowd pleaser as he performed a variety of stunts. Long free falls, riding atop speeding airplanes, riding fast moving automobiles to catch a swaying rope dangling from speeding airplanes overhead, and plane changing in midair, Grant was always on the lookout for new material to add to his dangerous repertoire. It was in August 1949 when Red got a chance to make his first batwing jump. A birdman friend had just witnessed the death of a close friend who was killed performing a stunt. Things were too dangerous he figured and he gave up the batwings, and passed them along to Grant. Red knew how dangerous these tricky devices were to use. It wasn't easy to control these cumbersome wings in the air because they were sensitive to the slightest movement. Another reason was the tremendous air pressure buffeting against the semirigid wing surface. Just being able to hold the wings apart in free fall required a painful endurance few could tolerate. Grant approached each attempt with caution, being careful not to over extend himself. He knew that in a split second he could be spinning out of control with the blood rushing to his head causing an unconscious blackout — it could be that dangerous! But the risk was worth a few chances and he accepted the odds on his own terms. Grant learned quickly, but carefully.

In short order he began looking for new ways to make this perilous activity a money maker. What he wanted most was a new stunt or gimmick that would attract larger crowds and help establish a lasting reputation for himself. There was big money and plenty of publicity for any man who could execute a stunt that was both difficult and original. Ever the crowd pleaser, Grant's creative juices began to flow. He hatched the idea of being the first person to glide in freefall from the United States to Canada. No one had ever attempted such a wacky flight before, but Red figured it to be a real money winner, and he committed himself to try and pull it off.

The big day came while he was performing for an aerial circus in Houlton, Maine. Advance publicity and promotional efforts had caught on and attracted much attention in that area. The newspapers played the story up big while the promoters were counting the money they expected to make. The international batwing flight was to be the center of attraction for the show. Suited up in his birdman apparatus, and two parachutes, Red lumbered aboard a Piper Tripacer and waited patiently as it slowly climbed to 14,600 feet. Exiting into the chilly air on the American side of the border, Red cooly controlled his wings until he was falling stable, and began a perfectly controlled glide. Maintaining a precise altitude for gliding, he estimated that by 8,000 feet he had flown over the Canadian border, and began looking for an open space to land. After cracking open his main parachute, he landed in a secluded area on the "Canuck" side. He gathered up his wings, folded his chute, and rejoiced with his friends who came to greet him. He set a new record for gliding. Pilots, spectators, and other official observers at the airport estimated Red had flown for a distance of over four miles, and had descended but three. It was a remarkable feat by even contemporary standards.

After Grant's spectacular gliding performance, newspapermen cajoled the cus-

Three of the last "birdmen" left to right, Tommy Boyd, Don Molitar & Lyle Cameron.

toms officials from both countries to engage in a tug of war match with his body. Astride the common border, the officials pretended to fight over who had official claim to his body. The newspapermen loved the act, and the publicity stunt made headlines in both countries. The promoters made money, the crowd was entertained with a new act, Grant set a new unofficial record, and parachuting had a new folk hero. His jump was one of the highlights of this eccentric business.

During the 1940's and 1950's many other erstwhile performing birdmen added to the folklore of this art. Men like Jimmy Goodwin; Cliff Rose, the youngest batman ever to perform; Tommy Boyd; Don Molitor; and Lyle Cameron.

Batwing Advice

In case you might be considering taking up this dangerous activity, Lyle Cameron, a noted authority on parachuting, and ex-batwing jumper and past editor of Skydiver Magazine, has some timely advice for you. "A simple physical examination is recommended. Spread two packing tables apart so you can reach them with your arms spread perpendicular from each side of your body. Next, place your toes on a chair and lay face down supporting your entire weight with your hands (one on each table) for seventy-five seconds. Few people can do it." He advises, "Until you can, don't think of jumping batwings, the strain is too much. The muscles can be developed by doing pushups with the hands being placed further and further apart until the total spread is accomplished."

Clem Sohn

The originator of batwing jumping is a barnstormer named Clem Sohn; he also has the distinction of being the first person killed with the use of such wings. In 1935 Sohn built a set of homemade wings which he attached to his body. His motivation was purely economical and he proved a box office sensation.

His fame as a birdman spread quickly and in 1937 he travelled through France to demonstrate this new entirely American oddity. The French had long excelled in parachuting and had a marked tendency to view American parachutists as oddball latecomers. But Sohn was a different story, the French aviation public took to this eccentric American parachutist immediately, but his good fortune was short lived. In April 1937, Sohn demonstrated his birdman gliding techniques to a crowd numbering in the thousands at Villa Vincennes. Using his homemade canvas wings, Sohn jumped from 9,000 feet and glided successfully to an opening altitude of about 1,800 feet. His feet became entangled in the suspension lines of the parachute because he had opened in a tumbling position. This is one of the greatest hazards of using wings. Sohn attempted to salvage himself by pulling his reserve chute; but it only fouled with the snarled lines of the first chute. Both of Sohn's parachutes had wrapped around each other producing a roman candleing effect and he crashed to the ground in a crumpled heap. Small wonder enormous crowds were always drawn to watch the birdmen perform — the spectre of death was always lingering close by.

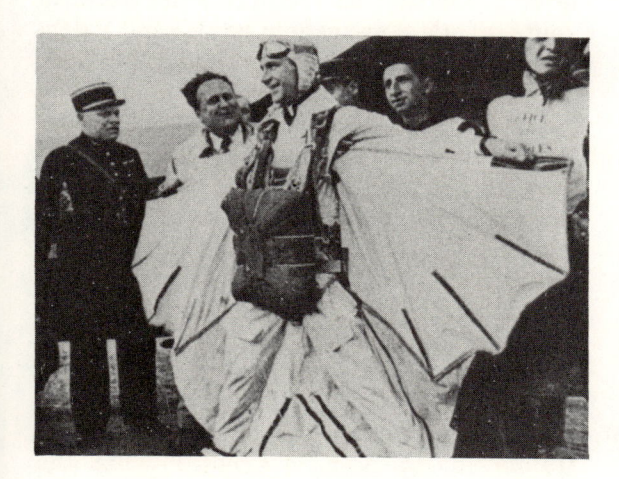

American Clem Sohn, the inventor of "Batwings," was the first to give his life flying these dangerous devices. This picture was taken just prior to his untimely death in France.

Leo Valentin

Perhaps the greatest birdman of all times was a Frenchman named Leo Valentin. This congenial parachutist has the distinction of advancing the knowledge and operation of batwing jumping by quantum standards. It is a fact that all of man's greatest endeavors start from primitive beginnings and progress to more exotic states. Batwing jumping was no exception. During Valentin's lifetime, his insatiable search for pure flight compelled him to advance the state of this art more than the combined efforts of all batmen. While most other birdmen were driven by financial motives, Valentin was obsessed with the concept of true independent human flight.

Valentin's interest in flying took a considerable time to develop. As a small lad of ten he was fascinated with flying and spent most of his spare time wandering around the hangars of Dogneville Aerodrome near the town of Epinal where he was born. Airplanes were like gigantic metal monsters to Leo and the pilots were practically gods. He left school at sixteen to become a butchers assistant and later a locksmith apprentice. Born into a poor peasant lifestyle, Leo never had the money to start flying, but his interest never faded. Any spare money young Leo had a chance to accumulate was spent attending aviation lectures at the Vosges Air Club.

Parachute Training

Like many French youths during 1938, the spectre of an advancing German army was compelling, and Valentin enlisted in the Armee de L'Air. In the wartime conditions, Leo soon became a corporal. Hoping to be enrolled in a pilot training course, he became impatient when he found out the aviation school lasted three years. Anxious to get into the air at any cost he volunteered for parachute training instead. Shortly thereafter, the naive corporal was transferred to the Maison Blanche Center at

Algiers to begin indoctrination as a parachutist. His friends thought he must be crazy to voluntarily ask for such duty, but Leo figured it might lead to flying. Things never did work out quite that way.

Actually, young Corporal Valentin had no idea what he was getting himself into. At Maison Blanche he and other soldiers began the strenuous training. Keeping company with cavalrymen, infantry, gunners, legionnaires, and other assorted hotheads and malcontents, Valentin was forced to deal with the realities of the life and death situations that would be his permanent companions.

Two days before he was scheduled to make his first jump Valentin witnessed the death of a fellow barracks friend. Raoule Sabe' and he had become good friends, and both shared their feelings often about their forthcoming jumps. Raoule was ready to make his first freefall and was anxious to prove himself capable. Freefall jumps at the parachute school were an electrifying event and many felt it took great courage to pass this ritual signifying manhood. Leo and the rest of the company watched anxiously as Sabe' prepared to jump from the airplane.

Tumbling from the overhead airplane, his parachute would normally have been deployed after three or four seconds — but it had not! His uncontrolled gyrations during freefall had streamered his parachute, and the onlookers watched in horror, waiting for the reserve to be thrown out. Seconds seemed like minutes as Sabe' fell faster and faster to the ground. A white flash appeared indicating Raoule's reserve was in the wind stream—but it also roman candled and snarled with the main. Valentin watched helplessly as his friend impacted with the ground at the far end of the field.

Leo learned his first lessons about parachuting, that death is a slut that honors no friendship or ties. Had Sabe' flung his reserve chute free and clear of the entangled main it probably would have opened and saved his life. Valentin was seized in the mighty grip of the mistress of fear, and unless he learned to overcome this obstacle, he would probably suffer the same fate as his friend. He learned to control his apprehensions and keep his fright to himself; this is the code of all parachutists.

Two days later, on October 15, 1938, and still wrestling with thoughts of death about his friend, Valentin made his first parachute jump. In subsequent jumps he learned to develop a confidence and willpower about his abilities. His instructors noticed him changing and to them it marked a mental maturing. This change in attitude also marked the difference between a mere novice and an experienced parachutist. Valentin had learned it all very quickly. Leo projected a coolness and a lucid state of mind about jumping which the French called "sang-froid." He also learned to know and trust his equipment. This helped free himself from the needless worry and anxiety which is an innate part of parachuting. With just a few jumps to his credit, Leo had earned the respect of his fellow parachutists many years his senior. He heeded the advice of his older and wiser companions when it was offered: "Learn your brolly and trust in yourself." It was excellent advice and Valentin was never to forget it during his career.

The veteran enlisted men at the parachute school helped Leo become an ardent learner and fervent leader. With their help he came to understand the brolly, a French term for parachute, was a simple device. Everyone joked that it must be simple so that commanding officers could understand its operation. Valentin helped instill in the students an understanding of the first rule of parachuting - the fate of each man lies in his own hands.

Valentin was undergoing mountaineering training on the Pyrean Frontier when the Armistice was signed. He managed to utilize the underground line to North Africa to escape, and found many of his friends in seclusion. From there he was sent to Fez where the first parachute school to operate since the French defeat, had been opened. With eighty jumps logged, Valentin was made an instructor. His vast experience with parachutes made him a valuable member of the jump school. The parachute was one of the weapons of war, and during the training of resistance forces, Leo was jumping from airplanes with greater frequency. He had been indoctrinated with the idea that parachute jumping is made in order to fight. But now that he was making more descents, he began to develop a real taste for parachuting as a pleasureable sport.

But war is not a sport and the pleasures he derived from parachuting would have to wait. On June 1, 1944, he and the rest of his parachute company found themselves under strict guard in a camp in Southern England. They were trained to jump under combat conditions, and all were sure their big day would come soon. Outfitted with the accouterments for war: metal helmets, camouflaged jackets and trousers, leggings, sten gun, revolver, explosives, ammunition, and survival supplies, the company waited nervously to do battle with the Germans.

Late in the evening of June 5, 1944, the first wave of troops was dropped by parachute behind enemy lines into Brittany. Their mission was to cut the main railway supplies that led to Paris. Reinforced with a stream of planes and gliders carrying additional combat troops, munitions, supplies, and first aid personnel, the countryside staggered under the onslaught of the advancing French troops. On the evening of June 9, Valentin and a contingency of six men were parachuted over Morbihan, far behind enemy lines. Landing approximately twenty miles from the coast of Brittany, and deep in German occupied territory, their mission was to blow up various railway lines.

After a fortnight of intensive fighting with the German forces, Valentin was wounded. His right arm was shattered by an explosive bullet, and fortunately he was taken to a neutral hospital in Issoudun. Side by side in this mutual sanctuary the doctors treated German and allied soldiers alike. As soon as he was able, Valentin was sent on convalescence to Marne. He subsequently stayed on sick leave after being refused to be sent back to the front. War ended in Europe on May 8, 1945, with the unconditional surrender of the German forces. Valentin was twenty six years old and more than ready to begin another adventure.

Making A Mayonnaise

Valentin was promoted to Sergeant Major after the war and was subsequently assigned as chief instructor of the newly established parachute school in Pau. Leo had ideas of a quiet and peaceful career in the military, but his restless creativity forced him to make other plans.

He enjoyed the regular hours, warm showers, and decent meals, all comforts he missed while in combat — but something wasn't right. While he jumped on a regular basis, Sergeant Major Valentin began to feel himself going stale. He was truly a professional parachutist now, and had made over 150 jumps, but he was bored. Leo was a master at his profession who was used to the challenges of breaking new ground. And there was little, if any, new ground to break that would excite and stimulate him. Valentin was bothered to no end about his situation, and often considered resigning from the army and giving up parachuting.

It wasn't that Leo was completely unsatisfied with his parachute jumping, but he came to believe he had much in common with a sack of flour when he made a jump. When he exited the airplane, he was usually out of control, somersaulting and falling head over heels. He had no control or technique. Leo had no style to his parachuting. Just like a bag of flour he had to fall away and take whatever happened to him; and this bothered him. Out of control in freefall, flapping about like so much dead weight at

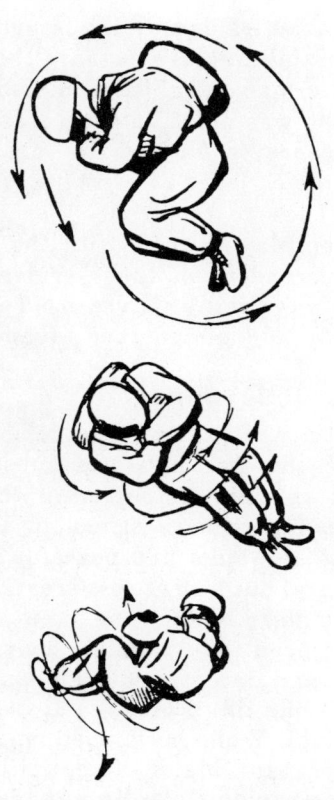

"Making a mayonnaise," a French term describing the tumbling, out of control position in common usage then.

120 miles an hour, was not his idea of professionalism. At those speeds the blood rushes to the brain quickly and can produce unconsciousness. The French call that experience, "Making a Mayonnaise." His lack of technique was a desperate problem.

These were conditions Valentin decided he could no longer tolerate. Once again fired with enthusiasm, he decided to devote his energies to developing a way of controlling his position in freefall, thereby making parachuting safer for himself and for others. It soon became evident to Valentin that many parachute malfunctions were directly attributable to poor body position during the opening sequence. Often times a foot or an arm would catch in the suspension lines causing the canopy to distort and open improperly, and on frequent occasions injure the jumper. Valentin was in a crisis, and it became crucial that he find some way to solve this dangerous problem.

In years past, Leo had been enthusiastic about helping promote parachuting as a sport, and he realized that different techniques would have to be developed for his dream to come true. To become a public sport, parachuting would have to be treated as an art. Otherwise, he felt parachuting would be no more than a means of transport to carry soldiers to the ground during times of war, or a carnival act to entertain people.

The challenge was implanted in Valentin's mind and he was obliged to accept it. He started studying aerodynamics and the laws that govern the forces of all falling bodies. Like Newton's discovery of the falling apple, Valentin learned how a cone shaped object falls point first through the air. A mental picture formed in his mind of an object in freefall being funnel shaped in order to remain stable. He grimly realized there was nothing funnel shaped about his body. An idea struck him that he could create an artificial center of gravity by extending his arms and legs while in freefall. by spreading the legs and arms, the reserve chute worn on the front of his harness, would give added weight and supply an artificial center of gravity. This in turn would make him more cone shaped, he figured, and possibly his stability problems would be solved. Like most visionaries, Valentin had only his gut feelings to bolster and support his theories. This all sounded well and fine on the ground, but the true test was to be met in the sky, where all problems must be dealt with.

Beautiful Freefall

On May 23, 1947, Valentin attempted to fall in a controlled manner. Exiting at 9,000 feet he knew how simple his task appeared to be. But once in freefall he found his simple theories of extending arms and legs was another thing. This position was difficult because he was not conditioned, or trained, to do these things in freefall. He was used to falling out of control. This was the normal way it was always done; this was Leo's instinct. On his first jump he could not bring himself to a mental state of awareness that allowed him to splay his legs and arms in the manner he envisioned. Leo opened his parachute at 1500 feet and rode his parachute to the ground dejected by his poor performance.

Drawing from a reservoir of inner strength, Valentin took off again an hour later the same day. More determined than ever to succeed he hurled himself once again from an airplane at 9,000 feet. This time it was do or die! He concentrated with every fiber of his mental being and forced himself to spread his arms and legs. Fully extended Leo experienced a strange quietness while in freefall. He was stable! He had found it! Motionless in sky, falling in a controlled face to earth position, Valentin knew his dream had been achieved. For over 150 jumps he had been conditioned to believe that uncontrolled tumbling was enjoyable. Now in the quiet, serene, beauty above the airfield he was falling in a perfectly controlled attitude; Leo was exhilarated!

Intoxicating as all this was, he experienced some fear because of how different this all made him feel. His freefall was a smooth, controlled fall; almost dreamlike. Exuberant like a child who has taken his first steps, Valentin made a third jump that day to make sure his jump was no fluke. The results were even better because he was more confident and aware. The third jump was actually fun.

On subsequent jumps Valentin learned how to maneuver his arms and legs that enabled him to turn. He learned how to do a back loop by bringing his arms and legs together into his body causing him to flip over. The more jumps he made only convinced him that most anybody could control himself in sustained freefall. It was simply a matter of controlling your mind and having the desire bad enough.

Now that his crisis was over, Valentin once more looked forward to making parachute jumps. He perfected his position to such a degree that low jumps no longer gave him any satisfaction. He was addicted to the sky and long freefalls. He was unhappy if many days went by without making a jump.

So excited with freefall and his ability to fall for long distances, Valentin became restless with an active imagination. If he was having pleasure in freefall, he reasoned, why shouldn't he be able to extend the time? Would this not make him live more intensely and more perfectly? Why shouldn't he be able to glide like the birds? Leo would answer these questions at a later date.

Valentin was now positive he could jump safely from any altitude. The key was body

The "Valentin Position," a method of controlled freefall.

control and he sat out to prove his theory was right. In February 1948, aided by fellow officers of the Armee de L'Air assisting him, Leo made a controlled freefall drop from 16,800 feet. This was not a world's record, which he had hoped, but it was as high as the school's old Junkers aircraft could fly. A month later in March, Leo secured a more powerful aircraft, in an attempt to set a new world's record altitude jump without respirator assistance. Valentin had prepared laboriously for this record attempt. With official army sanction he was able to use a pressure tank to practice making high altitude jumps to condition his body.

Outfitted with an electrically heated suit and boots, two pair of gloves, helmet, goggles, chronometer and altimeter, and two parachutes, Valentin looked like an overstuffed teddy bear as he prepared to make the jump. On March 22, he boarded a big Halifax airplane used at one time by the RAF for bombing raids on the Rhur. Stationed at Bordeaux, the powerful Halifax was equipped with four 2200 h.p. engines that gave a cruising speed of 250 mph. The airplane blazed its way over the Pau Airport on jump run straining with maximum rpm's. At 22,000 feet the plane reached its limit and would go no higher.

Full of confident expectations Valentin dropped through the tube of the bomb bay doors on the underside of the plane. Immediately he went into his stable position and remained in complete control during his record freefall. When the altimeter read 1,800 feet, he gave a healthy yank on the ripcord and was shortly nestled safely in his harness; he was ecstatic. This was Leo Valentin's first official record.

As a result of his record jump Leo realized the possibility of some military applications. He recognized the feasibility of training a corps of airborne troops to exit at high altitudes to jump behind enemy lines without being detected by radar. In the same vein, a corps of frogmen parachutists could be trained to jump into the sea to mine enemy warships. A decade later the United States Armed Forces established two such outfits. The army initiated a HALO unit (High Altitude Low Opening) consisting of small teams of reconnaissance troops. They could exit at very high altitudes, sometimes 40,000 feet, freefall in formation, and land behind enemy lines to carry out their mission. For awhile it was felt this concept might revolutionize airborne training, but other techniques were developed which made this concept obsolete. In addition, for many years, now, the U.S. Navy has had SEAL units (Sea Air Land) which can parachute into water for rescue and demolition operations. The navy also utilizes parachutists for their UDT units (Underwater Demolition Team) to help carry out their military missions. In November, the same year, Valentin established another world record. This time he jumped from 16,000 feet at night.

Both of these world record jumps attracted much publicity for Valentin. He was responsible for creating a new sport in France, and an admiring public was awestruck with his skill. The public wanted to see more of Valentin. The demand for his appearances at airshows was great. The "Valentin Position" was soon being taught at many military parachute schools. Parachuting was also beginning to catch on as a sport for civilians.

By this time Valentin's current enlistment with the Armee de L'Air was coming to an end and he decided not to reenlist. This was a gamble for Valentin on his part, but he was used to taking chances. His friends, military officials, and family begged him to stay in the army so he would be eligible for his pension in three years. But Leo had other ideas he wanted to start working on. Besides, he was finding military life was becoming somewhat stifling, and was having difficulties pursuing some experiments he was involved with. He was asking for more liberties than the army could possibly allow.

Leo decided the time was right for him to leave the military gracefully. Many men undergo a change of life, between the ages of 30 and 40, and as for Valentin, this change to civilian status would eventually vault him into international fame.

World's Most Daring Man

Since discovering his "freefall position" while in the army, Leo was convinced parachuting could be turned into a respectable sport. He left the army dedicated to the idea of promoting parachuting as an art; the art of human flying. Leo believed his falling position was a form of gliding and he intended to prolong the time in freefall by whatever methods he thought possible. In the meantime, the necessity of earning some money loomed paramount. Though he was now developing a budding interest in using gliding wings, he was forced to participate in many airshows around France to earn a livelihood that would pay for his experiments.

He shortly became a nationally known parachuting folk hero and responded to demands that he perform for his idolizing public. During the first year or so after leaving the army, he made exhibition freefall jumps at Nancy, Saarbrucken, Toulous, Neufchatel, Rouen, Meaux-Esbly, and Villa Coublay. Difficult as it may seem, it was painful for the creative Valentin to make these jumps. He considered himself an artist and his real interest was in other areas. But he had to perform for an insatiable public eager for more sensationalism. This type of exhibition jumping was leading nowhere for him except for some money and a few more entries into a log book. But Leo hung in there and did what he had to do. It was all part of being a hero.

Leo Valentin, "The Most Daring Man in the World", as he was usually billed, specialized in long freefall jumps with smoke bombs. High in the sky, with smoke trailing his plummeting body, Leo presented spectacular evidence that he could safely make the intrepid aerial journey. The press became infatuated with him and started playing him up as an eccentric. Valentin was neither an eccentric, nor a madman, though he probably seemed so to many, who could neither understand his motives nor his abilities. Leo had to tolerate his fame and good fortune, for this all provided him with much publicity. The old newspaper adage seems to apply this instance, "Bad press is better than no press."

Later on Valentin developed some specialized acts with other male and female partners. One of these exhibitions was called "The Aerial Duet" and sometimes "The Angel Jump" which he performed with Monique Laroche, a famous French female parachutist. After the "Aerial Duet" he concocted an "Aerial Trio" with two other female partners, Odette Geogel and Baby Monetti. This later act was a particular favorite and enjoyed popularity for quite some time.

L' Omme Oiseau

Now that he earned some funds for newer experiments Valentin turned his attentions to a concept which had engrossed him for some time. The concept of "Pure Flight" was intriguing, and just the sort of challenge the imaginative Leo would be attracted to. An ardent student of history, he read of the canvas winged exploits of the American birdman. Clem Sohn. Sohn was something of a parachuting folk legend in France, particularly since his untimely death in 1937 at Villa Vincennes. Valentin decided to carry on the work of this winged master. He had to learn from his mistakes and perfect the art of flying with canvas wings.

After studying all the available records concerning Sohn's exploits Leo determined he had made several vital mistakes. The first mistake was the rigid frame beneath the arms that prevented little freedom of movement. This was especially critical when it came time to open the parachute. It was difficult, if not impossible, to grab the ripcord without collapsing one side of the wings. It was not Sohn's wings that killed him, but bad body position, which tangled the chute upon opening. Valentin circumvented this problem by substituting whale bones for the rigid broomstick or metal rods which were normally used. The flexible supports were placed in such a fashion that would give his arms greater freedom to pull the ripcord and still remain in a stable position.

The second problem, though not as critical, was an aerodynamic imbalance with the distrubution of the canvas material. Leo redesigned the material which was normally placed between the birdman's legs. Hoping to achieve better stability, and a higher glide ratio, Valentin installed a series of vents between his legs, as well as vents on the outside between the legs and arms. It was hoped both these improvements would insure the success that eluded most birdmen.

"The new birdman" and "The new Clem Sohn", as Valentin came to be billed at various airshows, began making the rounds with his redesigned batwings. On April 30, 1950, over 30,000 persons gathered at the Villa Coublay Airport to witness Leo fly like a bird. His first attempt was hardly successful. Jumping from 12,900 feet, Valentin managed to fall in a stable position, and even glide across the ground. While the tremendous air pressure on the surface of the wings was an aid in freefall keeping the wings open, it was another matter when it came time to deploy the parachute. The new "Clem Sohn" found out very quickly that he did not have the strength in his arms to close them any time he wanted to. In a flash he realized the obvious — his arms must be independent of the wings.

To open his parachute, Valentin had to roll over on his back, thereby collapsing the wings. Leo barely had time to jerk the ripcord and open his chute before crashing to the ground. It now dawned on him why so many birdmen were killed by these treacherous devices. It was practially impossible to pull the ripcord without folding in the wings. And once the wings contracted, the parachutist would immediately begin to tumble out of control, greatly risking entanglement of chute and wings.

The first winged jump of birdman Leo Valentin.

On subsequent jumps this error was corrected so that he could reach his ripcord without having to risk folding his wings. On May 4, Valentin jumped from 6,000 feet at the Meaux-Esbly Airfield. This time the jump was an absolute success. He was able to maintain his position in the air, and three times during his freefall, was able to use his hands to make the wings bank a turn. Falling at an estimated speed of between 80 and 100 mph, instead of the terminal velocity of 120 mph., Leo proved he could glide and extend his time in freefall. This jump was a magnificent success and Valentin proved that he was indeed flying. The local papers reported in the headlines of the event, "Wings of the birdmen in the sky above Meaux" and "The birdman has flown, I saw it for myself."

Valentin's birdman demonstration was

Top photo: Vassard with early cloth wings. Center: Valentin with his first pair of rigid wings. Lower: Valentin riding to jump altitude to test his wooden wings.

successful in the eyes of the public, but he felt he learned a valuable lesson. He demanded perfection and was never satisfied with anything less. The results of the jump were encouraging but not up to his expectations. While he could glide somewhat, Leo figured at best, his wings did little except to break his freefall. The canvas wings were a mistake. What Leo wanted was to jump a wing that "generated its own lift." He was convinced the capacity of canvas wings to glide were severely limited. He wasted little time figuring out the details for a new project. All previous men in the history of batwing flying had trusted canvas wings; Valentin had a better idea.

In much the same manner as a rigid airplane wing is supported by a lifting suction above the wings, Valentin knew he had to develop a set of wings that generated this type of airflow. Canvas wings simply did not have the support of a leading edge to generate lift, nor does the human body. Neither has much potential for true flying. He set about to design and manufacture a pair of wooden wings with an aerodynamic lifting capability.

Valentin's new idea was a radical one, but with the help of an interested friend, M. Colligon, he began building his first pair of rigid wings. Built with three plywood, the wings were equipped with a longeron and internal strutting which paralleled the wings of an airplane. A lightweight steel tube framework which encircled his chest was fashioned to which the wings were attached by hinges. Total weight of the wings and tube framework was about 28 pounds. The final stages for testing the wings involved static tests in the wing tunnel at Chalais-Meudon. Permission was obtained to use this wind tunnel, but was later revoked when the director flatly refused to allow this contraption in his facilities.

Undaunted with this temporary setback, Valentin made the decision to use his untested new wings at an air show on June 8, 1951. This time a Hiller 360 helicopter was put at his disposal for the jump. Inclement weather, and a poorly operating aircraft, limited jump altitude to 4,000 feet. During his brief freefall a terrific gust of wind turned Leo on his back. No longer supported by the air, the wings slammed shut forcing Valentin on his back. Acting like a rudder, the wings threw him in a violent spin. Leo was barely able to open his parachute by 500 feet. Another lesson was learned. He must install a locking mechanism that would prevent the wings from closing once they were open in the air.

A month later the Epinal Aero Club organized an aerial show on the Dogneville Airfield. As a child Valentin had his first visions of flying at this airfield and he desperately wanted to make a spectacular flight. Unfortunately, things didn't work out too well for him. While waiting his turn to make a demonstration of his wings, somebody had mis-handled his wings, and accidently bent one of the locking mechanisms on the wings. During freefall, the left wing opened and locked in position, while the right side remained unopened. This produced another one of these raging spins that Valentin was learning to live with. With his latest misfortune he learned another lesson; never allow anyone to touch the wings except himself or his friend Colligon.

The aerial exhibition season opened in North Africa in 1953. Valentin continued his freefall exhibitions, and in the course of the year won a variety of cups and much money for his daring displays. Later that year, in September, Leo attended an air show at Lille for the benefit of children of fallen war heroes. The Air Ministry had asked him to give a demonstration of his wings and he gladly accepted. With new wings, a better corset, and a strengthened locking device, Valentin was ready to prove once and for all that he was able to fly like a bird. At the last minute government officials got wind of his performance and denied him permission to make the jump. They reasoned the wings

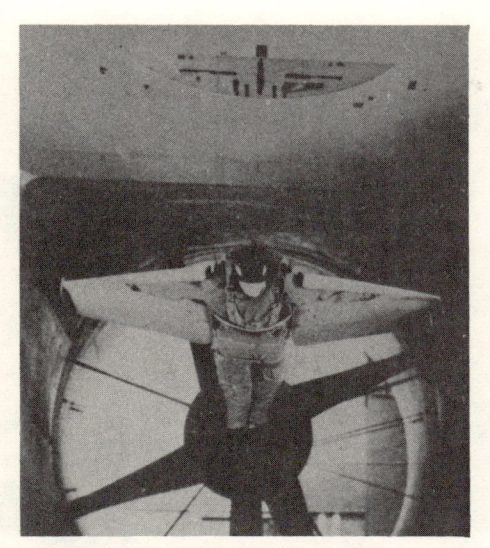

Wind tunnel testing of Valentin's redesigned wooden wings.

had not been officially tested. It was ironic, but the government had originally denied him permission to test the wings in their wind tunnel, and now they revoked permission because testing was not completed. From September 1953 to May 1954 Leo waited in vain while the government bureaucracy pushed papers deciding whether to allow him access to their facilities.

Tired and frustrated of waiting for the government red tape to run its clumsy course, Valentin decided to pay for the wind tunnel tests himself at a private facility. The Brequet Works at Villa Coublay housed a modern wind tunnel that ideally suited his needs. In order to determine how suitable the wings were for human use a dummy was substituted for the initial test. With the wings positioned properly, this impressive tunnel was capable of producing winds in excess of 60 mph. Lab technicians could get an idea of how the wings functioned without risk to its user. The results were quite encouraging and proved the wings were built well and capable of providing excellent lift. According to lab technicians, the wings were capable of generating a glide ratio of 3.3:1. Theoretically, this meant Valentin could glide over five miles before opening his parachute if he started at 9,000 feet. The following day Valentin replaced the dummy for live tests in the tunnel. This was an excellent experience and provided invaluable training for future live jumps. With practice, Leo found he could maneuver his wings at will, thereby producing turns. In addition, with the wings in a locked position, he could move his arms from the handhold and freely pull his ripcord, allowing him complete stability during the opening sequence. He was now ready for his greatest test. Valentin came away from the wind tunnel experience full of confidence and radiating with the knowledge that his dreams would soon be fulfilled.

On May 13, 1954 Valentin enplaned a DC-3 at Orly for the final test with his rigid wings. He was accompanied by an official witness, photographers, and his friend Colligon. The DC-3 flew on an easterly jump run over the

M. Colligon, assisting Valentin prior to his most successful birdman flight at Orly, France.

airport at 9,000 feet while Valentin nervously waited for his moment of truth. Exiting the huge doors the slip stream of the aircraft made the birdman tumble over on his back. Spreading his arms, rounding his back, Valentin rolled over to a face to earth position. Using his arms to control his flight direction and maintain stability, he began to glide. He was positive that he was now flying; witnesses on the ground confirmed this opinion. They estimated he covered over three and a half miles during his gliding descent. Not only could Valentin glide, but he could turn at will, and initiated several 360 degree turns to the right and left. At 2,000 feet he opened his parachute and proceeded to lower his wings and corset to the ground by rope. He landed uneventfully at the north end of Orly Airfield. Valentin's gliding birdman demonstration was perfect. His original concept of using wooden wings had worked as he knew they would. Leo flew with the wings further than any man had done before.

Already he began imagining where his next improvements would take him. He was mentally outlining plans he had to improve the wing profile, increase the lift, and streamline the body. Leo had visions of adding flaps to the wings that would enable him to turn and steer with greater ease. He knew he would have to go slowly, but his active imagination spurred him onward. Perhaps someday his wings could generate enough lift to fly about the sky at will. Who could tell where his efforts might lead: one day he might be able to land without benefit of a parachute.

Valentin could afford to take his time. He had reached the pinnacle of success. He proved he could jump successfully with his innovative rigid wings. It was now time to go slowly and methodically. For the next several years, he and his devoted companion Colligon, spent their time refining and manufacturing more effecient wings. Valentin was still in need of money and he continued making periodic exhibition jumps,

After his successful flight at Orly, a serious Valentin is already planning improvements to his wings.

but his primary interest and activity was directed toward building the ultimate pair of batwings.

Leo's Last Flight

By May 1956, Valentin was ready to try a newly designed pair of wings. He hoped his dreams of "pure flight" would take him a step closer to his mental expectations. A crowd of 100,000 spectators crowded into the Speke Airport near Liverpool, England on May 21, 1956. They had come to witness the world famous Leo Valentin fly. The activity was hectic and tense, and the air was scented with an ominous anxiety. The 37 year old Frenchman had spent a lifetime dreaming of flying. Everywhere the hopes and good wishes of success prayed for him. Valentin was scheduled to perform last for the airshow crowd. The drama continued to build in anticipation if his flight from 8,500 feet.

Valentin brought forth a newly fitted pair of balsa wings. Weighing just over twenty eight pounds, they measured over four feet wide, and nine feet from wing tip to wing tip.

Leo Valentin prepares for another daring flight.

Painted bright orange, the wings would add a colorful streak to the afternoon sky, permitting greater spectator visibility. The crowd anticipated that history would be made shortly as Valentin prepared to board the jump aircraft.

In what seemed like an eternity, but in reality was about 20 minutes, the huge Dakota airplane circled to altitude and prepared to come in on final jump run. Valentin sat nervously in the rear of the plane fidgeting with his gloves and giving a few last minute checks of his equipment. He forced a fair smile as one of his assistants patted him on the back and encouraged him with the remark, "Bonne Chance." Nervously, perhaps sensing this might be his last flight, Valentin lumbered toward the open hatchway of the plane. It was now 4:21 p.m. and birdman Valentin prepared to make his historic flight.

What happened after the exit is confusing. But apparently the slip stream from the airplane caught the wings prematurely, throwing him backwards, crashing on the fuselage and rudder sections of the airplane.

His wings splintered and Valentin was ricocheted into the air, spinning wildly in a vortex of turbulence, rushing towards the ground. A glimpse of white was seen as he apparently tried to pull his main parachute. The splintered remains of the wings snagged the nylon parachute fabric, hopelessly entangling the chute. Falling crazily in a heap of snarled equipment, a bare 1,000 feet above the ground, the spectators spotted another flash of white. Apparently Leo was still alive: struggling, fighting to deploy his reserve chute. The flailing body could be seen wrapped beyond escape in a white robe of nylon. Leo Valentin was last seen struggling to free himself from the tangled mess — but it was useless! The famed birdman crashed to the ground and died instantly upon impact. The long, distinguished, and sometimes frustrating career of Leo Valentin had come to a tragic end in a nearby cornfield. L' Omme Oiseau is dead.

Valentin's spectacular death was a prelude to the end of the winged birdman era. A few jumps were subsequently made by other enterprising birdmen with canvas wings, but the for most part, no one had the desire or motivation to continue in his footsteps. The price for fame and glory was not worth the risk any mortal was prepared to pay. Valentin was always ready to pay the supreme sacrifice in search of his dreams. He was aware of the risks he took. Since his early days as an army parachutist, Valentin knew death was always a constant companion. Anyone who tempts fate, is flaunting an unforgiving slut; ignore her and she will force you to pay the supreme sacrifice.

Among other things, Leo Valentin is credited with advancing the state of the art of batwing jumping to its highest level. He came as close as anybody in history in achieving pure human flight. Had he lived and continued his experiments, it just might have been possible men would be returned to the ground with stabilizing wings, instead of parachutes.

Valentin attempted to revolutionize mankind's relationship with the sky. Realistically though, he took his ideas about as far as was possible. His goals of true independent flight were probably a bit grandiose. The ultimate batwing experience may have been to land without a parachute, but it is very unlikely. Modern handgliding offers fewer risks and comes closer to the ideals of true human flight.

Nevertheless, Leo Valentin made a notable attempt, and perhaps others might follow in his path some day. Leo clearly established the dividing line between parachutist and birdman — a parachutist merely falls, but a birdman flies.

Batwing jumping — A search for the ultimate form of flight.

Chapter 5

Women In Parachuting

One of the longstanding folkmyths in parachuting, which has persisted to the present days, concerns the inherent weakness of females as parachutists. Most people have rigid expectations when they think of people who jump from airplanes, balloons, and the like. The stereotyped image of the he-man paratrooper type who has been painfully trained to endure the treacherous rigors of combat is so strong, most of us have a tendency to believe that only men are capable of risking the dangers and delights of parachute jumping.

The myth of the fragile, spaced-out female not being able, or wanting, to parachute is convenient because it locks in and solidifies our image of what we want a parachutist to be. By doing so, many of parachuting's prolific and daring folkhero's have been inadvertently cast into the dustbins of history. A close look into the history of parachuting reveals a folklore rich with glorious accounts of women parachutists. Their participation and contributions began, as we shall see, practically right from the inception of parachuting. Women parachutists have been bonafide members of the world's oldest aviation activity to the same extent as have men. Dazzling audiences with daring displays of courage and skill, or reaping the immense personal satisfaction that comes from using parachutes for fun and profit, women have added immensely to the folklore of parachuting. This fact is as true today as when the world's first woman parachutist cut herself away from a balloon in 1802.

During that year, only five years after Jacques-Andre Garnerin made his celebrated world's first parachute jump, he travelled to England for a series of balloon ascents and parachute drops. His wife,

Susan Joerns placed second in style at the 1972 World Parachute Meet held in Tahlequah, Oklahoma.

Jeanne-Genevieve Labroste, travelled with him, and in September (the date is not officially recorded) she dropped away from a hydrogen balloon to become the world's first female parachutist. She established a precedent for intrepid women who wanted to taste thrilling adventure. Her career was brief, and not particularly glamorous, but she paved the way for other women who followed in her path.

During several visits to Italy, Garnerin took along another female pupil by the name of Cecile Benoist. This 14 year old often made balloon flights and parachute descents. She descended by parachute at Torino on October 18, and at Florence on November 6, 1818. In 1820, this petite lady followed up her previous exploits by making descents at Milan in July, September, and at Verona on October 1.

Elisa Garnerin

Elisa Garnerin belonged to one of the most famous aeronautical families in history. She clearly established herself as the most prolific of all early parachutists. She was the niece of Andre-Jacques Garnerin and began her long career in aeronautics by learning to fly balloons at the early age of 15. Following closely in the footsteps of her famous uncle, Elisa went on to make a total of 39 parachute descents between 1815 and 1836. This talented young woman was the world's first professional female parachutist.

A large part of Elisa Garnerin's parachuting career, as proved by historical documents, took place in Italy. She made parachute descents at Milan on March 5 and May 9, 1824, in Rome on May 24 and November 20 and 27, 1825, in Venice on February 12, 1826 and at Moncalieri on June 25, 1827. Elisa recorded parachute descents in other European countries such as Germany, Spain, Russia, and France during her long and celebrated career. While parachuting was still in it's early embryo stage, women established themselves as highly competent practitioners in aeronautics.

Elisa Garnerin, the world's first female professional parachutist.

Katchen Paulus

The first professional parachutist in Germany was Fräulein Käthchen Paulus. During the late 1880's and early 1890's, she travelled different parts of Germany making parachute descents as part of a regular aerial exhibition show. She was carried aloft by a balloon while she was suspended underneath. Upon reaching an acceptable altitude, she cut herself away from the balloon in much the same manner as was popular by American smoke balloonists of the time.

She and Paul Letteman are credited with advancing parachute development by being the first to develop and use a "remote automatic attached sack type" parachute. The apex of the canopy was tied to the inside of a canvas bag, and then, the entire canopy and lines were folded and packed into the bag. The mouth of the bag was closed with breakcord and attached to her balloon.

**Fraulein Katchen Paulus,
German parachutist.**

Poster depicting the parachuting exploits of Katchen Paulus.

A ring knife was used to sever herself from the balloon. The weight of her falling body snapped the breakcord and started dragging out the parachute canopy. Once fully deployed she would descend to earth uneventfully. This basic design she helped develop is still used today for cargo drops.

Queen Of The Clouds

Just before the beginning of the 20th Century, a young woman named Ruby Deveau earned quite a name for herself as a daring smoke balloonist and parachute jumper. Born in Germany in 1877, Ruby immigrated to the United States at the tender age of four and shortly thereafter became an orphan. As a young woman she eventually found her way as a member of a vaudeville show troupe. In 1892, the troupe went broke and Ruby was stranded in Memphis, Tennessee. Here she witnessed an exhibition parachute jump, liked what she saw, and made application for employment. Almost hired on the spot, she made her first parachute jump in short order at the age of 15 years.

Miss Ruby Deveau was billed as the "Queen of the Clouds." She followed this exciting up and down career for over three years and made 175 exhibition parachute jumps in many parts of the country. The Nebraska State Journal of Lincoln, Nebraska, relates the exciting story of one of her jumps:

"The Grace Shannon Balloon Company was the attraction of Lincoln Park again yesterday. This company, it will be remembered, is the one that employs the nervy Ruby Deveau, known as 'Queen of the Clouds.' Yesterday afternoon she outdid all previous records as to the height of the ascent and furnished an emotional entertainment for over 4,000 people, who had come into Tom Hickey' fountain of pleasure. The ascension was not made until 5:00 owing to difficulties encountered in getting ready, but by the time the big air ship was cut loose the multitude looked on in wonder. Attached to the balloon were three parachutes, one for Mme. Deveau, one for Professor Krug, and also one for the dog that took a trip toward the happy hunting ground."

"Prof. Krug cut loose first, followed by the dog and then Mme. Ruby went like a flash through space. At times the big balloon would almost invert and swaying around in midair with the recklessness of an individual who has taken upon himself a jag. The height reached was estimated at 12,000 feet, and when Mme. Deveau came back to the park she was congratulated on the success of the ascension."

Miss Deveau made her last jump in 1895 in London, Ontario, as a result of breaking her back when she drifted into a chimney. After spending many months in a hospital recovering she decided it was time to retire from this business. In later years she studied typing and shorthand, became a legal stenographer, and eventually married.

Tiny Broadwick

Few parachutists can lay claim to having made more than 1,000 jumps. Even fewer can say to have played an instrumental role in bringing about the rebirth of parachuting. An even smaller number, less than a handful, could be considered to have been at the leading edge of the revolution in parachuting that occurred from 1910-1920. There was only one person who could claim to have done all of these celebrated feats and still be a female. Georgia "Tiny" Broadwick did all these remarkable feats. Amazing might be a better word considering she weighed a mere 85 pounds and stood only four feet tall during her jumping days.

Under the coaching of her foster father, Charles Broadwick, Tiny first donned a parachute in 1908 at the age of 15 and jumped from a balloon. She started a career that made her the sweetheart of all aerial carnival crowds and a pioneer in aviation. Oftentimes billed as "The Doll Girl", a name Tiny detested, her jumpsuit consisted of a white silk dress and ruffled bloomers. Beneath her diminuitive frame and dainty exterior was the soul of one who was a hardened veteran capable of dealing with the harsh realities imposed on her by the rigors of her profession. In the fourteen years she made a living by parachuting, such events as broken bones, dislocated shoulders, swamp landings, and being dragged over rough ground and rooftops, never dampened her enthusiasm in the least.

Back in those days the art and science of parachuting was a concept just beginning to develop. There were no high performance steerable parachutes to jump, where standing landings in front of a crowd would daz-

Tiny Broadwick, "The Doll Girl."

zle and entertain them. Parachutes were mainly the unmodified flat circular design made of silk or cotton. Fancy, snug fitting harnesses, would have to wait until later

Tiny Broadwick and Glenn L. Martin [1913 photo].

years. Though Tiny later helped develop and jumped a Charles Broadwick designed "coat harness", she mainly sat on a trapeze bar attached to a manila hemp rope which in turn was sewn to the canopy. Since there was no way to steer her parachute, she just jumped and let the wind take her away. She recalled, "If you landed in a tree you were all right - but if you landed on a rooftop and rolled off, you were hurting." Once Tiny missed, plummeting down a eight story gap between two sections of a building.

Tiny Broadwick is given credit for a number of firsts in parachuting. On June 21, 1913, in what is now the parking lot of the Los Angeles Zoo, in Griffith Park, she went aloft in a biplane piloted by Glenn L. Martin, who later became famous for his role in the aircraft industry. At the height of 2,000 feet, she released herself from a trap seat, thus becoming the first woman to make a parachute drop from an airplane.

Also in 1913, at the Perry Victory Centennial celebration, Tiny jumped from a "hydroaeroplane" into the cold water of Lake Michigan. She was the first person on record to make a parachute drop from a hydroplane (also piloted by Martin) and the first woman to make a water jump from an airplane.

At San Diego's North Island in 1914, Miss Broadwick gave the first official demonstration of a parachute to the United States Government, proving the success of the aerial invention developed by her foster father. This series of five demonstration jumps, of which the first four were static line activated, resulted in yet another innovation. On the fourth jump, the static line tangled with the tail section of the plane; so Tiny decided it would be safer to cut off all but a short length of line and pull this herself after leaping from the plane. On her fifth jump she became the first woman, and possibly the first person ever, to make a premeditated freefall parachute jump.

This daring series of demonstration jumps was witnessed by General George P. Scrivin, Chief of the Aviation Bureau of the U.S. Army Signal Corps. After these jumps, the army ordered its first parachute — a Broadwick "Coatpack," and thereby inaugurated a new epoch in aerial safety.

Clyde Pangborn [left], Tiny Broadwick, and Mayor Bimbo of San Diego.

In 1915 and 1916 Tiny jumped at the San Diego World's Fair. In a few years she married Andrew Olsen, a schooner master. "It was terribly hard for me to settle down. I had so much pep and energy", she remembers. "I was lonesome for my work and occasionally made a few jumps." Tiny made the last of her 1,100 plus jumps in 1922, flown by reknowned pilot "Upside Down" Clyde Panghorn, over San Diego.

Once ground bound, Miss Broadwicks interest in parachuting continued. She worked for an aircraft plant during the war years and was presented with the Pioneer Award in 1953. In her middle years Tiny kept in touch by belonging to aviation organizations like the Early Birds, OX5 Club, and the Southern California Aviation Breakfast Club. She is also a member of the Curtis Hall of Fame.

Perhaps one of her greatest honors came on November 16, 1972, when the Adventurers Club of Los Angeles, California, held a Tiny Broadwick Night. During the festive evening, attended by many aviation VIP's, she was presented a pair of "Gold Wings", which signifies 1,000 jumps. Norman Heaton of the United States Parachute Association made the presentation for her long and distinguished career in parachuting.

Georgia "Tiny" Broadwick ready to jump.

Bill Booth and "Tiny" Broadwick at the 1977 Zephyrhills parachute meet.

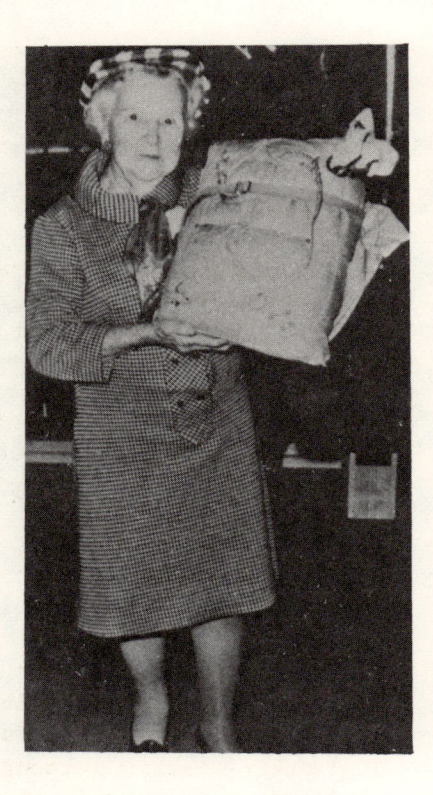

Tiny Broadwick, The First Lady of Parachuting, displaying one of her 1920 parachutes she donated to the Smithsonian Institute in Washington, D.C.

Georgia "Tiny" Broadwick passed away in 1979 at the age of 86. In her later years she became well known in skydiving circles. Tiny liked to visit many of the drop zones in Southern California and to attend many of the larger parachute meets held throughout the country. She oftentimes commented to the younger skydivers how easy and exciting modern jumping was compared to her time. Tiny is revered in parachuting circles for her contribution to the history and folklore of parachuting. She will always be affectionately remembered as "The First Lady of Parachuting."

Sisters Of The Silk

The role of women in parachuting during World War II was an indispensable one. Spurred on by patriotic motives, and a real shortage of manpower, women answered the call to duty by replacing men in critical jobs. In the field of parachuting, the job of a rigger is mainly a behind the scenes support position. Like the pilot who flies an airplane, each paratrooper in the U.S. Army requires the efforts of many supporting personnel to help him carry out vital missions. From the design and manufacturing personel, to the test jumper who evaluates the final product, to the parachute rigger who packs the chutes he jumps, all must work together and share the ultimate responsibility for maintaining the high standards required for victory. Women parachute riggers not only met, but exceeded, these expectations placed on them by the demands of wartime.

U.S. Army Paratroopers had a high regard for the small, but efficient, group of WAC's who packed their parachutes. Affectionately called the "Sisters of the Silk", WAC's performed the most noticeable of all safety operations. Trained to exacting standards at Fort Benning, Georgia, at the internationally famous Parachute School of the U.S. Army, female rigger applicants faced the same learning ordeal as any male.

Ask any in the airborne: paratroopers are made - not born. The same is true of the parachute riggers in the Women's Army Corps. The work is far from easy. The intricate techniques of packing and maintaining parachutes requires highly trained people. The WAC's at Fort Benning were sent through five weeks of gruelling and thorough indoctrination. They learned to master every phase of rigging: inspection, maintenance, and packing. Most important of all, they learned not to make mistakes. The life of every paratrooper depended on their precision.

The first week of training was devoted to

understanding the nomenclature, general functioning of the parachute, and rudimentry packing, tacking risers, and stowing suspension lines.

During the second week, the WAC's were taught the care, operation, and use of both the electric and manually operated sewing machine. Since these machines are used in a wide variety of applications such as the repair of harnesses, packs, and canopies, she must become an expert in their use.

The interpretation of drawings and blue prints, pattern layout, attachment of hardware, stitching patterns, patching of canopies, ripcord installation, and small fabric parts manufacture, occupied a good portion of the third and fourth weeks training. And if this wasn't enough, all WAC's were expected to maintain regular military proficiency in clothing and barracks inspections, close order drill, and special types of guard duty. Rigging school wasn't a bed of roses by any means.

Dedicated R.A.F. Sisters of the Silk.

The fifth week, and the last, saw the WAC's being subjected to a searching review of every detail learned in the preceeding four. She had to pack a chute that was to be "live jumped" by a paratrooper. This final practical test was a tense situation. Sweating out whether the rigidly packed and inspected chute would actually function properly and lower its jumper safely to the ground was the last hurdle.

Upon successful operation of "her own" chute, each "Sister of Silk" was awarded the prized silver, winged emblem of the parachute rigger. The personal satisfaction and pride of accomplishment was immense.

After graduation each new WAC parachute rigger was assigned to one of the many base parachute lofts at various military installations. Here the arduous, time consuming, and relentless quest for perfection continued. The total dedication of these female riggers, and the acceptance of them by their rugged paratrooper counterparts, formed a lasting alliance of mutual respect, admiration, and trust. Each Army Parachute Rigger believed totally in the pledge they were expected to live by:

The Rigger Pledge

I WILL - Keep constantly in mind that until men grow wings their parachutes must be dependable.

I WILL - Pack every parachute as though I am to jump with it myself and will stand ready to jump with any parachute which I have certified as properly inspected and packed.

I WILL - Remember always that the other man's life is as dear to him as mine is to me.

I WILL - Never resort to guesswork, as I know that chance is a fool's God, and that I, a rigger, cannot depend on it.

I WILL - Never pass over any defect, nor neglect any repair, no matter how small as I know omissions and mistakes in the rigging of a parachute may cost a life.

I WILL - Keep all parachute equipment entrusted to my care in the best possible condition, remembering, that little things left undone cause major troubles.

I WILL - Never sign my name to a parachute inspection or packing certificate unless I have personally performed or directly supervised every step and am entirely satisfied with all the work.

I WILL - Never let the idea that a piece of work is good enough make me a potential murderer thru a careless mistake or oversight. For I know there is NO compromise with perfection.

I WILL - Keep always a wholehearted respect for my vocation regarding it as a high profession, rather than a day-to-day task, and will keep in mind constantly, my grave responsibility.

I Will Be Sure—Always

The U.S. Army was not the only branch of the armed forces to recognize the talents of women in the field of parachuting. During World War II, the Parachute Rigger School at the U.S. Naval Air Station. Lakehurst, New Jersey, trained over 300 personnel each year to become parachute technicians. About 10% of this total were women.

Established in 1924, after the Navy issued regulations requiring all of its airmen to wear a parachute when flying, the first class had only 11 students and took but a few weeks. By the time the Second World War began, the course had grown to 15 weeks and included such technical subjects as oxygen usage in high altitude flying, life rafts and survival equipment, and even a 20 hour course in tumbling.

Why was tumbling required in a parachute rigging school? Because the Navy encouraged, but did not require, that all riggers actually jump a parachute they packed. It was their way of ensuring that it's rigger airmen understood the importance of their work. Tumbling helped condition each potential rigger for the task of making a live parachute jump.

There was an incentative for the riggers to jump. Not only did a live jump strengthen their confidence, but the extra $50 per month helped ease their financial strain. Males and females were given the opportunity to "live jump" a self-packed chute. Percentage wise, only a small number declined the offer. Once out the door of a fast flying R4D airplane, its ability and confidence that counts the most. Mother Nature can't tell the sexes apart falling through space.

Parachuting received a tremendous publicity boost as skydiving, called the "Sport of the Space Age," was refined during the late 1950's and early 1960's. Women were there contributing their enthusiasm, desire, and skills to promote this exciting sport.

Women have never taken to skydiving in large numbers. Estimates of their participation range from 5-10% during the 1960's, and as high as 15-20% during the 1970's. Perhaps the rigors of skydiving, the demands for performance, and social expectations, have a tendency to eliminate most women from considering sport parachuting as a legitimate athletic alternative. Perhaps not! But modern skydiving is mostly a male sport. But don't be fooled into believing that women who do skydive haven't done it as well, and some as we shall see, much better than males. Women who skydive follow closely in the footsteps of other female jumpers, and carry on a long tradition of excellence.

In 1956 the United States sent it's first parachute team to Moscow for the 3rd World Championships. Five parachutists and one alternate composed this meager delegations. The U.S. Team finished 6th overall out of ten countries competing. This was an adequate showing for such a new U.S. sport; but they would have to do better. This first team was composed entirely of males. In order to compete to the fullest, in the overall country standings, female jumpers would have to be included. It wasn't until 1960 that women met the challenge of competing internationally.

Bobbie Gray

U.S. Parachute Team tryouts for 1960 were held at Fort Bragg, North Carolina. Captain Bobbie Gray of the XVIII Airborne Corps Club was one of three females entered in the women's division. Jumping along side male competitors, she placed an incredible 12th overall to earn a place as the only female on the team that would compete in the world meet being held in Sophia, Bulgaria. A year earlier, Miss Gray had become the first female in the U.S. Army to make a freefall parachute jump. Later that year, Miss Sherrie Buck, a civilian, was selected as the second member of the 1960 U.S. Parachute Team. Both would be the first women's team, and the first U.S. women to compete in international competition.

Unfortunately, Bobbie Gray suffered a broken left leg during the world meet while trying too hard to reach for the target panel, and had to withdraw. Sherrie Buck went on to finish 10th out of 24 women competing in the individual accuracy event. The results by these two women, and the entire U.S. Team was the best ever.

1962 Overall World Champion Muriel Simbro looks on as Joe Crane kisses Nona Pond. Dagmar Kuldova of Czechoslovakia placed second.

Muriel Simbro

World meets in parachuting, for the individual events of style and accuracy, are held every even year. The 1962 women's team competing at Orange, Massachusetts, surprised, even startled, everybody by delivering brilliant performances. Of the five world titles won by the U.S. Team, the women brought home four of them. The women's team accuracy championship from 1000 meters was won by Muriel Simbro, Nona Pond, and Carlyn Olsen. Pond, Simbro, Olsen, and Kim Emmons, combined to win the Overall Women's World Team Championship event. Muriel Simbro captured the Women's World Championship in Individual Accuracy from 1500 meters. Muriel also combined that score, with scores in the style event and team accuracy event, to capture the most prestigious of all the women's competition trophies, as she won the Overall Woman's World Championship.

Members of the 1960 U.S. Parachute Team: kneeling, Bobbie Gray, left, and Sherrie Buck. Standing, left to right, Richard Fortenberry, Jim Arender, Loy Brydon, James Pearson, and Harry Arter.

Muriel Simbro

Now Muriel Simbro is a very special woman because of her competitive achievement in being the first U.S. woman to ever win a gold medal in a world meet. She is also the first female in the United States to earn a "D" license.

The Class "D" license is not easy to obtain, and was never meant to be. It requires a minimum of 200 freefall jumps, plus demonstrating proficiency in accuracy, spotting, style, jumps into water and at night, and jumps from as high as 12,500 feet. Small wonder the United States Parachute Association has named this their Expert license. Muriel was only the 78th person to be awarded this highest of licenses. After receiving her "D" license in September, 1961, at Livermore, California, the only comment from this very talented and capable woman was, "My only grievance is that more women don't participate in Sport Parachuting." As it turned out, more women did get into skydiving. No doubt many were influenced by the high standards set by Muriel Simbro.

This pattern of competitive excellence continued during the 1964 world meet held at Leutkirch, West Germany. The U.S. Women's Parachute Team of Thelma Taylor, Maxine Hartman, Anne Batterson, Gladys Inman, and Susan Joerns, placed third in team accuracy, and took a first place overall team gold medal. Maxine Hartman took home a 3rd place bronze medal in the style event, and "Tee" Taylor brought home gold medals as the World Style Champion and Overall World Champion. In just five short years, United States women skydivers came from nowhere to completely dominate international competition.

Nona Pond — member of the 1962 U.S. Parachute Team.

Susan Joerns

In terms of competitive excellence and longevity in parachuting, the absolute master, male or female, belongs to Susan Joerns. Few competitors in any individual sport have attained a peak of excellence, and stayed at the top for such a long period of time, as the remarkable record of this attractive young woman proves. From 1964, when she was first selected as an alternate on the U.S. Woman's Parachute Team, until 1978, when she was again a U.S. Team member, Joerns competed in 12 U.S. Nationals and went to 4 world parachute meets.

She has amassed an amazing total of 30 trophies and medals for her competitive

Susan Joerns — A tenacious competitor.

achievements. Twelve of her awards were for first place performances. This record total would have been higher had she chosen to enter the nationals in 1969, 73, 74, and 79. Also the United States boycotted the 1966 world meet by not sending a U.S. Parachute Team. Suzie was a team member by virtue of placing 1st in Style, and 2nd Overall.

Suzie Joerns competition record per year looks like this: 1964: 1st in Style, 3rd Overall 5th in Accuracy, 1965: 1st in Style, Accuracy, and Overall, 1966: 1st in Style, 2nd Overall, 1967: 1st in Style, 1st Overall, 1968: 1st in Style, 2nd Overall, 1970: 1st in Accuracy, 1971: 4th in Style, 1972: 2nd in Style, 1975: 1st in Style, 5th Overall, 1976: 2nd in Style, 5th Overall, 1977: 5th in Style, 3rd Overall, 1978: 5th in Style, 7th Overall.

1980 will be a year for holding another World Meet. Suzie Joerns missed the 1979 U.S. Nationals because she was attending medical school in Houston, Texas. If she finds time to attend, it's probably a good bet she will continue to add to her already record number of competitive laurels.

Maxine Hartman-Nellen

The U.S. Parachute Association issues "Gold Wings" to its members who have made 1,000 freefall parachute jumps in accordance with their Basic Safety Regulations. The plain facts are that it takes a lot of money, time, and dedication to reach one of skydiving's highest milestones. Maxine Hartman-Nellen became the first U.S. female to receive this prestigious honor when she made her 1,000th jump on October 1, 1967. She celebrated this historic occasion by skydiving from an AX-5 hot air balloon at Steve Snyder's Ripcord Para-Center, Lumberton, New Jersey. She was only the 105th person in the U.S. to be so honored.

Barbara Roquemore, a California jumper who has been a member of several U.S. Parachute Teams was the second female to receive "Gold Wings," and the first to be presented "Diamond Gold Wings" by USPA. She was presented this award on November 19, 1979. Gold Wings with one diamond signifies the completion of 2,000 freefall parachute jumps. Barbara was the 26th U.S. jumper to earn this award.

In case anybody is wondering if there is still yet another plateau to be achieved by a woman skydiver, the answer is absolutely yes. If the mind is boggled by 1,000 or 2,000 skydives, then 3,000 jumps is even more staggering. The U.S. Parachute Association issues "Double Diamond Wings" to mark the occasion.

Patt Valley

Petite, pretty, and a very talented Patt Valley made parachuting history by becoming the first female in the United States, and the free world as well, to make 3,000 skydives. This historic event took place at the Greene County Drop Zone in Xenia, Ohio, on July 15, 1978. Patt began her jumping career in 1963 at Gainsville, Georgia. A USPA member for 14 years, she now lives in Xenia and spends much of her time at the drop zone instructing, jumpmastering, and fun jumping. Her next goal in a long and distinguished career is to be the first woman to make 4,000 skydives.

When not attending to her responsibilities around the drop zone, Patt spends much of her time with the Falling Angels, a Xenia based all female exhibition skydiving team. The "Angels" consist of Nancy Kurlin, Karen Dean, Suzanne Sherer, Patt Valley, and team manager, Jack Fitzwater. The "Angels" travel to many of the air shows in the Indiana, Ohio, Kentucky, and Michigan areas where they have established themselves as crowd pleasing favorites.

There is something about watching four lovely women jump from an airplane, perform intricate aerial maneuvers in freefall, and make standing landings, that really turns the spectators on. Perhaps it's the perceived danger, their aerial precision, or

Official poster of the 1968 World Parachute meet.

Patt Valley, first woman in the free world to amass 3,000 freefall parachute jumps.

maybe people just can't quite believe women can do all these things. Whatever the reason may be, their continued success speaks well for them. As far as can be determinded, the Falling Angels are the only active all female demonstration team in the United States.

A specialty of the Falling Angels, and a genuine mind-blower for the crowds who watch, is Canopy Relative Work (CRW). The "Angels" exit the airplane about 5,000 feet, open their ram-air parachutes immediately, and proceed to fly each canopy together so they are connected by each other's feet in a vertical stack. After a four-way canopy stack is completed, they circle around for several minutes, and then fly the stack directly towards the spectators, separate at near ground level, and each "Angel" performs a standup landing. The crowd goes wild with appreciation.

The Falling Angels exhibition parachute team. Standing, Jack Fitzwater, team manager, kneeling, left to right, Patt Valley, Suzanne Scherer, Karen Dean, and Nancy Kurlin.

Members of the Greene County world record canopy relative work 12-Stack," completed at the 1979 U.S. National Parachuting Championships on July 6th, held in Richmond, Indiana.

The Angels obvious expertise in this newest phase of skydiving led them to form a larger team in an attempt to break the world's record for canopy stacks. In July, 1979, the current record was 9-stack. During the "Boogie", or open jumping portion of the 1979 U.S. Nationals, held in Richmond, Indiana, their persistence paid off big rewards. Composed entirely of Greene County Skydivers, they assembled a new world's record 12-stack on July 6th. Momentary contact by a 13th jumper was made, but not held long enough to qualify as legal by existing rules.

The record setting jumpers in the 12-stack, in order of entry were: Karen Dean, Don Bucklin, Nancy Kurlin, Patt Valley, Andy Spurlock, Terry Burris, Jeff Saunders, Brian Barrett, Jim Fangmeyer, Roger Gardner, Chris Milliken, Jayne Marchant, and Scott Haslam.

Ardath Evitt

Generally speaking, people would agree that being young is definitely an advantage when it comes to making intentional parachute jumps. Youth have the edge in terms of stamina, tend to be less cautious, and incline more towards daring activities. For the most part these basic assumptions would be correct. But don't be mislead! Just about anybody could make a parachute jump given the correct situation, proper training, and a genuine desire to do so, regardless of age.

Take the example of Ardath Evitt, a 74 year old great-grandmother who calls Paris, Illinois, home. She had a dream about making a parachute jump. Her family thought she had gone just a little bonkers. Her grandson, 30 year old Clyde Taylor, who originally put the bug in her ear, didn't think so and agreed to help her.

After being turned down at several drop zones, the persistent grandma found her way to Kelly Field, home of the Parachutes and Associates Drop Zone in Mooresville, Indiana. Bob Branch, the owner and operator, agreed to let her go through his First Jump Course training and make the jump, but only if the weather conditions were perfect. The wind was the key consideration; too little or too much and the jump would not take place.

After completing the rigorous training, Ardath had to wait for two weeks until the right conditions prevailed. On Sunday, August 6, 1978, Grandma Evitt, Clyde Taylor, and instructor/jumpmaster, Karen Hymbaugh, felt the time was right. Outfitted in jumpsuit, helmet, goggles, boots, and two parachutes, the intrepid grandmother said she was ready to go.

Everybody climbed aboard a single

Great-Grandma Ardath Evitt, oldest person in the world to make their first parachute jump.

engine Cessna 180 and broke ground to fulfill her dream. Circling in at 3,000 feet, Karen put out Taylor and made ready for another pass over the drop zone. Several minutes later Mrs. Evitt followed with a perfect exit. Her chute opened perfectly and she steered it to a flawless landing on the drop zone.

It is believed that Ardath Evitt is the oldest person, female or male, to ever make a parachute jump, eclipsing the record of another 69 year old woman who jumped in May 1977. After making her historic jump, grinning broadly and sopping wet with perspiration, the brave grandma had this to say, "I'll do it again, but I'm gonna do it in cooler weather." And chances are pretty good she will. The moral of this jump? You're only as young as you think you are!

Cheryl Stearns

It should be obvious by now, but women have played a highly significant role in the folklore of parachuting. And there is no doubt they will continue to do so because they have come a long way. The final woman discussed in this chapter will help make this point even more obvious.

The acknowledged performance masters in Sport Parachuting are without question the "Golden Knights", of the United States Army Parachute Team (USAPT). In the individual competition events mentioned throughout this chapter, the "Golden Knights" figured prominently. There has hardly ever been a national championship, or a U.S. Parachute Team, that hasn't been dominated by members of this elite unit. Becoming a member of the USAPT is probably one of the most difficult assignments any soldier could attempt. Being airborne qualified is only the first step. Each applicant is strictly evaluated during team tryouts, held once a year, on military bearing, attitude, leadership, discipline, and parachuting ability. Needless to say, but very few persons are selected to join this traditional all male team.

This all male tradition went by the wayside in 1974 when Cheryl Stearns was selected to become the first female to join the "Golden Knights." Nobody did her a favor by any means—she earned her slot just like anybody else. In the next six years, while a member of the USAPT Competition Team, Sgt. Stearns did a lot more than just earn the respect of her fellow team members - she rewrote the record books for women.

At her first nationals competition in 1974, Stearns placed 17th in Style, 7th in Accuracy, and 9th Overall. A year later at the 1975 nationals, she started staking out her territory in the women's division by taking a 1st in Accuracy, 11th in Style, and a 7th place Overall.

1976 was a very good year for this dynamic woman. At the nationals competition she placed 1st Overall, 2nd in Accuracy, and 3rd in Style. As a member of the U.S. Woman's Parachute Team at the world meet, she took home a Gold Medal as a member of the 1st place team in Accuracy, 1st place Overall Country, 2nd place Silver Medal in individual Accuracy, and 11th in the Style event. Not too shaggy for her first World Meet!

In 1977, Sergeant Stearns placed 3rd in Style and 2nd Overall. But at the 1978 nationals she swept every event by placing 1st in Style, Accuracy, and Overall. This was followed up by a superb performance at the 1979 World Meet, held in Zagreb, Yugoslavia, where she literally knocked'em all dead! She took a 1st in Style, a 2nd in individual Accuracy, was a member of the first place accuracy team, 2nd place for overall country, and a very big 1st place gold medal as the best overall individual jumper. Cheryl

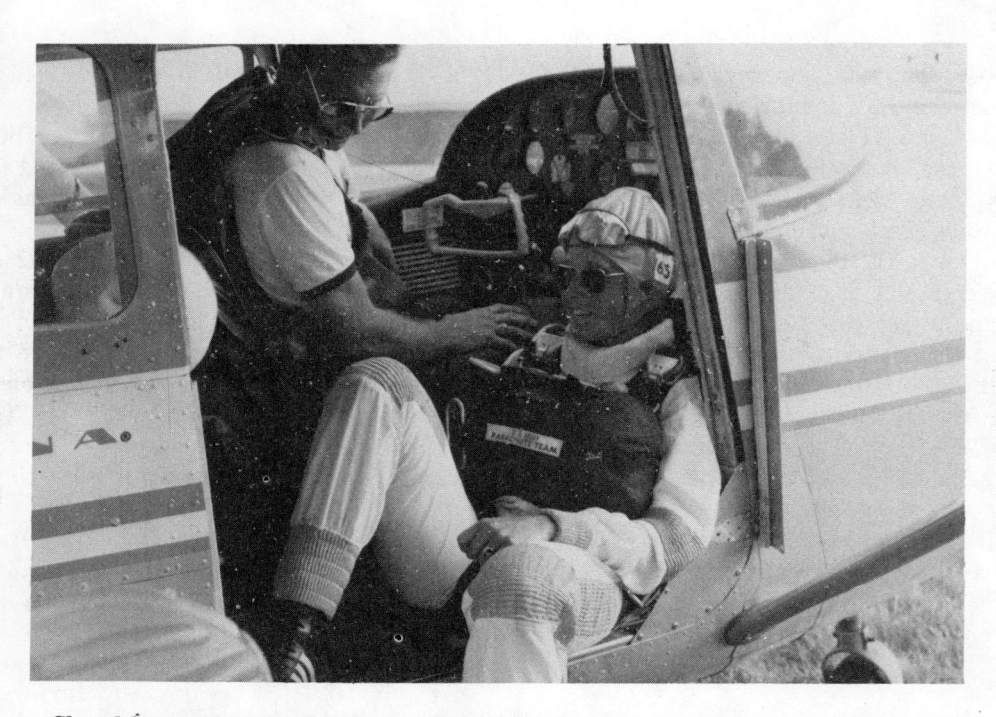

Cheryl Stearns boards an aircraft at the 1979 U.S. nationals for an accuracy jump, as the pilot, Skip Giles, observes.

Stearns clearly established herself as the best woman skydiver in the world. But wait, there's more!

The 1979 U.S. Nationals were held in Richmond, Indiana. Once again she swept all three individual women's honors by taking 3 1st place finishes. Interestingly enough, when her scores were compared to those of the top male competitors, consisting entirely of fellow USAPT members, she beat everyone of them. For the first time in the history of U.S. Parachuting competition, a woman was the best individual skydiver. And that ain't too shaggy anyway it's sliced as most males will tell you!

For Cheryl Stearns, there isn't too much for her left to accomplish in skydiving, ex-

The best individual skydiver in the United States for 1979 — Cheryl Stearns.

Bob Von Derau, USAPT member and 1978 national parachuting champion, congratulates Cheryl Stearns for her winning skills.

cept of course to repeat her record performances. Her 20 medals in national and international competition during six years of tough jumping since 1974 is a record. She has rewritten every female parachuting record possible. Most suspect that whatever she eventually gets into will be done with the same fervor. Hers is a grand story and exemplifies the standards by which modern women are constantly striving for.

In the 178 years since the first woman donned a parachute and tasted thrilling adventure, Cheryl Stearns is the best to date by far. Her part in the continuing evolution of women parachutists only confirms what people have been saying about them for years, "you've come a long way indeed."

J. Floyd Smith — His original concepts led to the development of the first manually operated parachute.

Chapter 6

Dayton: Cradle Of U.S. Parachuting

Across the "western front" the skies became a blazing battleground ignited by the firepower of Sopwith Camels, DH4 British de Havilland's, Bristol Fighters, and the Vickers FB5 Gunbus. World War I was the first major war to utilize the airplane as an instrument of power. The military quickly realized the awesome potential of aircraft, and immediately began frantic efforts to develop airplanes with more speed, manuverability, and armaments. Interestingly enough, the parachute was all but forgotten in this race for destruction. After the Great War, men would have to gather at Dayton, Ohio, where the airplane was born, to reinvent the parachute.

Up to this time, parachutes were still considered the unreliable tool of crackpot stuntmen and not a suitable device any respectable pilot would be caught dead with — and none were! The almost total lack of use of parachutes by World War I airmen is one of the greatest tragedies in aviation history. There are some plausible explanations why an acceptable parachute wasn't designed and utilized. But considering the time and money that went into training pilots, and the availability of some parachutes, it has to be a mystery why something wasn't done to stop the senseless death rate of U.S. airmen.

The attitude of the pilots themselves certainly didn't encourage and speed the development of parachutes along. Many pilots had a fetish about their use, feeling it was a sign of cowardice and a lack of confidence in one's ability and equipment. A pilot would rather take his chances in a broken down, fire-gutted plane, than place his trust in a flimsy piece of silk that was less than 100 percent reliable. Ironically, many pilots actually jumped from burning airplanes to escape the inferno, only to meet sure death impacting the ground. Strange as it now seems in retrospect, less than one hundredth of one percent of the flights made during the first World War were made by pilots wearing parachutes.

Balloon Chutes

In the latter days of the war, aviation leaders began to look for a method of cutting down the terrible death toll of these pilots. Their attention soon turned to the American Balloon Section. Balloonists were used in the war as artillery spotters and observers. These large sausage shaped balloons used were easy prey for enemy aircraft firing incendiary bullets. Since the balloons were filled with hydrogen gas, a single hit resulted in instantaneous combustion.

Records of the American Balloon Section revealed the lives saved by utilizing parachutes. It was found that 117 emergency jumps were made during World War I. A total of 76 men made the jumps, 26 of whom made more than one jump. One balloon commander is credited with using a parachute five times in a single day.

J.V. Mumma, in *Parachutes*, describes their application. "The use of parachutes in balloons was the first practical use of the invention as an aid to saving life. The old free balloon type parachute was used for this purpose with the canopy attached to the balloon basket and connected by shroud lines to a harness worn by the observer. When the balloon was fired upon, the observer fastened the shroud line ring to his harness and jumped overboard. The parachute automatically released itself as the retaining cord broke."

Taking a lesson from the success of these wartime balloonists a great deal of thought was given to designing a parachute for airplane pilots. The only parachutes in existence, those developed by the aeronauts, were much too large, heavy, and unwieldly, to be carried aboard the frail airplanes of those early days. Still the carnage of death of American pilots continued. Squadron leaders came to realize the stark reality of their situation. Pilots could not be expected to live more than six weeks after they reached the front. A pilot might not last his first flight and a pilot who went through the entire conflict was rare. One commander had his group of pilots replaced four times because of combat losses. Slowly, but surely, the truth became more obvious to everybody: if a plane was shot down, the pilot was almost always killed.

Another agonizing fact came to light during the last days of the war. It was observed that German pilots were beginning to wear parachutes and quite often used them to save their lives. In the Spring of 1918, a German pilot bailed out of his plane at 18,000 feet using a German built Heinecke parachute. This was the first instance of any airman using a parachute to save his life in combat.

Mumma describes the chute this way: "This Heinecke parachute was packed in a cylindrical sack, 16 inches in diameter and 10 inches deep. The top of the sack was closed by a draw-wire. The pilot used the sack as a seat cushion, to which was attached his harness. The draw-wire was secured to six or eight feet of 50-pound cord, the other end being tied to the fueslage of the plane. When the pilot jumped over the side this cord disengaged the draw-wire and pulled the parachute from its sack. The cord was then broken by the weight of the man's body."

Capitalizing on information made available from parachutes recovered from German airplanes and pilots, the Allies developed several crude types of chutes. The English came up with the Mears and the Guardian Angel; the French with the Orrs and the S.T.A. models. All of these, including the German built Heinecke, were unduly heavy, weighing 20-35 pounds without the harness. None were strong enough to withstand opening at speeds in excess of 100 miles per hour. Despite the continued urging of military men like General Billy Mitchell, Commander of American Air Forces in France, the U.S. never developed a suitable parachute for its airmen to wear during World War I.

If World War I accomplished nothing else, it clearly established the utility of parachutes, and the urgency of perfecting one for use by pilots. After the Armistice was signed in 1918, the challenging work began in earnest.

Floyd Smith

The United States Goverment authorized a board of experts to be set up to begin the work of developing an emergency parachute in 1918. The technical experts assembled at McCook Field, Dayton, Ohio, to begin their arduous task. Included in the group were Major E.L. Hoffman, Guy M. Ball, J.J. Higgins, J.M. Russell, Floyd Smith and Sgt. Ralph W. Bottreil. Hoffman was chosen to supervise this unit.

McCook Field was originally established as a research and development facility for the U.S. Army Signal Corps Aviation Section on October 18, 1917. Orville Wright, and two prominent Dayton citizens, Charles F. Kettering, and a Mr. Smith, selected this tract of land located west of Troy Pike and east of the Miami River. The land was owned by the heirs of Anson McCook. This acreage was eventually bought and leased to the city of Dayton, which in turn leased it to the U.S. Government. A flying field was built and named after the "Fighting McCooks", whose record for courage and bravery during the Civil War was legendary around Dayton.

Being favorably located within the U.S. industrial complex, McCook Field became the engineering and development station and proving ground for airplanes during World War I. Engineers and mechanics gathered at McCook Field to pool their aeronautical resources so they could measure the performance and adaptability of new airplanes for use by U.S. forces in Europe. Among other things a major portion of the R & D work on the Liberty engine took place at this historic field.

Almost forgotten by the U.S. Air Service,

The original Smith Pack.

Floyd Smith had been previously authorized to begin experiments at McCook Field just prior to the signing of the Armistice. Due to the efforts of a Colonel Willard, who was closely associated with General Mitchell, Smith had been transferred from South Field, Dayton, where he had been a final inspector of all aircraft production. Smith managed to locate in an abandoned hangar at McCook Field where he continued his early experiments with parachutes. In the tremendous demobilization effort, his little unit was completely overlooked and he continued unmolested.

His early work at McCook Field would prove of great value later to the panel of experts. Smith's idea was to develop a parachute system capable of being operated independently of an airplane. A "free" type parachute, he argued, could be operated entirely by the pilot once he fell clear of the airplane, and therefore not have to worry about the static lined rig becoming entangled on the airplane. The sad truth is that

Floyd Smith's ideas were a little ahead of their time. His ideas were scoffed as being ridiculous.

Various objections were raised to counter Smith's concepts. Most argued, and very persuasively, that an airman was incapable of making even the shortest of freefalls. Wouldn't he lose consciousness? Wouldn't fear freeze his reactions? Could he keep cool long enough to pull the ripcord? Others suggested that if an airman were injured he would be unable to operate a ripcord. With an automatic, or static lined parachute, all the pilot would have to do is fall out of his plane, and the chute would open on it's own.

A common argument heard and voiced often, actually concerned the integrity of pilots. They argued that if a pilot had a reliable means of escape he might be tempted to abandon his plane when the going got a little rough, or when there was a chance he still could make a landing. This line of reasoning completely misunderstood the psychological motivations of Air Service pilots and the relative importance of his life and his machine. In later years, the universal use of parachutes enhanced pilot performance by the knowledge that even if their plane was shot down, they could escape to fight again.

Startin' From Scratch

As work continued by members of the McCook Field crew, it became painfully obvious that very little accurate data was available about parachutes. The state of the art was woefully limited. Theories had to be developed, tested, and confirmed or rejected during the early going.

All known types and makes of parachutes were tested. Most of these were shipped to McCook Field from other countries. Dummies were used to drop test every parachute from every conceivable position; upside down, climbing, diving, and spinning. The German Heinecke parachute proved to be the weakest and most unsafe of all those tested. It was a simple canopy, made with

The German built Heineke parachute — the first to be used for life saving from an airplane.

cotton fabric that had grommets placed around the skirt, to which 70 pound lines were tied. Using a 200 pound dummy at 100 miles per hour all the lines were snapped. Silk lines were later attached and the canopy disintegrated at 110 miles per hour. Similar results were obtained when testing other models. These tests only confirmed what everybody suspected: there was no entirely satisfactory parachute for use from an airplane.

The early experiments did produce some notable advancements. Most noticeable was the use of habutai silk lines being substituted in place of hemp cord. Hemp lines had a tendency to snag when coiled for long periods. The use of silk eliminated this discrepancy, saved space and weight, was flame resistant, and was a more versatile product. Silk was universally used until World War II when it was replaced by a lighter and stronger man-made product called nylon.

Design Imperatives

After extensive research tests and compilation of the data, the McCook field experts knew they didn't have the kind of reliable parachute they needed; but they now had a clear idea of what they wanted. They decided to encourage further development by inviting interested parachute designers and manufacturers to come up with their own models based on criteria they were given. The requirements were very stringent for the times. Each parachute would have to meet or exceed the following expectations:

1. It must be possible for the aviator to leave the aircraft regardless of the position it might be in when disabled.

2. The operating means must not depend on the aviator falling from the aircraft (not static line operated).

3. The parachute equipment must be fastened to the body of the aviator at all times while in the aircraft.

4. The operating means must not be complicated or liable to foul, and it must not be susceptible to damage through any ordinary service conditions.

5. The parachute must be of such size and so disposed as to give maximum comfort to the wearer and permit him to leave the aircraft with the least difficulty or delay.

6. The parachute must open promptly and must be capable of withstanding the shock incurred by a 200-pound load falling at a speed of 300 miles per hour.

7. The parachute must be steerable to a reasonable degree.

8. The harness must be comfortable and very strong and designed so as to transfer the shock of opening in such a manner as to prevent physical injury to the aviator. It must also be sufficiently adjustable to fit the largest and smallest person.

9. The harness must be so designed that it will prevent the aviator from falling out when the parachute opens, regardless of his position in the air, and at the same time it must be possible to remove the harness when landing in the water or in a high wind.

10. The strength "follow through" must be uniform from the harness to the top of the parachute-bearing in mind the old axiom -"No chain is stronger than its weakest link."

11. The parachute must be so designed that it is easily repacked with little time and labor.

"Sky-Hi" Irvin

About this time an enterprising young engineer named Leslie "Sky-Hi" Irvin arrived at McCook Field with a parachute of his own design. His parachute incorporated some novel ideas, but for the most part, it was very similiar to previous types used in balloons. After looking over Floyd Smith's unique design, he liked what he saw, and became an instant convert.

Irvin brought a great deal of practical experience with him. Though only a young man of 22, Irvin had made over 200 static line jumps from balloons and airplanes, and had never noticed any loss of breath. Even as a circus high diver, where he often jumped from 75 feet above the ground into a net, he never came close to losing consciousness. One other time he witnessed a parachutist falling to his death and saw the man flailing his arms and legs frantically until impact. Since the jumper was still conscious, Irvin figured he still was able to pull a ripcord, or to use another chute if he had one.

With this aerial background, Irvin quickly

Leslie "Sky-Hi" Irvin prior to making a static-lined jump from a balloon. His mother wishes him well.

realized the ultimate potential and value of Floyd Smith's radical designs. There wasn't any doubt in his mind a pilot could open a parachute in freefall. Floyd and Irvin worked closely as a team to combine the best features of both their parachute systems. What emerged was a refined design that gave the engineering test group much reason to be hopeful.

The combined design featured a 28 foot canopy, block constructed of 1.6 oz. Habutai silk, a small 24 inch, spring loaded pilot chute that would act as a drag to pull the main canopy out and into the air. The main canopy, pilot chute, suspension lines, and connecting risers, were all neatly stowed in a new compact container. The container was attached to a comfortable and adjustable harness, giving the airman sufficient room to perform his flying duties. Also featured was a ripcord mounted on the front of the airman's harness. The ripcord consisted of three steel pins welded to a steel cable. The pins secured the pack with a locking cone that fit through a grommet. To open the pack and release the pilot chute, the user had only to pull the cable which withdrew the pins. This model was designated as the Army Airplane Parachute Type "A".

Even though the Type "A" was vastly superior to any previous parachute assembly, the skeptics still sounded off, voicing their disbelief. The parachute had been tested eleven times, once with a 235 pound dummy going 118 miles per hour. The rate of descent was a mere 9 feet per second, more than enough to meet the stringent expectations. But still nobody had yet to "live jump" the parachute.

First Freefall

On the morning of April 28, 1919, the grapevine around McCook Field buzzed with excitement. The gossip going around said the newly designed freefall parachute was going to get its first practical test. Major Hoffman had given Les Irvin permission to make the jump, and a chance to make history. For some reason Floyd Smith, whose basic design concepts started this whole experiment, would not make the jump. Just why Irvin was chosen over Floyd, who also had some jumping experience, is a mystery. It's a good bet that the decision was based on politics or personalities. Smith was, of course, very disappointed. More aggravating to him was the fact he had been chosen to pilot the plane that would carry Irvin to meet destiny.

As the time drew nearer for Irvin to make the jump, everybody who could do so went to see the sight. Almost everybody figured Les Irvin would be killed or maimed; a martyr to aviation. An ambulance waited nearby, motor running, ready for the worst.

Intuitively, however, Irvin knew better. In a put-up or shut-up situation, Irvin climbed into a DeHavilland DH-9 biplane on that same day. Despite last minute warnings from friends and professional associates, he decided it was time to settle this whole issue. With Floyd Smith manning the controls of the airplane, Irvin took off, and climbed to 1,500 feet above the field. Circling in on jump run Irvin smiled and exited the airplane. He fell for several seconds, and completely in control, gave a healthy yank on the ripcord and watched as the canopy blossomed open perfectly.

His parachute had worked as he knew it would, but in his jubliation he didn't concentrate on landing, and broke an ankle. At this point no one really cared. Not only had he proved to some skeptics that his parachute could do what he said it would, he also became the first person to officially make a premeditated freefall parachute jump. All in all, it was quite an historic day.

The jump was a convincing one to some, but not to everybody. A discussion still centered on the idea about how far a man could fall before he would lose his senses. So, on the morning of May 14, 1919, Floyd Smith walked over to Jimmie Johnson, who at the time was the chief civilian test pilot at McCook Field, and asked if he would fly him to make a freefall jump. Johnson was dubious about this, but finally agreed to take Smith up.

Smith leaped from the airplane, fell about 500 feet, and opened his parachute. The system worked perfectly and he landed uneventfully. Within the next several days more freefall jumps were being logged. The age of freefall had truly arrived, and the rest is history.

Leslie Irvin reaped the enormous benefits from being the first to make a freefall parachute jump. As he lay in the hospital two weeks after his historic jump, he learned of Smith's jump, and others being made by volunteers. To him there was no longer any doubt a man could safely jump from an airplane in distress and operate his chute in freefall. Shortly thereafter, the U.S. Army Air Service put their official stamp of approval on the chute by placing an order for 300 of the systems. It still would be several years before pilots were required to wear parachutes, and more years before pilots completely overcame their distrust of using them. But the ice had been broken and substantial headway made in this important area. With the initial order placed by the U.S. Government, the parachute manufacturing industry was created. Irvin rushed back to Buffalo, New York, to start his business.

Irving Air Chutes

Over the years Irvin's parachutes would gain world wide acceptance by surviving the most rigid tests. The U.S. Government conducted over 50,000 live and dummy tests, under every conceivable condition, before it was adopted as standard equipment. The English Royal Air Force made an additional 7,000 tests to convince themselves of the parachutes value. In time, other governments bought Irvin's parachutes. Success came swiftly to the business minded Irvin. Within a few years, the demand was so great for his aerial lifesavers, he opened other factories in Glendale, California, Fort Erie, Canada, and in Letchworth, England.

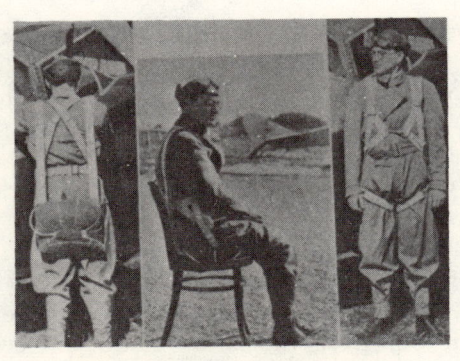

Les Irvin wearing a seat type parachute his company built.

The Irving Air Chute Company, as it was now officially called, owes its name to an interesting mistake. When the Articles of Association were being drawn up, a "g" was added to his last name by mistake. It was found out too late and the name remained. It would cost some money to change the papers. Irvin was parachute rich and cash poor, so the "g" remained on the title. From then on, all Irvin parachutes were manufactured by the Irving Air Chute Company.

Under Les Irvin's personal supervision, the I.A.C. produced the first biased cut parachute canopy, the first ring slot parachute, and the first quick connector emergency reserve chute. Irvin is also credited with inventing the first practical quick release fittings and the first quick release harness ever used. He developed the first successful automatic barometric ripcord opener, and the first para-brake used to slow down airplanes. I.A.C. produced the first parachutes used by the British Airborne forces and the Russian Paratroopers, and later made chutes for the French government. The last government to start using paratroopers was the U.S. government. The American parachute used by U.S. Paratroopers was a design patented by Irvin in 1920.

Until his death, in 1966, in Los Angeles, Leslie Irvin had been at the helm of his continually growing organization. The company, whose stock is traded on the American Stock Exchange, operated divisions in Denver, Colorado, Raleigh, N.C., Cortland, N.Y., Glendale, California, and Lexington, Kentucky. Subsidiaries also operated in Canada, Sweden, France, South Africa, and affiliated companies operated in Spain, Italy, Germany and Australia.

Floyd Smith, who designed the original freefall parachute system, never got the recognition he deserved. Though an inventive and brave individual, Smith didn't have much savvy as a businessman. His patents were often infringed upon, and though he won a few court cases, things just didn't work out for him. With minor improvements, his designs were to remain the basic standard model for a great many years in the parachute industry. Smith worked at designing parachute systems for Switlik and Pioneer Parachute Companies in later years. Over 100,000 pilots and passengers have survived emergency bailouts since those early years, giving the best testimonial to his creativity. The history of parachuting owes a debt of gratitude to men like Floyd Smith whose vision reached far beyond the horizon, when others couldn't see pass their noses.

The Irving back type parachute.

Major E. L. Hoffman

By the end of 1924, most of the original McCook Field experts had gone their separate ways. Their mission had been completed to the fullest extent possible. Major E.L. Hoffman, who supervised those historic tests, received the Collier Trophy in 1927 for his efforts in helping develop what is still considered one of the safest and most reliable types of parachutes. In one form or another, the basic design his crew put together, is still used today. The inscription on the Collier Trophy reads for "the most distinguished contribution to the science of flight."

Hoffman's efforts are often overlooked, but he was the first to scientifically deal with the question of the speed at which a man falls. His theoretical calculations established that the speed would not exceed 120 miles per hour when the air resistance of the average human being would equal the acceleration due to gravity. His classic calculations were subsequently confirmed by practical experiments. To this date the "terminal velocity" of humans in freefall is still considered to be 120 miles per hour.

The Hoffman Triangle parachute.

In later years Hoffman owned the Triangle Parachute Company in Cincinnati, Ohio. Formerly the Safe Aircraft Co., his firm built the Hoffman Triangle parachute. This innovatively shaped personnel canopy gained some popular acceptance in military and civilian applications. Civilian parachutists liked its slow rate of descent and steerability. The military utilized this canopy as part of their A-1 assembly, a manually operated quick attachable chest parachute, and in the S-3 model, a manually operated seat parachute with a 23 foot Triangle chute. However, the complexities of the design and production difficulties eventually forced the Army to discontinue its use.

Major E.L. Hoffman.

The "Russell Lobe"

James M. "Jimmy" Russell, also of the orginal McCook Field group, continued his involvement by designing and manufacturing parachutes. In 1924 he designed a canopy with scoops ("Russell Valve Type") which assisted openings. In 1926 he designed the famous Russell Lobe parachute which was his major contribution to parachuting. Dissatisfied with the unstable descent characteristics of the flat-circular canopies, Russell produced a mushroom shaped parachute that was extremely stable. This

The "Russell Lobe" parachute.

unusual design obtained a good measure of acceptance and popularity, particularly among civilian parachutists, because of it's stability, reliability, and slow rate of descent.

The Russell Lobe canopy was not deployed by a pilot chute; Russell didn't like their use. Instead the canopy was deployed into the air by means of an "ejecto" strap. This strap was tucked in the last fold of the canopy during packing. A jerk on the ripcord would remove the pins, pull off the entire cover from the pack, and throw the canopy into the airstream behind the jumper. This method of deployment was possible because the internal rigging lines and center lines were relatively short and packed very small with less folds than round canopies. Using this unique "ejecto" strap, the Russell Lobe canopy opened in less than one and three-fifths seconds from the moment the ripcord ring was pulled.

The Russell Parachute Company was formed about 1926, in San Diego, California. Later another branch was opened in England. The Company suffered a serious reversal of fortunes when it lost a hotly contested patent lawsuit to the Irving Chute Company. The company went out of business in 1935.

McCook Field remained the "Cradle of Aviation" for ten years. As the development of faster and heavier airplanes progressed, this 254 acre field soon became inadequate. A huge sign warned aviators "This field is small, use it all." The citizens of Dayton donated over 4000 acres for a new location. On October 12, 1927, Wright Field was dedicated and that site became the new center of U.S. military aviation experimental efforts. McCook Field was returned to the city of Dayton and later renamed after Charles F. Kettering, a doctor, inventor, engineer and influential citizen. Kettering Field is still located in north Dayton a short distance from innerstate 75, off the Keowee Street exit. A low income housing development and a home for the elderly sits next to a variety of baseball diamonds, football and soccer fields. A historical marker has been

James M. "Jimmy" Russell, one of the original McCook Field pioneers.

erected by the Montgomery County Historical Society to remember the site of this famous airfield.

The Final Test

The parachute system designed by the McCook Field engineers had come a long way in use and acceptance. Missing was the ultimate test which would prove beyond a doubt the parachute's value. Everybody had to wait until the fall of 1922 before an Irving parachute received its first baptism in emergency conditions.

Lieutenant Harold R. Harris, a 27 year old pilot assigned to McCook Field as Chief of the Flight Test Section, Engineering Division, was very well known for his skills in airplane racing and testing. On the afternoon of October 22, 1922, the young, good looking pilot became the first person in the world to save his life by using a Irving freefall parachute.

Flying in mock combat with fellow pilot

Lt. Harold R. Harris, the first to save his life with an manually operated parachute.

Muir Fairchild at 2,500 feet, the two men began maneuvering for position. Harris, flying a Loening monoplane fighter equipped with experimental ailerons, and Fairchild, in a Thomas Morse MB-3 biplane fighter, continued their practice at full throttle. Circling near the center of Dayton, Harris turned to pursue Fairchild when his airplane began to shudder violently. The ailerons were unbalanced and Harris was unable to control the monoplane.

With the control stick vibrating wildly against his legs and the plane speeding to the ground at about 150 miles per hour in a 30° dive, the aircraft began shedding parts of its structure. Harris quickly realized the inevitable. He had only one option available if he wanted to continue flying. He had to leave the aircraft and open his parachute.

Unbuckling his seat belt and standing up into the tremendous air pressure, he was literally blown clear of the disabled airplane into freefall. Three times Harris pulled what he thought was the ripcord that would arrest his rapid fall. He was actually tugging at the leg strap fittings on the harness, located about three inches below the rip-

Marker erected by the Montgomery County Historical Society to commemorate the site of McCook Field — The Cradle of Aviation and Parachuting.

cord. The fourth attempt at yanking the ripcord succeeded and Harris found himself swinging under a beautiful white silk canopy in seconds.

Harris later recalled, "At no time did I have any sensation of falling. I had perfect control of my arms and could move them up and down my body at will." Observers of the bail-out estimated Harris opened his parachute a mere 200 feet above the ground. Seconds later he landed in a grape arbor with his canopy drapped over the side of a fence. He was the first person to save his life with a manually operated parachute while escaping from a disabled aircraft.

Caterpillar Club

Several days after Lt. Harris' successful leap, two members of the McCook Field Parachute Section gathered up some souvenirs of the bail-out and decorated their loft walls with them. Parts of the aircraft, photographs of Harris after he landed, and the parachute he used, became part of a makeshift museum. The publicity surrounding this jump, and the collection of mementos soon attracted visitors.

Milton St. Clair, one of the parachute men, was showing two newspapermen from the Dayton Herald, Maurice Hutton, the Herald's Aviation Correspondent, and Verne Timmerman, a photographer, around the museum shortly after it was put together. Timmerman made a casual suggestion, "Why not start a bail-out club? There was already one member, and there would surely be more that could join in time."

The thought clicked in their minds. Maybe it was a good idea; it had definite possibilities. What should the club be called? After thinking for several minutes the suggestion of "Sky Hookers" was offered; another mentioned "Crawlers" - but neither name seemed just right.

Browsing through some literature several days later, St. Clair read material about the Caterpillar Tractor Company. In an inspired moment he thought of the silk spun by a caterpillar which lowered itself to the ground. The caterpillar was a great symbol to use he figured. Hutton and Timmerman also liked the name immediately and the Caterpillar Club came into existenance.

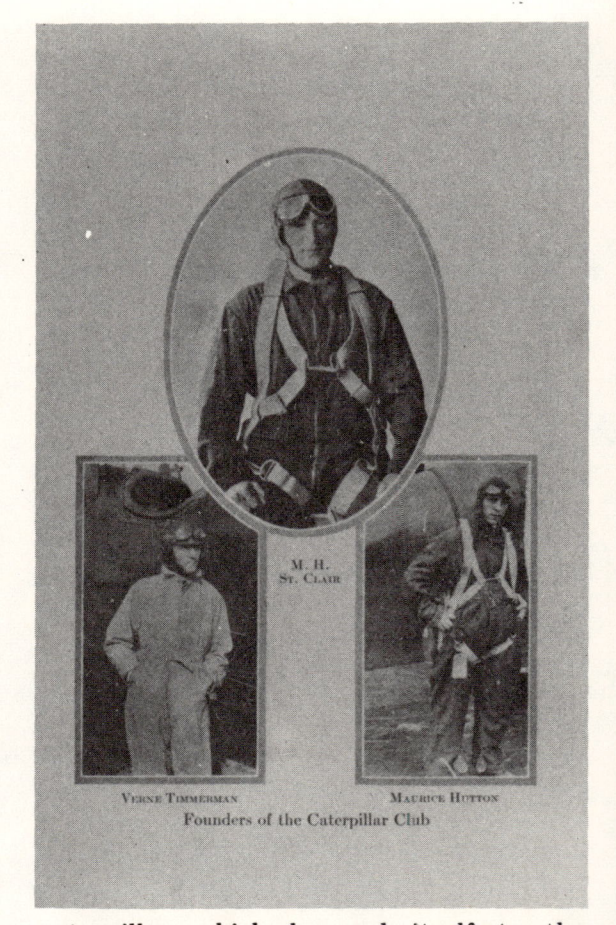

Major Hoffman thought the whole idea was great! The same went for Floyd Smith, Guy Ball and James Russell. They were all enthusiastic, especially Leslie Irvin. Since his factory in Buffalo was churning out hundreds of these new chutes, the idea of a club for satisfied customers, had a special appeal to him.

A special pin was designed from a hastily put together committee composed of Irvin, Smith and Ball. Made by a Buffalo jeweler, the small Caterpillar pin was made of gold, had small ruby eyes and the recipients name and rank was engraved on the underside. Irvin stated from the outset he would give a caterpillar pin to every person, no matter where he lived, who saved his life in an emergency with one of his parachutes. It was a promise he never broke.

Shortly after the formation of the Caterpillar Club, Lt. Frank Tyndall bailed out of a M.B. 3A in distress on November 11, 1922 and became the second member of the elite Caterpillar Club. Technically speaking, and to be historically correct, Harris and Tyndall are not officially recorded as the first recipients of the gold caterpillar pin. They were the first two to escape from a disabled airplane and save their life with an Irving parachute. In 1929 the official roster of the Caterpillar Club was back dated three years to include Henry Wacker, John Boettner and William O'Conner, all civilians, as the first three members of this exclusive club.

Wingfoot Express

These men gained entry due to a controversey that arose shortly after the club was formed. The question was raised concerning the use of parachutes from other than a disabled airplane and their use as a life saving device on intentional jumps. Wacker and Boettner made static-lined excapes when the blimp they were helping to crew, the Wingfoot Express, burst into a orgy of flames over Chicago in July 1919. Hardly anything is known about O'Conner, the third member, except that he was a civilian and he made his qualifying jump on August 24, 1920 over the city of Dayton.

Why members were included of this nature, who neither used a Irving freefall parachute, or made their jumps from a disabled aircraft, is open to speculation. Perhaps it was due to the tremendous publicity surrounding the crash of the Wingfoot Express. Prior to the start of the Caterpillar Club, there were countless static-lined parachute jumps being made in emergency situations from both balloons and airplanes. Despite this pecularity of the Caterpillar Club, Lt. Harris is recognized by most aviation people as the first member of this club.

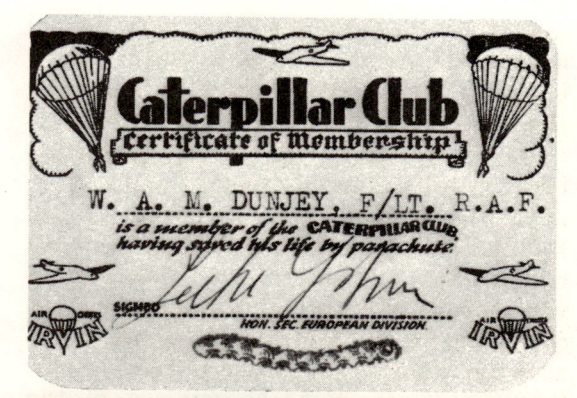

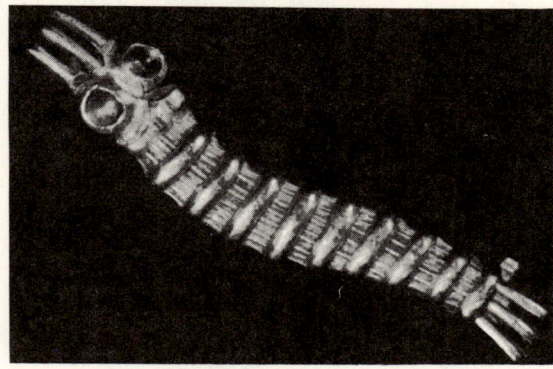

The official Caterpillar Club pin.

An interesting feature of the Caterpillar Club, and one that every member surely appreciated, was the absence of any traditional organization. The club had no entrance fees, dues, meetings, committees, social premises, and no officers. Membership was for life and according to Irvin, "The only privilege of membership was it's continued enjoyment." Irvin undertook to maintain club records at his Buffalo factory. The only club property was the filing cabinet which housed membership applications.

Aviation's most exclusive fraternity grew steadily after 1924 when ten new members would join the club and bring the total membership to 15. At the end of 1925 it stood at 27, by 1926 it was 40, 1927 there were 78 and at the end of 1928 there were 120. By 1930 membership in the Caterpillar Club was over 210 persons.

By 1955, the Caterpillar Club had enrolled over 40,500 members who had saved their lives with Irving parachutes. And through the years, more persons obviously were saved by Irving chutes, but never bothered to apply for membership. Though not as in vogue as in earlier times, the Caterpillar Club is still active, if only in principle. The club will always remain a tribute to the man who made it all possible.

The parachute is so universally used that an emergency bail-out doesn't bring that much attention. But the folklore of the Caterpillar Club is remembered vividly by modern skydivers and others who parachute for fun, profit, and defense reasons. The safety of parachutes is taken for granted these days, but most can recall how difficult things were "back in the good old days", when a parachute jump was filled with much more danger and insecurity. The annals of the Caterpillar Club are filled with thousands of exciting stories of men and women who used a parachute to save their lives. Interested readers are encouraged to read about these exciting, unusual, and sometimes hilarious accounts in such books as *Jump!* by Don Glassman, and *Into the Silk*, by Ian Mackersey.

The course of history often takes a stange turn here and there. Irvin's name being misspelled is one example. In another curious twist of fate, Irvin never had to use a parachute in an emergency situation, even though he had a lifetime of flying and owned many airplanes. He could never become a member of the club he helped nurture for so long. Leslie "Sky-Hi" Irvin was never to be a Caterpillar.

Oldtimer Bob Kiehfuss

Hot and muggy afternoons are a common occurrence in July around Cincinnati. In an effort to arrest his boredom, Bob Kiehfuss drove to Dayton to look over a new shopping center in 1971, and perhaps buy a few items. It wasn't merchandise, but the resurrection of many fond old memories and experiences about parachuting, that Kiehfuss carried away with him that day.

Walking around the complex of stores, Bob noticed a small shop whose owner's last name was Klink. This rang a bell! After talking with the owner, Jim Klink, for a couple of minutes, he found that Jim was the son of Bob Klink, an old friend and parachute buddy he used to jump with during the late 1930's. The younger Klink, of all things, was a pilot and skydiver at the Greene County Parachute Center in Xenia, Ohio.

Later that afternoon, Kiehfuss drove to the drop zone at Xenia, and introduced himself to many of the jumpers. He asked numerous questions about the airplanes and the equipment used by the skydivers; everything was so new and different from anything he ever imagined. Bob was amazed at how the jumpers could control their

Countless pilots owe their lives to parachutes. This lucky pilot lived to fly again.

1938 photograph of Bob Kiehfuss preparing to jump from a Waco biplane.

bodies in freefall, and how they could steer their parachute once opened. It didn't take long for the local boys to realize they were talking with a man who made numerous parachute jumps before they were born, and during a time in parachuting, when many still considered it to be a dangerous stunt.

They learned, for instance, that in 1937 Kiehfuss was a member of a flying club called the Cincinnati Albatross Birdmen. The club flew regularly out of the Western Hills Airport, a small grass strip about fifteen miles west of Cincinnati. It was during this time some of the pilots began making parachute jumps. Shortly thereafter, the Cincinnati Parachute Club was formed. It looked interesting and Bob decided to give it a try.

After spending a few hours being checked out by another fellow pilot and jumper friend named George Schmiedeke, Bob was ready to make his first jump. Wearing a 28 foot Triangle parachute for his main chute, and a seat pack for a reserve, he was carried aloft in a Waco biplane on January 23, 1938, to begin tasting a new kind of adventure. His first jump was a freefall, as were all of his subsequent jumps. The instructions were simple: when you get feet first, yank the ripcord! Well that's what Bob did, and after a successful jump, Bob was hooked on parachuting. This was the first of close to a hundred jumps he would make in the next several years.

Bob recalls how difficult parachute jumps were to come by in those days. "About the only persons making a lot of jumps were those performers connected with travelling airshows. Parachute equipment, if you were lucky to find it, was usually very expensive. Also it was difficult to find a pilot who wanted to take a chance and fly you. In those days one or two jumps per weekend was something to talk about."

National Air Races were the big aviation spectaculars during this time. Parachute jumpers usually played a featured role either by doing exhibition jumps or competing in spot landing contests. The Air Races attracted many of the finest precision pilots and expert parachutists who competed in these three day events. With just seven jumps to his credit, Kiehfuss managed to qualify for the 1939 Cleveland Air Races. And though he didn't win anything, he had a great time and gained some valuable experience. He met and talked with many of these famous pilots and jumpers, including Joe Crane, who was the driving force in establishing the National Parachute Jumpers Association.

Kiehfuss continued to be a semi-regular at many of these kinds of aviation events throughout Ohio, Indiana, Kentucky, and Michigan. Oftentimes he figured prominently in the spot landing contests. When not

Bob Kiehfuss [center with rig] and members of the Cincinnati Parachute Club. 1939 photo.

competing he would make exhibition jumps. His specialty was flag jumps. On other occasions he carried a large umbrella and jumped while holding onto it. The crowds loved this exhibition because they were sure he was going to be killed when it collapsed on opening. A parachute was always hidden in the airplane so the spectators couldn't see it. It helped build the drama. After falling several thousand feet with the broken umbrella, Kiehfuss yanked open his main chute and landed safely. The crowds were always entertained and everybody was happy. And that was important to Bob and the other jumpers. Jumping was exhilarating fun, and the club liked sharing their experiences with others.

During these years the hottest canopy for competition jumping was the Hoffman Triangle Parachute, then manufactured in Cincinnati by Carl Noelcke. Kiehfuss regularly tested these chutes for Noelcke, and promoted their use in his exhibition and spot landing jumps. When not busy with these activities, Bob spent time promoting and developing interest in parachuting as the president of the Cincinnati Parachute Club.

Eventually these happy days became troubled times for a nation engulfed in war. In 1942, Kiehfuss was drafted into the armed forces, and this all but put an end to his parachuting activities. After returning home in 1946, he attempted to generate some activity for parachuting, but the interest wasn't there. Most of his old buddies were either married or had sold their equipment. It just wasn't the same; enthusiasm was difficult to arouse. The years after World War II were mostly inactive ones for parachuting. The 1950's witnessed a resurgence of activity, but by this time Kiehfuss was married, settled down, and retired from active parachuting.

Years later, in 1971, after hanging around the Greene County Parachute Center for several weeks, the old juices began to flow. He wanted to experience one more time the surge of adrenaline rushing through his body, and the quiet feeling of gently floating down under a parachute canopy. With the help of Jim West and Jack Fitzwater, Kiehfuss made another parachute jump, his last, at the age of 57.

The hard core jumpers at Greene County, and there are many, can relate to oldtimer

Bob Kiehfuss very well. He has a engaging personality, and like most jumpers, has his share of jump stories and experiences he likes to swap with them. He has noticed how friendly and open the modern jumper is about helping those with less experience. Bob says that, "In the old days there were few jumpers. It was difficult, if not impossible, to learn anything from most parachutists. They tended to be a secretive lot, and not inclined to share their knowledge with others. This attitude made learning more difficult and a lot more dangerous than it had to be." Bob is very glad to see the sharing and openness, which he feels enables today's newer skydivers to learn and progress much more quickly than he did. And this he feels is the best thing that can help promote skydiving as a sport.

As senior jumper, in terms of longevity at the Greene County drop zone, Bob has earned the respect of students and skygods alike. Not solely because of his age, but the fact that he doesn't live in the past. He has taken the time to know all about the advances made in parachuting. Says Bob, "If I were 20 years younger, I'd probably be jumping my buns off."

Kiehfuss still spends many of his Sunday afternoons at the drop zone. He enjoys the atmosphere, the people, and of course is still attracted to the exciting world of freefall skydiving. Though he no longer jumps from airplanes, Bob spends his time photographing and watching the jumpers. He can still be coaxed into talking about the good old days when anybody who leaped from a perfectly good airplane was a genuine folkhero. He can usually be located in the vicinity of his brown Cadalliac, which he drives to the drop zone crammed with Gatorade, munchy foods, fruit and his scrapbooks. The jumpers who know him come up and talk with Bob, while taking a few slugs of cool, liquid refreshment to slake their thirst. He is staying involved with a sport he loves almost as much as life itself. To the Greene County skydivers, oldtimer Bob

Jim West [right] poses with Bob Kiehfuss after his last jump in 1971.

Kiehfuss is more than a folkhero; he is part of their tradition. And tradition cuts a wide and deep furrow at this drop zone.

Greene County Is Skydiving

The Greene County tradition started in April 1963 with a $1500 loan, the friendship of Jim Shearer, and a dream. After his discharge from the U.S. Army 101st Airborne, where he had been an instructor with 320 military jumps, Jim West decided skydiving was the thing to do. Together with Shearer, they started a parachute center where skydivers could call home, and have a drop zone that wasn't ruled by pilots. They bought student gear, trained new jumpers, rented planes, and worked very hard. Eventually their dedicated enthusiasm on behalf of jumpers began paying dividends.

In four short years the center owned four jump aircraft. The on-field facilities included a lounge area, inside packing tables, office, dressing rooms, hangar, concession stand, and bunk room. In those early days West had the dedicated help of Al Gordy, Ken Glover, Jay C. Pugh, and the Loudakis brothers, George and Mike. The work was far from easy, the hours were long, but the rewards were many. There were lots of skydives to make and good times to share. During this time the Greene County club slowly evolved into a major center of skydiving activity, attracting jumpers from a five-state area.

Greene County is no ordinary parachute center. From the start, this was, and still continues to be, a family oriented parachute center. Home is where the family stays. Many jumpers bring their families and plan on staying a day or two so they can skydive with some of the best. This operational philosophy has continued to reap rewards for those who call Greene County their family. Over the years this dream has expanded into a family of affiliated drop zones.

Another principle underlying this concept in drop zones, is West's desire to help people. For instance, a young, energetic young man will find his way to the drop zone one day. He desires to jump out of an airplane, but doesn't have the money. "No problem," says the Boss. "We got plenty of work just waitin' for somebody to do it." In short order the kid might be sweeping out the hangar or loft, picking up the trash, mowing the 22 acre field, or "gunking down" one of the many airplanes. If the kid is really serious about skydiving he will eventually learn to become a skilled jumpmaster, instructor, pilot, rigger, and earn his jumps by becoming part of the crew that trains first jump students.

A Helping Hand

Most of these young men and women just

Skydiving Billboard.

Kathy Adams and "the Boss" fuel the Twin Beech on a busy day.

want a way to pay for their jumps, and be part of the exciting world of skydiving. A few want to continue with parachuting as a vocation, and will want to run their own drop zone. When the time is right, the Boss will be there to help them reach for their dreams. He helps these young people become squared away businessmen by helping them start their own operation. Whatever it takes to get them started, usually equipment, airplanes, money, legal help, and lots of extra training, is always gladly given.

Ken Heissman was the first to branch out and do his own thing. He went to Bardstown, Kentucky, in 1971, and started his own Greene County tradition. Since then other affiliated centers have opened up throughout the United States. Bob Von Derau and Ralph Hartman went to Atlanta, Georgia, Phil Lura opened a center at Covington, Louisana, Rusty Young went to Kansas City, Kansas, Chuck Leonard to Sarasota, Florida, and Jeff Sanders to West Point, Maryland. Other centers opened for a while in Dallas, Texas, Cleveland and Marion, Ohio. The experience of running your own company is a dream as old as the United States itself, and one which West has helped others to realize.

The crew at the home center in Xenia, Ohio is typical of all Greene County drop zones. Everybody pitches in to do a job. Practically all of the team have a pilots license, scads of skydives, USPA licenses, Instructor/Jumpmaster ratings, a FAA riggers ticket, and tons of hours logged mowing the grass, gassing planes, and training students. On any given day, "Super Joe" Gebhardt, Scott Haslam, Kathy Adams, Harvey Seaman, Patt Valley, Wilbur Ryle, Jim Fangmeyer, and Brian Barrett are busy with their duties, while the Boss goes where he is needed. During the very busy times,

Jim's wife, Lee, pitches in by running meets and organizing parties.

Nobody gets lost in the shuffle. Students are the life blood of any parachute operation, and there is a genuine feeling that somebody cares. Students always have somebody to talk to when they are feeling a little insecure about making that first freefall, or how to pack a new canopy. People helping people, doing what they like, and doing it to the best of their ability, tends to cultivate a breed of unique and dynamic skydivers. This quality instead of quantity attitude works. The Greene County system of parachute centers is the largest in the world, and getting bigger.

Everybody at Greene County is justifiably proud of their accomplishments, especially those in competition. A third place bronze medal in the 4-way relative work competition in 1970 at U.S. Nationals, a second place silver medal in the same event at the 1971 nationals, and a first place gold medal in 4-way at the 1972 nationals. At the 1978 U.S. Nationals Bob Von Derau, transplanted owner of the Atlanta, Georgia center on active duty with the U.S. Army Golden Knights, took a gold medal for first place Master Overall Champion, and a silver medal in Master Accuracy. At local levels, the Greene County skydivers almost always figure prominently in conference meets. Steve Adams, Craig Walko, Alan Godfrey, Kenn Heissman and Bob Boswell have collected enough gold medals to fill a small book. The same can be said of Patt Valley in the women's events. Like the boy sez, "if it's worth doing, it's worth doing well."

Anniversary Skydive

Many honors have come the way of Greene County over the years. One of the greatest was the chance to celebrate the 50th anniversary of freefall in 1969. The U.S. Parachute Association sponsored a skydiving exhibition into Kettering Park (originally McCook Field) in Dayton, Ohio, on April 27, 1969. With the help of the Dayton Chamber of Commerce, Ken Glover, Mideastern Conference Director for USPA, Kress Lochridge of the Air Force, and twelve selected parachutists, this historic event captured the attention of Dayton residents. Over 5,000 spectators came out to help celebrate the 50th anniversary of Leslie Irvin's historic freefall. The twelve skydivers were; Ed Drumheller, test jumper and aeronautical engineer for Irvin Industries; Karen Roach, Martha Huddleston, and Dave Sauve, all members of the 1968 U.S. Parachute Team; Doug Metcalf, the National Collegiate Parachute Champion; and Jim West, David Ellis, Bob Hieatt, Donald Bonner, George Loudakis, Paul Fayard, and Steve Crussett, all members of the Xenia based Greene County Parachute Club.

The day of the jump was bright and sunny, but the skygods drove the winds to over 20 mph. Even the intreprid test jumpers of the original McCook Field crew knew when to stay on the ground. After a test load of jumpers landed successfully at the Xenia drop zone, it was decided to go ahead with the exhibitions. Afterall, everybody figured, "If Irvin could leap into the jaws of death..." An old skydiver axiom explains this situation, "It's never too windy to jump - maybe a little windy to land, yes, but never too windy to jump." So everybody began loading up the airplanes.

To make a long jump story shorter, the first plane load of Drumheller, Loudakis, Fayard, and Crussett, landed in the middle of the park under some very marginal conditions. The second load of Roach, Huddleston, Sauve, and Metcalf, all U.S. Team Members, weren't so fortunate. They got caught in a dramatic wind lull, and opened up too far away to make the target area. The final load of Bonner, West, Ellis, and Hieatt, got ideal conditions and landed practically deadcenter on the target panels. The crowd ooohed and aaahed during the festive celebrations. Ken Glover presented Jim West with Diamond Gold Wings marking his 2,000th jump. Everybody got a warm ova-

Dayton: Cradle of U.S. Parachuting

tion for their efforts. Leslie Irvin would have been proud of everybody that day.

The Big "Woohaa"

Every year on the first Saturday of December, the Greene County skydivers from all the centers gather in Xenia to celebrate Christmas. Just like the swallows returning to Capistrano, or the buzzards returning to Hinckley, the "family" returns via airplane, automobile, and weather permitting, by parachute. There are enough airplanes flying in to make a small air force, and enough good vibes to go around for everybody. The newest jumpers have heard about Xenia, and the Boss, and plan on taking larger doses of some of the best skydiving available anywhere.

Now the Greene County jumpers pride themselves on doing everything the best. Their Christmas party is no exception. "Super Joe" calls it a "woohaa." The term comes from taking a slug of booze and saying "Woohaa, sure do taste good." The 1979 edition of this traditional event was the 16th consecutive year; and it was a real "Woohaa." This once a year feast brings everybody together to celebrate the achievements of its members. Each center owner takes a turn at presenting recognition awards to those persons who were most instrumental in furthering the cause of sport parachuting at their DZ.

Least everybody think these good ole boys are perfect, the Findleson Award is presented annually to the person who made the biggest "screw up." This is a fun award, and there are usually lots of prospective nominees being considered for the honor. But only one is selected as being the best of the worst. As the Boss says, "Anybody can win it, even the best among us." Jim has won this coveted award three times. The 1979 Findleson Award was fondly presented to Bill Moran. His dirty deed: running up a Cessna 180 with the wind, causing the aircraft to tip over and bending the prop, while he was instructing a new student in such manuevers.

This year the curiosity of the jumpers drove several persons to keep track of the number of jumps each person had who attended the party. The number must be fantastic; West had over 6,000, Von Derau had over 3,800, Valley over 3,300 and Adams over 3,200. There were many with over 2,000 skydives, and a bunch with over 1,000 jumps present. When everything was totalled up, it was a staggering 120,698 skydives! Of the 179 jumpers present, the average was a shade under 675 skydives per person. Terry Pierson summed everything up after the total was announced, "Nobody likes sitting on the ground, ain't no action there."

And to think this whole business of freefall parachuting started in Dayton, over 60 years ago. It's too bad Leslie Irvin, or Floyd Smith aren't around to see the changes they helped foster. The advances made in sport parachuting would stagger their imagination. But if there are spirits in parachuting, it's a good bet they are cavorting around Dayton. Imagine Leslie Irvin or Floyd Smith saying, "Wish I was alive, so I could skydive!"

Chapter 7

Bustin' New Sky

The sky is a relentless master. Those who would challenge its dominion should consider the lethal dangers that cannot be avoided. Man is confronted with a variety of complex physiological handicaps which must be surmounted to survive any ascent beyond 15,000 feet. The gravest threats to survival arise from a marked decrease in breathless oxygen and sub-zero temperatures.

If man dares to venture into the thin, frigid, and hostile atmosphere, elaborate precautions must be taken. Special flight clothes and pressure suits will help defend a parachutist against the chilling effects of -69 degrees F temperatures at altitudes of 36,000 feet and above. Sophisticated pressurized oxygen systems must be used to prevent the effects of hypoxia — a lack of sufficient oxygen in the body cells or tissues. Above altitudes of 40,000 feet life sustaining oxygen must be forced into the lungs. At these extreme altitudes blood boils quickly without supplemental oxygen and a person's Effective Performance Time (EPT) is 15-20 seconds. The environmental characteristics of extreme altitudes turn the sky into a formidable adversary.

Yet despite these inherent dangers, high altitude parachuting has long been a favorite quest of American parachutists. To successfully perform these daring jumps requires more than a realization of the risks involved. Powerful airplanes, detailed planning, and a dedicated desire to overcome the natural elements are crucial. The vast majority of parachute jumps made in the United States are made from below the altitude of 15,000 feet. It is not surprising then, that those few who have made very high altitude parachute jumps, are often regarded as somewhat of folk heroes in their

Art Starnes fully suited up for his record freefall in 1941.

own right. Many would dream of busting new sky, but few accept the challenge.

This chapter deals with the efforts of several men who accepted the challenge and defied their natural instincts. Each of these men, in their own way, and for their own reasons, contributed significantly to man's knowledge of himself and his environment. Whether their reasons were scientific or personal, all increased the distance man had been in extended freefall. For to be able to take command of the air, to be godlike, to own the sky as do the birds, might be the ultimate reason that attracts men to freefall. Human freefall represents the last frontier for aviation minded men. To fly without wings or any mechanical contrivance is the ultimate aviation experience.

This conscious ability to freefall and to plan high jumps has not always been possible. The sky was generally considered to have limited access during the formative years of parachuting. One of the longstanding folk myths about parachuting was that men would be rendered unconscious while making even the shortest of freefall drops. This attitude in the 1920's was shared by the general public, most aviation people, and many parachutists as well. Fortunately, not all persons were bound by these folk myths. The psychological fear of falling, helpless, into a void at incredible speeds, stopped most from even considering freefall. Intuitively, many parachute jumpers knew from their own experiences, that such attitudes only served to retard the progress of aviation safety.

Early Freefalls

The quest to freefall from higher and higher altitudes was compelling for some. It all started with Leslie Irvin. He made the first official freefall parachute jump on April 28, 1919. Two weeks later, on May 14, 1919, Floyd Smith fell 500 feet testing a new pilot's rig. Harold L. Whitby increased this record on April 4, 1928 by freefalling 4,400 feet at the Pensacola Naval Air Station. An Iowan named Kohlstedt is said to have regularly fallen longer distances as early as 1920. Most of his exhibition jumps were completed in the Middle West. The contract he wrote with each promoter stipulated he make a delayed freefall of at least 5,000 feet, open up less than 500 feet above the ground, and land in the infield, or no pay.

For early jumpers who knew their environment, the danger was not in doing long freefall, but the punishing openings. They hadn't figured out how to reduce the opening shock, which could easily daze a jumper and do considerable damage to the parachute. Modern day skydivers jump with deployment devices encasing their chutes that retard the opening slightly. Sleeves, bags, and packing straps allow for easy opening by staggering the opening sequence, instead of getting the jolt all at once. Oldtimers figured a crushing opening was a lot better than no opening.

Probably the first official, and verifiable, world record for freefall jumping belongs to Spud Manning. He jumped with a certified barograph strapped to his body at 16,665 feet, and fell 15,265 feet before opening his canopy. Manning's jump took place over Los Angeles, California, on March 1, 1931. A French parachutist, James Nieland, is said to have made three high altitude freefalls, in the middle 1930's, equipped with medical instruments and oxygen. The highest jump was from 37,000 feet. When and where he jumped, and how far he fell before opening, is not documented.

Despite public ignorance, freefall parachuting was to become a fairly common occurence in aviation during the 1920's and 1930's. Folk myths die hard, and in the case of those about freefalling human bodies, they continued to persist, even to present times, in a limited sense. Freefall jumps were of a relatively short duration. Several practical reasons limited high freefalls during these years. The power limitations of early airplanes was a major factor. Also, there was no genuine reason, other than

Harold L. Whitby, standing on the wing of the airplane which carried him to his record freefall of 4,400 feet.

perhaps stunt jumping, to travel to very high altitudes. Little scientific research was conducted that would have contributed to man's total knowledge of this domain.

Alien Sky

With the passage of time, airplanes being built were larger, more powerful, and capable of climbing higher and higher into the sky. As commercial and military aviation progressed, so did the interest in high altitude parachuting. Traveling at greater altitudes, these early pioneers began to realize the inherent dangers associated with their new world. This alien domain forced man to search for new answers to complex questions. Out of the practical necessity of saving lives, scientific interest and inquiry into the effects of high altitude had now become a prime issue.

Pilots flying at great altitudes, and oftentimes in combat conditions, were at the mercy of nature in emergency situations. World War II brought to the forefront not only the use of more sophisticated airplanes, but also the use of paratroops as well. By this time parachutes had been proved and accepted as a reliable lifesaving device; and it was required equipment for all military flying personnel. But the eternal sky still remained as a threatening and destructive force which had taken the lives of too many unprepared pilots already. It was an environment few relished visiting, no matter what the reason.

There were many questions the Army, as well as aviation scientists, wanted to know about the atmosphere. Would a flyer's heart stop, or his lungs burst? Could he think? What happened to his circulatory system when he plunged earthward from a disabled aircraft? Was it possible, they all pondered, for a pilot to abandon his disabled aircraft at high altitude, and freefall as long as possible so he could escape enemy gunfire, and get into the warm, breathable air at lower altitudes? The greatest minds were perplexed by these unknown quantities.

Many had jumped at high altitudes; but none had ever ventured a long precarious freefall journey. Like many folk myths about aviation, there were many skeptics who said it was impossible. A few believed otherwise.

The "Aerial Maniac"

One of the earliest parachuting pioneers who attempted to answer these kinds of questions was Arthur H. Starnes. Circumstances demanded an experienced jumper who could make experimental jumps to ascertain the physiological effects of high altitude parachuting. Art Starnes was just the kind of man to accept the challenge.

His career in parachuting had already eclipsed close to twenty years. During the barnstorming days of the 1920's, Starnes had been a stunt jumper, wing walker, and skilled pilot. He was billed as "The Aerial Maniac" and everywhere he performed, crowds were thrilled with his death-defying maneuvers. Some of his famous stunts, like swinging beneath flying airplanes on a ladder and dropping into automobiles, plane-changing in midair, and jumping into lakes from flying airplanes, allowed thousands upon thousands of spectators to vicariously experience the thrills of this amazing individual. He was admired by his fellow jumpers because of his cool nerve and his unusual ability.

His dangerous appearing acts often gave the impression that death was imminent; but in reality the details of his show were intricately planned and precisely coordinated. In the years he traveled the eastern, midwestern and southern parts of the United States, he regularly had gotten himself into many tight spots. He always planned on giving the appearance of living

Early photo of Art Starnes taken during his barnstorming days.

on the ragged edge of disaster. And his audiences were never disappointed. This famous "Aerial Maniac" was a professional barnstormer in the strictest sense of the meaning. In every respect, Art Starnes was a folk artist in parachuting.

During his years as a barnstorming stunt jumper he performed regularly for many of the more famous flying circuses of the times. Joining forces with the Gates Flying Circus in 1925, he coordinated his stunts with featured pilots "Loop King Brooks" and "Upsidedown Clyde Pangborn." Later, he formed his own flying circus. He met and became personal friends with Roscoe Turner, who at that time was a fledgling pilot. Working together, they formed the Roscoe Turner Flying Circus. Their acts included airplane acrobatic flight, parachute jumping, wing walking, passenger rides, and Starnes' most famous of all stunts — "The Swing of Death."

"The Swing of Death" was a particular favorite of spectators who came to watch the barnstormers. It was also one of the most dangerous of all aerial stunts. The stunt involved Starnes to appear to accidentally fall off of the airplane and to swing from the landing gear under the fuselage, dangling helplessly, attached only by one shock cord. Starnes had a way of always appearing to be just able to save himself from this apparent accident; by being barely able to climb back onto the fuselage. Starnes was one of the few men during the barnstorming days who had the skill and daring to complete this very hazardous stunt. But then Starnes was no stranger to dangerous activities.

Starnes' interest in barnstorming and stunt jumping began to wane over the years. He continued an active involvement in parachuting and by the late 1930's began to center his efforts in the name of science and national defense. His enormous amount of experience, which included over 300 jumps, made him the ideal candidate to test the effects of long delays from high altitudes.

Working with scientists from the University of Chicago, he became immersed in this high priority project.

As a stunt, high altitude jumps were one thing; but to rely on them as a standard procedure for airmen was another question altogether. The stratosphere was now owned by the airplane. Could the pilot rely on his mental capacities and parachute to save his life in emergency situations? This whole question was shrouded in mystery despite previous experimental high jumps. But there was enough speculation to indicate that stratosphere jumping was not only possible, but probable.

Lifesaving Research

The project called for Starnes to make a record breaking freefall from over 30,000 feet. As nearly as possible, he was to simulate an emergency exit by a military pilot leaving a crippled airplane. Pilots opening their parachutes at high altitudes encountered two fatal problems. The first was the lack of life-sustaining oxygen and the second was the fact that they were easy prey for enemy aircraft. This would necessitate the pilot making a rather long freefall jump to a much safer altitude. Starnes was acutely aware of the impact his test jumping would have on the lives of all military pilots.

To prepare Starnes for his record-making jump, he was equipped with a variety of scientific instruments and gauges. Starnes carried over one hundred pounds of equipment during the jump. Besides his main and reserve parachute, he wore a breathing mask and a sufficient supply of aviators oxygen. To protect himself against the estimated -46 degree F temperatures at jump altitude, he wore an electrically heated suit of coveralls. Starnes also wore a 16 millimeter movie camera strapped to his right hip and pointed to the ground. The camera was to record the spin of the body while in freefall. On his right forearm he wore an altimeter so he could gauge his altitude while descending and know when to struments to record his heartbeat and respiration rate, as well as the altitude. This information was relayed by a small radio transmitter wired directly to electrodes over his chest for the broadcasting of his heartbeat. And finally, he had a device so he could transmit his voice to the ground while in freefall.

To practice wearing and using this sophisticated, as well as cumbersome gear attached to his body, Art made numerous practice research jumps in the high altitude chamber at Northwestern University. Many of them more exacting than the real intended jump. One test jump in the practice chamber was from the theoretical altitude of 40,000 feet, which is the highest altitude man can survive without special pressurized flight suits. Later Starnes would make several live practice jumps from altitudes to familiarize himself with his parachute equipment. Starnes' cool nerve and reliability under stress gained the respect and admiration of all those who worked with him. The stamina and endurance expected of him was extraordinary. His own body weight of 190 pounds, plus all of the equipment he was to wear during his jump, brought his combined weight to over 300 pounds.

Record Freefall

On October 24, 1941, Art Starnes boarded a Lockheed Lodestar in the name of science, national defense, and publicity. The Lodestar was one of the few commercial planes in the country at that time capable of flying above 20,000 feet. For approximately an hour and forty minutes the silver monoplane climbed higher and higher into the sky. At 31,400 feet above sea level, Starnes exited into the cold thin air of the stratosphere.

Starnes began a world's record freefall jump of 116 seconds. He describes this epic making jump, "I was conscious all the way down and comfortable, too," he told newsmen. "I could see the earth whirling by me, for I was in a fast body spin. Then I

Starnes fully equipped prior to making his historic jump. The 16 mm camera strapped on his side recorded his body spin during freefall.

open his parachute. A zippered pocket inside his coveralls held a battery of in-

Arthur Starnes [center] being congratulated by his mother and son after his record freefall.

whipped through a fragment of cloud and my goggles frosted up. I raised one side of the goggles and glanced at the sensitive altimeter."

"I had only two moments of fear," Starnes told the crowd afterwards. "The first was as I stood in the open door of the plane, trying to get enough oxygen inside my helmet and wondering if my equipment would clear the door frame. But the second, more frantic sensation, was when my goggles frosted up in a cloud bank at 23,000 feet and my body went into a series of violent spins and somersaults."

"I threw my legs far apart and then crossed them alternately. That usually pulls me out of a body spin. But it had no effect this time. My head was clear and I began counting to myself. I knew I was falling about 250 feet a second."

"When almost a minute and a half had elapsed, I felt I must raise my goggles and look at the altimeter strapped to my wrist. This was at 15,000 feet. At about 5,000 feet the frost evaporated, leaving my goggles clear." "I knew the worst was over then," he said.

When his altimeter read 1,500 feet, Starnes pulled his ripcord and opened his main parachute above the hard ground of the Chicago Airport. As an extra safety precaution, he opened his reserve parachute to slow down his rate of descent. He landed safely in a cow pasture on the south side of Chicago.

This record-making freefall jump, after months of elaborate preparation, was eminently successful. Starnes' only injury was to his lower lip, which he bit when his parachute opened and jolted him into a temporary blackout. Aside from this minor incident he had proved to scientists, flight surgeons, and to the hordes of skeptics, that a human could survive a long freefall without losing consciousness. Starnes' greatest contribution to the advancement of aviation medicine and safety was that he proved a stratosphere combat pilot, with proper training, could bail out of a wrecked airplane and freefall to a safer altitude where life-giving oxygen was more accessible, and low enough to avoid enemy gunfire.

More Records

The psychological barrier had been broken! Like many great men of our time who break insurmountable barriers, their records are soon eclipsed. In short order, and in less dramatic fashion, Starne's record was broken. Major Boris Kharakhonoff, a Russian Army officer, jumped from a height of 40,813 feet. This was a full two miles higher than Starnes. There is some dispute among historians as to when Kharakhonoff made the jump. Some say he made the jump in August, 1940, others contend the leap was made in 1942. At any rate the jump was not as widely publicized as was Starnes', and is difficult to verify with complete accuracy.

In 1943 Lieutenant Colonel W.R. Lovelace of the U.S. Army Air Corps stepped out of a B-17 Flying Fortress to test exposure at high altitude. His was not a long freefall; he chose to have his parachute opened immediately. He was a skilled flight surgeon who had never made a parachute jump before. But at 40,200 feet he was prepared to risk his life to test the elements in the icy cold atmosphere a different way. His mission was to simulate a pilot opening a parachute at high altitude and having to ride the canopy to the ground. After dropping through the bomb bay doors, his chute was opened by a static line. For twelve harrowing minutes, Colonel Lovelace was tossed about in the air until he finally descended to an altitude where oxygen was more plentiful, and his parachute more stable in the denser air.

Parachutes don't function as well, nor are they as stable, in the rarefied air at higher altitudes. Lovelace was wrenched into unconsciousness from the violent oscillations of his canopy, but somehow managed to hang on. Many minutes later he landed helplessly in a wheat field suffering from a combination of severe shock, oxygen starvation, and frostbite: but he did recover completely.

Art Starnes and Lt. Col. Lovelace's historic jumps provided the necessary scientific data to support the development of future high altitude exploration necessitated by the ever increasing technological advances being made. Man's insatiable desire for speed and performance required new sky to operate within. Starnes busted new sky and helped open the gateway to the stars.

The Jet Age

As predicted, the 1950's witnessed the development of ever more highly advanced and complicated supersonic aircraft, which travelled at incredible altitudes. The survival needs of the pilots who commanded these airships would be even greater. Starnes contribution provided an invaluable beginning to a story that has yet to be finished.

Due to the great strides made in rocketry, and with the advent of the jet engine late in the 1940's, man had the capacity to fly at altitudes in excess of 100,000 feet. And though flights above this height were the

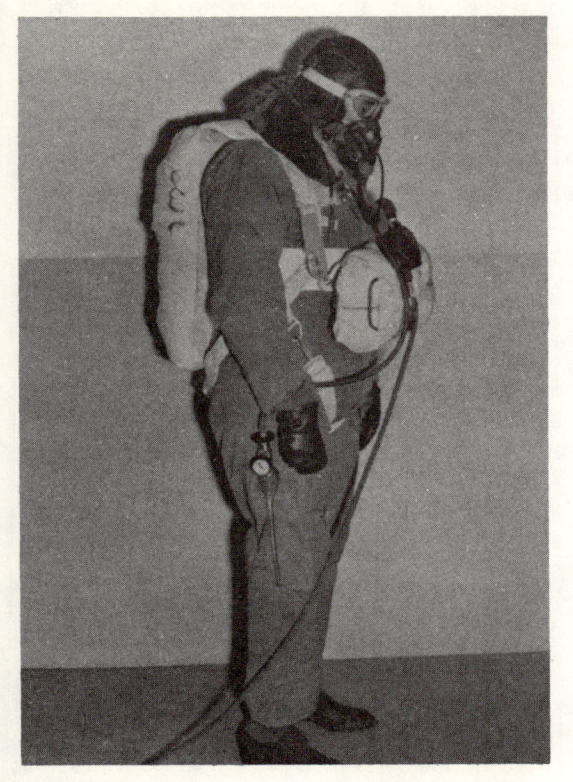

Colonel Lovelace prior to his record-breaking canopy ride.

exception, there were a variety of aircraft capable of operating within the range of 75,000 to 80,000 feet.

At these extreme altitudes there is no air to speak of. Any airman forced to eject from a damaged airplane would incur the wrath of this alien sky. Without specialized breathing apparatus and specially built pressure suits that compensate for the lack of gravity, his blood and other body liquids would quickly boil, and the effects of hypoxia would be fatal. The Time of Useful Consciousness (TUC), or survival time is measured in seconds. Experience had already shown that the greatest chance for survival is to freefall to lower altitudes, into the thicker air. Opening a parachute in these high altitude situations is to invite disaster. The lack of oxygen and pressure, coupled with the powerful opening shock on the airman's body, and the freezing coldness, is a combination of forces which is practically impossible to survive.

By the late 1950's, pilots, flight surgeons, and aviation engineers alike, were acutely aware the performance of modern aircraft had far outstripped the capacity of their parachuting survival and ejection equipment. There was no way the lives of airmen could be assured during an emergency bail out. Man's conquest of the sky had raced far ahead of his ability to safely protect himself. As in earlier years it was now critical that higher altitude survival gear be developed. Pilots and crew members required years and many thousands of dollars to prepare themselves for carrying out a national defense responsibility. To risk losing this expertise for lack of an adequate escape system was a waste of human life and resources. Airmen needed the confidence of knowing their lives could be saved in time of danger. Without that confidence, any pilot would find difficulty in adjusting psychologically to these environmental stresses.

Project Excelsior

To meet this critical need, the United States Air Force initiated a series of projects in 1958. The projects were called Excelsior. The purpose was to test the new Beaupre parachute system and related components to be developed by this team. The men of Project Excelsior were to send a man to the very edge of space as their primary task. Excelsior hoped to prove that a pilot could abandon his aircraft and survive the elements during a lengthy freefall. Live test jumps were the only effective way to prove the reliability of this emergency equipment.

The project officer for Excelsior was Captain Joseph W. Kittinger, Jr. As a USAF crack test pilot experienced in emergency ejection systems, a balloonist, and parachutist, he brought much needed experience and enthusiasm to his teammates. Kittinger would need a great variety of skills and expertise to successfully manage Project Excelsior. Kittenger was in charge of this project; but more importantly he was to be the test jumper!

After several years of intensive research and preparation, Kittinger, aided by the help of his Excelsior teammates, prepared themselves for the final stages of this historic project. His third jump for Excelsior, and his most famous, took place on August 16, 1960. His gondola was lifted from the New Mexico desert by a helium filled balloon measuring over 360 feet in height. Carrying Kittinger and a payload of data-gathering instruments of just over 1,200 pounds, the balloon ascended at 1,200 feet per minute. Kittinger was carried aloft to an altitude of 102,000 feet above the earth. He was above 99.2 per cent of the earth's total atmosphere sitting on the edge of space. He stayed at float altitude, as high as the balloon could go, for approximately eleven minutes.

Seated in the gondola, on the edge of space, Kittinger gazed at the grandeur and beauty of the fantastic world he was about to leave. He could see the earth for a full 400 miles, its curvature and the stark beauty of the clouds rolling in and out below him. As

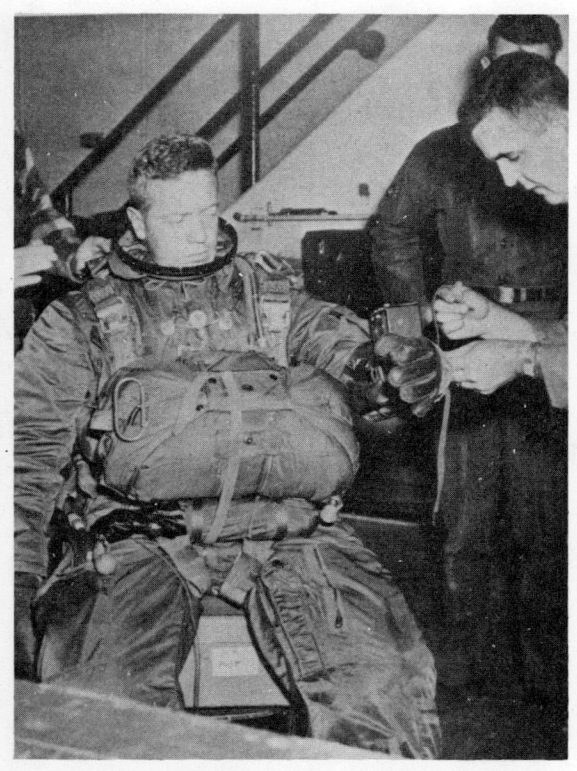

Captain Joe Kittinger "suiting up" for his record descent from 102,800 feet.

he stood up and moved toward the open hatchway of the gondola he whispered to himself, "I've beaten you so far . . ." A safe environment was about twenty miles straight below him; and there was but one path to take. The moment of truth was ever so silently catching up with him — now was the time to begin the journey through the hostile air to reach safety.

Twenty Miles Up

With full confidence in his own abilities and those of his fellow teammates, and utilizing the finest emergency parachute ever devised, he was prepared to bust new sky. After a final instrument check, Kittinger turned on the eleven cameras aboard the gondola, and grabbing both sides of the hatchway, took a final breath and silently prayed, "Lord, take care of me now." He stepped from the confines of the gondola 102,800 feet above planet Earth.

Someone once wrote that man lives life the fullest when he experiences the extremes. For Joseph Kittinger the extremes of his life were just beginning. During his descent from twenty miles above the earth, he freefell almost four and a half minutes and reached speeds in the thin atmosphere of over 600 miles per hour. The Beaupre parachute functioned perfectly during the harrowing descent.

After exiting the gondola, the first of his two timers fired in 16 seconds. He felt the stabilization chute deploy as it tugged at the straps of his harness. The stabilizing drogue chute was to prevent Kittinger from spinning too much out of control during his 600 mile per hour trip through this alien sky. His peak speed of 614 miles per hour at 90,000 feet, had now been slowed down to a mere 250 miles per hour as he continued falling through the thicker atmosphere from 60,000 to 50,000 feet. All systems functioned smoothly as he was maintained in a perfectly controlled position. As he passed through the altitude of 30,000 feet on this epic voyage, he had been in freefall for three minutes and thirty seconds. Between 17,000 and 18,000 feet the main chute deployed perfectly and began checking his descent to a safe 18 feet per second. The long descent was over, and Kittinger once again found himself in the safe confines of a friendly environment.

This world record parachute jump culminated in a successful landing in the New Mexico desert. With the exception of some swelling to his right hand, due to a malfunctioning heating system in his glove, the jump is an absolute success. Kittinger had proved by the ultimate test: man can escape at extreme altitudes and lower himself safely to a friendlier environment. Even the most critical evaluations of the Excelsior crew acclaimed the jump a total victory.

For Capt. Joe Kittinger and the members of the Excelsior crew, their search for a safer sky was filled with many personal rewards. But it also meant their work would be used to save untold lives of future generations of aviation personnel. Kittinger followed a tradition of aviation pioneers who were willing to risk the spectre of the unknown, so that others could follow more safely. His efforts and sacrifices were indicative of the highest and most noble of man's idealistic search for a safer way to live.

Kittinger's jump from 102,800 feet is an unofficial world's record that stands to this date. Since the purpose of the jump was to develop and test emergency parachute equipment, no attempt was made to obtain official sanction from the Federation Aeronautique Internationale (FAI) as a world record. Excelsior was not a self-serving project: there wasn't time or room. The jump would never have gotten off the ground, to say the least, without the unified efforts of the entire Excelsior crew.

Yet obviously it could not have been completed without Kittinger — the results speak for themselves. He was the driving force that demanded perfection and dedication. Kittinger is a legend to his contemporaries in the Armed Forces and in the parachuting circles around the world. He dared to venture into an environment anything but friendly, and returned safely to tell his own personal account. His historic jump will be remembered as long as there are books being written about parachuting. Kittinger successfully busted new sky as no one has been able to do since.

Nick Piantanida

However, success doesn't always come so easy to others. Both Art Starnes and Joe Kittinger, each in their own way, contributed vastly to the advancement of scientific knowledge and aviation safety in their attempts to bust new sky. Each answered a call to public duty; risking their lives more

20 miles high above the planet Earth, Kittinger begins his famous freefall.

out of a sense of dedication then obsession. Time was short and the need critical — those were the factors mandating their famous plunges. During the mid 1960's, Nick Piantanida was mandated by an inner need that only he could understand. It was a personal obsession that drove him to the edge of space and into higher altitudes never visited by a parachutist since.

Perhaps mankind's greatest and most noble achievements have been dreamed about and brought to completion by the dynamic and singleminded purposefulness of the most independent of personalities. If anyone ever defied classification and understanding it had to be Piantanida. Here was an individual who scorned playing by the rules.

Rules, he believed, were only useful if they served his purpose. Lest Nick be classified as some sort of nut or sociopath, which he wasn't, you might get the idea that he was not a useful and positive contributor to society — which he was. It was just that Nick liked doing things his own way; sort of the American Dream and all that stuff. Once his mind was made up, little could be done to deter him from achieving his goal. This pattern of lifestyle was set early in his childhood.

During Piantanida's teenage years he lived in Union City, New Jersey. He was tall, lanky, and very awkward for his age. Nick lacked the coordination most kids his age are blessed with. For years a silent pain deep within his spindly legs hampered his participation in a variety of sports. Not knowing better, he endured the suffering and assumed they were typical growing pains. Later Nick was diagnosed as inflicted from osteomyelitis — a crippling bone infection.

The bone infection was checked with medication, but it looked like young Nick would have to spend the rest of his life on crutches. The doctors and his family had adjusted to this fact. Nick couldn't handle that attitude at all! There were other things he wanted out of life besides walking around on crutches. Living a full and vibrant life was important to this young man.

Instinctively, Nick devised his own rules to solve this problem: he couldn't play by the rules that thought he should be a cripple. After hobbling to school on crutches for several days he figured this was one hell of a way to learn to walk. On his way to school one day, with his crutches under his arms giving support, Nick ventured into a secluded alley. When he left the alley the crutches were in a pile of garbage. And step by excruciatingly painful step, he forced himself to school. This agonizing routine was repeated on the way home. And it continued until he was satisfied he could walk like normal kids. Nick relearned to walk through willpower. He drove himself to do things this way because that was the only way he knew. This grueling determination set a pattern for Nick and hardened his ability to believe in himself.

Shortly thereafter Nick began to reap the rewards of his suffering. He started taking flying lessons and pretty soon began to solo and discovered the beauty of the sky. Later, while a member of the armed forces, he fought eleven bouts as a heavyweight boxer and won them all. In subsequent years Nick was a member of a national Catholic basketball championship team, a mountain climber, and survival expert.

Years later, in 1963, after he was married and settled down in Union City, Piantanida drove past a parachute center in Lakewood, New Jersey. Stopping to watch the activity, he became fascinated by the crazy people hurling themselves out of airplanes and loving every minute of it. And on top of that they were paying to do it! Nick couldn't believe his eyes. He was so intrigued by what he saw he returned the next day to make his first parachute jump. The Lakewood Parachute Center was a growing hub of skydiving activity on the east coast during those years and their three hour course taught the basics for thirty-five dollars. It was a lot of bucks to Piantanida, but he decided to take a risk.

Like many who experienced the sensations of their first jump, Nick could tell even before his chute blossomed open he liked what he was doing. His early sensations with skydiving were thrilling, and more rewarding than anything he had ever done. These early thrills were ones that would alter the direction and purpose of his life drastically.

Beat The Russians

Compelled by his inner determination and abundance of skills, Nick soon became an experienced freefall parachute jumper and instructor. One day, during a lull in activity at the Lakewood Parachute Center, he overheard several other instructors talking about the world freefall record of 83,520 feet currently held by a Russian parachutist. Something clicked and an idea was soon planted in his mind. In a way he could never articulate or understand, Nick was compelled from that day forward to try and better this world mark.

The more he talked about it, the more he realized it was not just another pipe dream. His thoughts lingered on the jump continually. Ever so gradually, Nick developed a mental picture of himself making the actual jump. Once he saw himself make the jump, he feverishly set out about planning and organizing every detail for this project. Of course, he could do everything by himself. After all, it was his idea wasn't it? And wasn't he supposed to be making the jump? Nick soon found out things weren't so simple.

Piantanida was anything but an organization man. He was a basic loner type who had little need to be involved with others: unless, of course, he had to. He soon realized others would have to be involved to help handle the logistics, research, and planning. Nick needed skilled persons who had talents. Without their help this jump would be a rudderless mind trip. Nick became a team man in short order.

His individuality remained intact while he carried an enormous share of the burdensome responsibility during the initial stages of the planning. He wrote reams of letters requesting financial and technical backing. The enormous expense and sophisticated equipment required of the project was staggering. Nick never thought about giving up — he couldn't. His travels carried him all over the east coast, to Washington D.C., to encourage people to support his efforts to return the world freefall record to the United States. His pleas had a patriotic ring about them that gained him many ardent supporters.

Days passed into weeks, the months passed into years, and gradually Piantanida began acquiring the financial and technical support he needed. The cost for such a jump was staggering. Normally, projects of this caliber were only possible by military people who had the financial resources and backing of the United States government. Capt. Kittinger's famous leap in earlier years had the logistical and financial backing that cost millions and millions of dollars. Piantanida had neither the financial resources nor the total expertise required for such an endeavor. However, his persistence gradually overcame these deficiencies.

Help Arrives

Pioneer Parachute Company, the nation's largest manufacturer of military parachute equipment, would provide the technical support and outfit Piantanida with the best freefall system available. Raven Industries built the polyethylene balloon and gondola that would carry Nick to a world record altitude. Support, guidance, and finances was the specialty of Jacques Istel. As president of Parachutes Incorporated, a leader in developing freefall skydiving instruction, and a leader in modern skydiving, Istel was already well known in the United States. With Hal Evans joining the team, Istel and Piantanida formed a company to help assist this effort. It was called SPACE, INC., which stood for Survival Programs Above a Common Environment.

Now that he had the financial and moral backing of Istel and Evans many doors were opened when otherwise they had been slammed in his face. Nick began to receive cooperation from all branches of the armed forces which had previously discounted him as a crackpot. As a result, Nick underwent physiological training at Tyndall Air Force Base in Panama City, Florida, and at the FAA Civil Aero Medical Research Center in Oklahoma City, Oklahoma.

By mid 1965, Project Strato Jump was beginning to take the shape of a serious endeavor. In preparation for this attempted world freefall record, Piantanida underwent numerous practice jumps from altitudes of 15,000 to 36,000 feet AGL. The jumps were made possible by a donation from the National Aeronautics and Space Administration (NASA) who loaned Nick a high pressure suit built especially for the U.S. Space Program.

Now that Project Strato Jump was moving along, extra support was forthcoming from a variety of civilian corporations. Raven Industries, originally contracted to provide balloon and gondola, assumed the technical responsibility for directing the launch operations and manning the tracking and recovery instruments. Ed Yost of Raven was delegated by Piantanida to be the overall balloon project director. Nick would have his hands full preparing himself for the jump.

General Electric Re-Entry Systems was contracted to furnish a team of engineers and technicians at the launch site to monitor Piantanida's freefall velocity during the jump. This was accomplished with the aid of a transmitter mounted on the back side of his reserve parachute. A mobile van utilizing a high powered receiver would capture the signal while he was falling and automatically print and store the data into a computer.

Project Strato Jump

By December 1965 Project Strato Jump was a reality, and all support systems were in place. The five million cubic foot helium balloon had been manufactured and attached to the 4 x 4 x 5½ foot gondola which would house Piantanida on his ascent skyward. On board instrumentation, included an electrical control panel, absolute pressure gauge, numerous temperature gauges for the inside and outside, and a clock, were all tested and sealed. Nick's main parachute was furnished by the Pioneer Parachute Company. Since he was a sport jumper by training, Nick figured he couldn't use a better canopy than a Paracommander; a highly steerable and reliable

Nick Piantanida, wife Janice, Bill Jolly, and Jacques Istel discuss the upcoming flight.

sport canopy. His reserve housed a 28 foot flat circular military parachute. Both the main and reserve canopy were to be activated by a model FF-1 automatic opener furnished by U.S. Gauge. The main parachute was set to open at 6,500 feet and the reserve for 4,000 feet.

On board the gondola "Second Chance" was sufficient oxygen for the journey. Electrical mitts and socks provided heat in the dark, high altitude cold. In the event of an emergency at high altitude, a firing device could be initiated from the ground that would release the gondola from the balloon. Then a parachute would be deployed when it reached a safer altitude. This would help insure Nick's survival in the event a serious malfunction occurred. Nick also carried a tape recorder in his leg pocket to record his reaction during freefall, and he had a camera attached to his right arm to photograph the gondola as he jumped.

Nick had a personal thing about wanting to make this jump to set a new world freefall record. But it wasn't all passion that drove him — there were a variety of scientifically valid reasons to make the jump. Project Strato Jump had four primary objectives; (1)

to establish that a trained parachutist could freefall from altitudes in excess of 100,000 feet without the use of stabilizing devices, (2) to investigate the effects of transonic speeds on the human body in freefall, (3) to gain for the United States the world's freefall parachute record currently held by Eugene Andreev of Russia, who had jumped from 83,520 feet on November 1, 1962, (4) to surpass the manned balloon altitude record.

Piantanida planned to make his world record attempt without the aid of a drogue chute. At extremely high altitudes a stabilizing device is normally used to prevent the suspected fatal effects of a flat spin. Sport jumpers were trained in precise body control. Nick was positive he wouldn't need the drogue chute. The engineers of Pioneer Parachute Company had calculated a freefall from an altitude of 120,000 feet would result in the jumper reaching a maximum speed of over 750 miles per hour near the vicinity of 90,000 feet. Piantinida was expected to fall faster than the speed of sound — an incredible feat; and with little to protect him but the thin nylon of his pressure suit. It took guts to plan such an epic adventure. Small wonder Piantanida was obsessed with idea of being the first man to break the sound barrier in freefall — no average neurotic would get within 100 feet of the "Second Chance."

Two Attempts

October 22, 1965, Piantanida lumbered aboard the gondola on his first attempt to set a world record. At 22,700 feet, over St. Paul, Minnesota, the 3.7 million cubic foot balloon hit a 6 knot wind shear and shredded. Piantanida made an emergency exit from "Second Chance", but had to open his chute at 10,000 feet in order to avoid landing in downtown St. Paul. He missed the crowded inner city; but ended up on the outskirts of town in the city dump. So much for Nick's first attempt to fulfill a dream.

Approximately three months later, on February 1, 1966, Project Strato Jump lifted off the ground at 12:11 a.m. It was a perfect launch for balloon N4799T and gondola "Second Chance" ascending at a rate of a thousand feet per minute in the 13 degree below zero weather.

With Piantanida manning the controls of "Second Chance" the balloon entered an altitude of 40,000 feet. Gradually, jet stream winds of 100 miles per hour began carrying the balloon into northwestern Iowa. At

The final stages of launching as the enormous helium filled balloon slowly fills. Piantanida sits in the gondola "Second Chance."

46,000 feet, the outside temperature was -61 degrees below zero. At 60,000 feet Nick opened the doors of the gondola and began to enjoy the view. The curvature of the earth was evident and the sky began to take on a darkened effect. Piantanida continually monitored his position with the instruments on the control panel. Every fifteen minutes he had to reset a timer to prevent the gondola from automatically disconnecting the balloon.

Fiction was turning into reality for the anxious passenger. Like intricate pieces of a large and complex puzzle, the balloon slowly rose to 70,000 feet, then 80,000, 90,000, and then to 100,000 feet above the windswept frozen ground.

At 100,000 feet Nick reported to ground control there was a cloud like powder falling off his balloon. Ground control replied, "It's OK, Nick, expansion is shaking off the cornstarch." Nick replied, "The sky is as black as coal. What a beautiful sight."

At the same time, Hal Evans and Dick Wagaman, USPA North Central Conference Director, were monitoring the conversation between Nick and ground control flying in a Piper Tripacer. Both were trying to stay under the balloon, while the winds at altitude were over 140 miles per hour, and drifting the balloon across and into Iowa.

At 1:52 p.m. Nick gave an altimiter reading to ground control of 120,000 feet.

At 1:56 p.m. at jump minus 2 minutes, Nick began releasing his seat belt at 123,800 feet. Just a few pieces of the puzzle remained to complete years of passionate planning, hoping, and dreaming. The moment of truth beckoned! But it was not to be!

At 1:57 p.m. Piantanida discovered the oxygen disconnect valve for "Second Chance" was frozen. Try as he might, he could not loosen the fitting because of the awkwardness of wearing his pressure suit and gloves, causing him limited use of his hands. During the next eleven minutes the conversation between Nick and ground control went something like this:

1:58 N.P. - "Disconnect, having problem with oxygen. . .disconnect. . .going overtime."

1:59 NP - "Ground control, do you read me? We've got problems, I can't. . ."

1:59 NP - "Isn't this a bitch. . .Can't disconnect oxygen. Don't make me talk."

2:00 NP - "I don't believe it, I can't separate the hose."

2:00 NP - "Oh God, let me get this hose."

2:02 NP - "Don't make me talk. I don't believe it, I just don't believe it."

2:03 NP - "How in the hell can this thing be stuck? — crescent wrench."

2:04 NP - "It's getting so damn hot. God, I just don't believe it."

GC - "Nick reconnect your safety belt."

2:06 NP - "I can't hook up the belt. There is no way of making it. Nobody will believe it."

2:07 GC - "Try, Nick, try."

NP - "I've no control with the gloves. . ."

2:08 NP - "Can't do it."

2:09 NP - "I just can't release this gadget. . .let me know if you're going to cut me down."

GC - "Nick, I'll give you a countdown from 10. Brace yourself against the seat, put your feet on each side of the door and hold on tight."

NP - "Roger."

Ed Yost - "Nick, do you read me?"

2:10 NP - "Who's going to cut me down?"

EY - "I will, Nick, make sure you have a good hold."

NP - "Can't hear you, Ed. Let Souix Falls take it."

Souix Falls - "Nick, we're cutting you down on Yost's signal."

NP - "I have high temperature and no vent." (heaving breathing. . .Yost explained cut down effects.)

NP - "Okay, Roger."

2:12 NP - "When it comes I'm braced."

EY - "Okay, Nick, Mark. . .10, 9, 8, 7, 6, 5, 4, 3, 2, 1."

At 123,800 feet Nick was cut away from his balloon and went into freefall while inside the open gondola. The 46 foot parachute was not timed to activate to open until 97,000 feet. In the 35 seconds he would fall with little to secure him, except his brute strength, Piantanida and the gondola would fall over 26,000 feet with speeds in excess of 600 miles per hour.

The worst type of tragedy had occurred, and Nick had no choice but to ride "Second Chance" down until the 46 foot drogue chute would open. The next 35 seconds would be the most terrifying event Nick had ever experienced.

Buffeting through the rarified atmosphere in the uncontrollable gondola, Nick was lucky not to be thrown out. Luckier, yet, when the chute opened at 97,000 feet, he managed to stay inside the gondola. He descended through the thin air for the next 31 minutes, during which time the gondola was subjected to violent oscillations in excess of 180 degrees.

A frustrated and angry Piantanida banged down at 2:45 p.m. on the cold soil of northwestern Iowa. The oxygen hose was still frozen shut. Nick managed to pry it open with a knife as three recovery aircraft circled overhead in search of a place to land.

Project Strato Jump II had ended after coming agonizingly close to success. For weeks Nick would relive the jump in every detail. If only he would have been able to loosen the disconnect he could have made his historic leap. If only! The sense of frustration and agony continued to swell in his mind. So close - but so far from realizing a dream he had passionately sought.

One More Time!

The team did not give up! Project Strato Jump III was rescheduled for early May 1966. Hopefully, the experiences learned in Project Strato Jump II would be an invaluable resource to the dedicated team members. After analyzing the frozen valve to determine why it stuck, no positive

The Gondola "Second Chance" which carried Piantanida to an altitude of 123,800 feet.

reason could be found. It was speculated some foreign substance had gotten inside the valve grooves and crystalized in the frigid air, sealing the fitting. No one ever knew for sure. Trying not to whip themselves too hard for their failure in the almost successful jump, the engineers, technicians, and a dejected Piantanida, busied themselves with the preparations for the third record attempt. Confidence ran high the third time would result in the success they all ached for.

On May 1, 1966, Piantanida began this third attempt to freefall from 125,000 feet. His shapely brunette wife Janice, watched as the five million cubic inch gas bag inflated with Nick aboard.

Ascending at a rate of a thousand feet per minute, "Second Chance III" slowly climbed higher and higher into the sky. An hour later, Nick had reached an altitude of 57,000 feet. All sensors indicated a perfect launch, and all systems were "go" as the ascent was moving along according to schedule. The weather was perfect - there seemed to be no problems.

Suddenly, the ground crew monitoring Nick's conversation in the control shack heard a rush of escaping air! Woosh! "Emergency!" an anguished grunt yelled through the microphone. "Emergency!" Puzzled and confused, the ground crew final-

The final flight of Nicholas J. Piantanida.

ly began to realize Nick's oxygen supply had been blown out of his pressure suit in the thin atmosphere eleven miles high. The balloon was still ascending, taking Nick towards the 60,000 foot level where the air is so thin, the lack of oxygen can boil a man's blood in a matter of seconds.

Realizing the intensity of the situation, the ground crew cut loose the tiny gondola from the helium balloon. By this time, the unconscious Nick was freefalling in "Second Chance III" to an altitude of 43,000 feet where his lungs could have a chance to pull in much needed air to maintain his life.

Horror-stricken with panic, the ground crew waited till Nick's parachute opened the freefalling gondola. From the ground they witnessed the chute opening, carrying the unconscious Piantanida closer to earth. The gondola landed in an open field near Worthington, Minnesota 25 minutes later. By the time rescuers could reach Nick, he was just barely alive. Laying on the ground, with the pressure suit oxygen tubes still in his mouth, he fought for every breath to stay alive.

Nick's Last Battle

Nick was in the greatest fight of his life. Rushing him in a helicopter to Worthington Municipal Hospital, doctors made an opening in his neck and inserted a breathing tube to his throat. Still unconscious a day later, Nick was flown to Hennepin County Hospital in Minneapolis, and placed in one of the new high pressure oxygen chambers, forcing some of the vital gasses back into his exploded lungs.

Piantanida was still alive, but unconscious. Doctors reported he was breathing better - but the prognosis was anything but encouraging. He had undergone the most rapid decompression ever experienced by any human being; it was a miracle he was still alive. Though unconscious, Nick was fighting for his life in his usual characteristic style.

What happened to Piantanida at 57,000 feet to cause such an emergency? The dejected crew could only speculate. Nick was the only one who knew for sure, and the secret was sealed in his mind. Trying to second guess this accident was difficult at best; but speculation was better than nothing at this point. One theory suggested Nick had somehow been slowly deprived of oxygen due to a leak in his suit, causing narcosis, a deep stupor for lack of oxygen. His confused state might have caused him to open a valve to let in outside air into the suit. Others speculated his face mask had become fogged while passing through the troposphere, thus preventing him from seeing beyond the gondola. On numerous occassions, Nick experienced similar difficulties, and lifted his face mask visor and closed it rapidly to clear off the goggles. Perhaps this time the visor didn't snap shut so securely, and Nick was robbed of precious air escaping from his pressure suit.

Reasoning and theorizing was of little use to Nick as he lay unconscious in a hospital, his life supported by a variety of sophisticated medical instruments. He never improved, and during the following months became gravely worse. Nick died peacefully in a coma.

So ended the story of Nicholas J. Piantanida, a brave, fearless, rugged individual whose quest to bust new sky had cost his life. His dream came agonizingly close to success. Many unsung dreamers and pioneers who failed paid the ultimate price -their legion forgotten.

Piantanida surpassed the world's altitude for a manned balloon flight, as well as having descended by parachute from 97,000 feet. Both epic feats could have been records by themselves; but not under these circumstances. FAI requirements to establish a world class record for manned flight required a pilot to land with his balloon. Further, record attempts must specify which record the parachutist will try to break. Since Piantanida was attempting a freefall record, his descent by parachute was not recognized by the FAI.

Some small success came from Nick's efforts, though. In Piantanida's mind he felt he proved a stabilizing chute was unnecessary during freefall from altitudes greater than 100,000 feet. His high speed opening at 97,000 feet was not fatal as previously believed by the Air Force. He also proved he was one hell of a man.

Piantanida entered into this project fully aware of the dangers he would face attempting this extraordinary freefall. Assuming risks was his nature. He did things his way, as he always tried to do them. His final effort was just not good enough.

Nick Piantanida's memory lives on in the folklore of his contemporary skydivers. Not so much because of his failure, but due to his ironwilled determination to strive for a goal he felt worthwhile. His failure was an inspiration to many who admired and respected this man. Perhaps some day another rugged individual will follow in Nick's footsteps successfully. That person will have learned from Nick's mistakes and he will have learned how to be the kind of man to make such jumps. Future generations of men who strive to bust new sky will have to possess the willpower and determination that brought Nick Piantanida to the foreground of public awareness; and so close to victory.

BIBLIOGRAPHY

Caidin, Martin, *Barnstorming*, New York. Duell, Sloan & Pearce. 1965.

Caidin, Martin, *Silken Angels*, New York. J.B. Lippencott Co. 1964.

Conover, C.R., *Dayton, Ohio*, New York. Lewis Historical Publishing Co., Inc. 1932.

Davis, K.S., *The Hero*, New York. Doubleday & Co. 1959.

Dollfus, Charles, *The Orion Book of Balloons*, New York. Orion Press. 1961.

Dwiggins, Don, *Flying Daredevils of the Roaring Twenties*, London. Arthur Barker Ltd. 1969.

Glassman, Donald, *Jump!* New York. Simon & Schuster. 1930.

Greenwood, James R., *The Parachute From Balloons to Skydiving*, New York. E.P. Dutton & Co. 1964.

Horan, Michael, *Index To Parachuting*, Richmond, IN. Parachuting Resources. 1979.

Kittinger, J.W., *Long Lonely Leap*, New York. E.P. Dutton & Co. 1961.

Low, A.M., *Parachutes In Peace and War*, London. The Scientific Book Club. 1942.

Mackersay, Ian, *Into The Silk*, London, Robert Hale Ltd. 1956.

Mosley, L., *Lindbergh — A Biography*, New York. Doubleday & Co. 1976.

Mumma, J.V., *Parachutes*, California. The Campbell Co. 1930.

Poynter, Dan, *The Parachute Manual*, Santa Barbara, CA. Parachuting Publications. 1977.

Rolt, L.T.C., *The Aeronauts*, New York. Walker & Co. 1966.

Sellick, Bud, *Parachutes and Parachuting*, Englewood Cliffs, N.J. Prentice-Hall, Inc. 1971.

Valentin, Leo, *Birdman*, London. Hutchinson. 1955.

Wise, John, *Through The Air*, New York. Arno Press. 1972.

In addition, the following sources were used: The Chronicle-Headlight-Enquirer, The Indianapolis Star, Nebraska State Journal, The New York Times, Let's Talk Parachutes, Ballooning, Parachutist, Skydiver, & Truth News Trends Magazines.

WHERE TO SKYDIVE!

Interested in jumping out of a perfectly good airplane? Want to experience the exhilerating sensations of falling at speeds of 120 MPH, and faster? Do you have a desire to be part of the most thrilling evolution in aviation? Literally thousands upon thousands of people are discovering Sport Parachuting each year. During the last twenty years, there has been a revolution going on in the field of parachuting. Advances in training techniques and equipment have completely changed this dynamic sport. Go out to your local drop zone and take a look. Meet the jumpers, talk with them, and discover the personal satisfaction that comes from making one jump or a thousand. Skydiving is a lot easier than you probably think; and it's great fun.

The following Sport Parachute Centers are affiliated with the United States Parachute Association. They follow USPA Basic Safety Regulations and Doctrine for student and advanced skydivers. Affiliated Centers also offer first jump courses taught by USPA certified instructors. For more information about this exciting sport, and the United States Parachute Association write to: USPA, 806 15th st. N.W. Washington, D.C. 20005.

CENTRAL CONFERENCE
(Iowa, Illinois, Missouri, Kansas, Nebraska)

Archway 227 N. St., Sparta, IL 62286, (618) 443-2091 or 9020
Cargo-Air SPC, Prairie Lake Lodge, Rt. 2, Marseille, IL 61341
Expert SPC, 4220 N. 11th, Lincoln, NE 68521, (402) 477-5577
First Church of Skydiving, 504 W. Elm St., #5, Urbana, IL 61801, (217) 384-7272
Greene County SPC/Kansas, Rt. 2, Wellsville, KS 66092, (913) 883-2535
Mid-Missouri SPC, Box 206, Moberly, MO 65270, (816) 263-3969

EASTERN CONFERENCE
(New York City and Long Island, New Jersey, Pennsylvania, Deleware, District of Columbia, Maryland, Virginia, West Virginia)

Hartwood SPC, Rt. 6, Box 3698, Hartwood, VA 22471, (703) 752-4784
Maytown SPC, 722 Basler Ave., Lemoyne, PA 17043, (717) 255-2292
Parachute Associates Inc., 145 Ocean Ave., Box 811, Lakewood, NJ 08701, (201) 367-7773
Parachutes are Fun, 280 W. State St., Millsboro, DE 19966, (302) 934-8562
Pelicanland Air Sports, RR 1 Box 17, Ridgely, MD 21660, (301) 634-2997
Quantico Skydivers (USMC), Box 344, Quantico, VA 23134
Ripcord Paracenter, Burlington County Airport, Medford, NJ 08055, (609) 267-9897
Southern Cross SPC, Box 366, Williamsport, MD 21795, (301) 223-7541
Sport Parachuting Inc., 300 N. Military Hwy., Norfolk, VA 23502 (804) 461-1500
United Parachute Club, Rt. 663/Swamp Pike, Gilbertsville, PA 19525, (215) 323-9667
West Wind SPC, Box 912, West Point, VA 23181, (804) 785-9990 or 9994

EUROPEAN PARACHUTE LEAGUE

Hassfurt SPC, 167 A Zollner St., 08600 Bamberg, W. Germany, 0951/3218Z
Illesheim Aero Center, Box 193, APO NY., NY 09140, 09841-8716
Special Forces Europe SPC, Flint Kaserne Bad Toelz, W. Germany, APO NY, NY 09050, 09041-30-616

MIDEAST CONFERENCE
(Kentucky, Ohio, Indiana, Michigan)

Air Sports Inc., Branch Airport, Coldwater, MI 49036, (219) 562-3406
Greene County SPC/Gallipolis, Box 91, Bidwell, OH 45614, (614) 245-5011
Greene County SPC/Kentucky, Rt. 2, Box 140, Bardstown, KY 40004 (502) 348-9981
Greene County SPC/Xenia, 1790 Foust Rd., Xenia, OH 45385, (513) 372-6116
Mulenberg County SPC, Box 391, Greenville, KY 42345, (502) 338-0556
Parachuting Service Inc., 197 Burt, Tecumseh, MI 49286, (517) 423-7879
Skydiving Inc., Box 346, Wilmington Air Park, Mason, OH 45040, (513) 398-2955
Waynesville SPC, 4925 N. St. Rt. 42, Waynesville, OH 45088, (513) 897-3851

MOUNTAIN CONFERENCE
(Colorado, Wyoming, southeast Idaho, Utah)

Ogden Sky Knights, Box 9343, Ogden, UT 84409, (801) 392-1557
Reynolds Air Service, Littleton Airport, Sedalia, CO 80135, (303) 794-9390

NORTH CENTRAL CONFERENCE
(Wisconsin, Minnesota, South Dakota, North Dakota)

Green Bay Skydivers, Carter Airport, Rt. #3, Pulaski, WI 54162, (414) 497-1983 or 822-3644
Kapowsin SPC, 27921 Ort-Kap Hwy., Kapowsin, WI 98344, (206) 893-2907
Minnesota Skydivers, 1200 Tiller Ln., St. Paul, MN 54162, (507) 645-8608
Para Naut, 9096 Hwy. 21, Omro, WI 54963, (414) 685-5995
Sky Knights, Box 817, E. Troy, WI 53120, (414) 642-9933
St. Croix Valley, Box 363, Osceola, WI 54020, (715) 294-2433
So. Wisconsin Skyhawks, 18300 Winfield Rd., Bristol, WI 53104, (414) 857-2007
Valley Parachuting Inc., 630 7th St. W., West Fargo, ND 58078, (701) 428-9088
Wisconsin Skydivers, W. 204 N. 5022 Lannon Rd., Menomonee Falls, WI 53051, (414) 252-9996

NORTHEAST CONFERENCE
(Massachusetts, Rhode Island, New Hampshire, Maine, Vermont, Connecticut, and parts of New York)

Albany Skydiving, Duanesburg Airport, Box 131, Duanesberg, NY 12056, (518) 895-8140

DZ Parachute Club, Fulco Airport, Rt. 67, Johnstown, NY 12095, (518) 762-4900
Frontier Skydivers, 3316 Beebe Rd., Wilson, NY 14172, (716) 751-9981
Gift of Wings, 4539 McKinley Pkwy., Hamburg, NY 14075, (716) 457-9719
Le Jump Pepperell, Rt. 111, Box 601, E. Pepperell, MA 01450, (617) 433-9948
Seneca SPC, RD 2 Box 2632, Seneca Falls, NY 13148, (315) 568-2423
Taunton SPC, 45 Howard St., S. Easton, MA 02375, (617) 823-3682
Wyoming County SPC, RD 1 Box 174A, Arcade NY 14009, (716) 457-9680

NORTHWEST CONFERENCE

(Montana, western Idaho, Oregon, Washington, Alaska)

Issaquah SPC, 2617 271st St., S.E., Issaquah, WA 98027, (206) 392-2121
Ozmo SPC, Rt. 1, Box 63-S, Athol, ID 83801, (208) 683-2821

PACIFIC CONFERENCE

(northern Nevada, northern California)

Yolo DZ, 626 Arthur St., Davis, CA 95616, (916) 758-9098
Corning DZ, Marquerite Ave., Corning, CA 96021, (916) 824-9909

SOUTHERN CONFERENCE

(Florida, Georgia (Columbus area), Alabama, Tennessee, Mississippi, Kentucky (Ft. Campbell area), Louisiana, Arkansas)

Central Arkansas SPC, 103, Carlisle, AR 72024, (501) 982-4692
Fayard Aviation/Alabama, Box 219, Elberta, AL 36530, (205) 986-8117
Greene County SPC/Louisiana, Rt. 1 Box 677E, Covington, LA 70433, (504) 892-6311

SOUTHEAST CONFERENCE

(North Carolina, South Carolina, Georgia, Florida)

Astroid SPC, Box 295, Clemmons, NC 27012, (919) 765-9204 or 622-3618
Carolina Skydivers, Box 786, Shelby, NC 28150, (704) 482-1988
Carolina SPC, Box 21584, Columbia, SC 29221, (803) 798-4346
Central Florida SPC, St. Rt. Box 498A, Eustis, FL 32726, (904) 357-7800
Deland Air Sports, Deland Airport, Box 1657, Deland, FL 32720, (904) 734-5867
E. Carolina Military PC, Box 2032 MCAS, Cherry Point, NC 28533, (919) 466-2667
Fayard Aviation/S. Carolina, Box 236, Moncks Corner, SC 29461, (803) 899-2885
Flying Tigers SPC, Tiger Airport, Clemson, SC 29632, (803) 654-1386
Ft. Gordon SPC, 1924 N. Leg Rd., 8-G, Augusta, GA 30909, (404) 738-0487
Franklin County SPC/Louisburg, Hwy. 56, Box 703, Louisburg, NC 27549, (919) 496-9223
Franklin County SPC/Midland, Midland Field, Hwy. 601, Midland, NC 28107, (704) 888-5479

Greene County SPC/Atlanta, Rt. 4, County Line Rd., Jenkinsburg, GA 30234, (404) 775-9067
Raeford SPC, P.O. Drawer 878, Raeford, NC 28376, (919) 875-3261 or 5626
Skydive Inc., 28700 SW 217th Ave., Homestead, FL 33030, (305) 759-3483 or 274-7526
Swamp Hollow SPC, Rt. 6, Box 13, Quincy, FL 32351, (904) 875-2767
South Florida Parachute, Circle T Ranch Airport, Indiantown, FL 33456, (305) 597-2736
Zephyrhills PC, Box 1101, Zephyrhills, FL 33599, (813) 782-2918

SOUTHWEST CONFERENCE

(Oklahoma, Texas, New Mexico)

American Parachute Center, Box 2653, Bryan, TX 77801, (713) 279-2161
American Parachuting, Ent., 5250 Professional Dr. #54A, Wichita Falls, TX 76302
Houston SPC, 19815 Becker Rd., Hockley, TX 77447, (713) 351-0194
N. Texas SPC, Barber Airport, Box 2, Mansfield, TX 76063, (817) 473-0051
Skydance Inc., Tahlequah Municipal Airport, Tahlequah, OK 74464, (918) 456-5114
Skydivers of Texas, 5301 Parkland Ave., Dallas, TX 75235, (214) 824-3540
Spaceland SPC, Houston Gulf Airport, 1525 Pearl, League City, TX 77573, (713) 337-1713

WESTERN CONFERENCE

(Arizona, southern Nevada, southern California, Hawaii)

California City SPC, Box 2178, 6284 Curtis Place, California City, CA 93505, (714) 373-4659
Coolidge Parachute Center, Box 1807, Coolidge, AZ 85228, (602) 723-3753
Elsinore SPC, 20701 Cereal Rd., Elsinore, CA 92330, (714) 674-2141
Marana Skydiving Center, Marana Airpark, Marana, AZ 85238, (602) 682-4441
Perris Valley SPC, 2091 S. Goetz Rd., Perris, CA 92370, (714) 657-3904 or 8727
Taft SPC, 500 Airport Rd., Taft, CA 93268, (805) 765-6159

First And Only Service Of Its Kind

PARACHUTING PR RESOURCES

INFORMATION SPECIALISTS IN THE FIELD OF PARACHUTING

- **Searches**
- **Reprints**
- **Consultation**
- **Book Sales**

WRITING? RESEARCHING? CURIOUS about the field of Parachuting? Many people are these days because Parachuting is more and more being recognized as a field of serious study, in addition to being a popular aviation activity. Parachuting Resources, the first and only information specialist for all of Parachuting, wants to save you time, work, and most importantly MONEY!

The field of Parachuting is nearly 200 years old. A wealth of information is available but it is scattered everywhere. This field overlaps with many other technical disciplines such as Medicine, Psychology, Aero-space Engineering, Law, Manufacturing and Quality Control to name a few.

Are you writing a Masters or Doctoral thesis on some aspect of Parachuting? Perhaps you are a lawyer in search of information on TSO requirements, automatic openers, or student instruction. You could be a writer looking for historical material for a short story or a book. Have an interest in high altitude parachuting? Need the latest information about skydiving, the most exhilerating and colorful aspect of aviation? If you are trying to track down reliable information, do you know where to start your information search? Most people don't know-Parachuting Resources will!

Put our 20 years of experience in this field to work for your project. We have the largest library and storehouse of information on Parachuting anywhere! You won't be disappointed. Satisfaction Guaranteed!

SEND FOR A FREE DESCRIPTIVE BROCHURE OF SERVICES & FEES TO:

MICHAEL HORAN
P.O. BOX 1333
RICHMOND, IN. USA 47374
(513) 456-4686

INDEX TO PARACHUTING
1900-1975

By
Michael Horan
A Readers Guide To Parachuting Literature

This is the first comprehensive work that has attempted to collect and organize the biblography of this sizable body of literature. More than 2700 entries from American and foreign periodicals are included.

The ultimate reference that tells you all you need to locate written material about:

Aerodynamic Decelerators
Aerospace medicine
Equipment
Exhibition parachuting
High altitude parachuting
History
Instructing
Judging
Jumpmastering
Military parachuting
National championships
Photography
Psychology
Relative work
Rigging
Unusual jumps

Plus 44 other major categories

"Recommended for all public and academic libraries" — *Library Journal*

"An outstanding, detailed bibliographic reference to every writing important to sport parachuting. This reference is long overdue, and will be valuable to all from novice parachutist to Ph.D. candidate." — Russ Gunby, author of *Sport Parachuting*

"As an aviation writer, I find *Index to Parachuting* second only to a dictionary in usefulness. This book is an absolute must for anyone writing on parachutes or parachuting. Where was this book when I needed it?" — Dan Poynter, author of *The Parachute Manual*

Now Available In Soft Cover

To Order Send $7.95 + $1.00 for
Surface Shipping Anywhere To:
Parachuting Resources, P.O. Box 1333
Richmond, In. USA 47374

INDEX

A

Adams, Kathy, 131
Adams, Steve, 132
Adriatic Cup, 31
Aerial Duet, 85
"Aerial Maniac", 139
Aerial Trio, 85
Aeronautics, 11
Aero Squadron (94th), 33
Aerostation, 10
Alma, Kansas, 64
American Balloon Section, 114
American Legion, 26, 28
Americus, Georgia, 62, 64, 67
Andreev, Eugene, 150
Arender, Jim, 103
Army Air Service, 66
Arter, Harry, 103
Atlantic Parachute Company, 45

B

Bahl, Erold, 55, 56
Ball, Guy M., 115
"Ballooning Magazine", 29
Balloon (ing), Smoke, See Chp. 1
Barnstorming, 35, 36, 37, 54, 56, 60, 139, 140
Barrett, Brian, 108, 131
Batterson, Anne, 104
Bat Wings, See Chp. 4
Beaupre Parachute, 144
Benoist, Cecile, 95
Biffle, Ira (Biff), 55
Billboard Magazine, 16
Billings, Montana, 61
Birdcity, Nebraska, 60
Blanchard, J.P., 12
Bled, Yugoslavia, 48
Boettner, John, 125
Bonner, Donald, 132
Booth, Bill, 99
Boswell, Bob, 132
Bosworth, George, 47
Bottreil, Sgt. Ralph W., 115
Boyd, Tommy, 78
Branch, Bob, 108
Bristol Fighters, 113
Broadripple Park (Indpls.), 16
Broadwick, Charles, 98
Broadwick, "Coatpack", 98
Broadwick, Georgia "Tiny", 97, 98, 99, 100
Brooks Field, Tx., 66, 67
Brydon, Loy, 103
Buck, Sherrie, 103

Bucklin, Don, 108
Burns Flying Circus, 35, 36
Burris, Terry, 108
Bushmeyer, Buddy, 39

C

CAA, 47
CBS Sports Spectacular, 77
Cameron, Lyle, 78
Campwood, Tx., 64
Canopy Relative Work, 107
Carlinville, Ill., 33
Caterpillar Club, 69, 70, 124, 125, 126
Cessna, 180, 109
Chanute Field (Illinois), 66
Chronicle-Headlight-Enquirer, 26
Cincinnati Albatross Birdmen, 127
Cincinnati, Ohio, 127
Cincinnati Parachute Club, 127
Civil War, 15
Cleveland, Ohio, 33, 38
"Cloth of Gold", 18
Collier Trophy, 121
Colligon, M., 88, 89, 90
Coolidge, Calvin, 72
Corbin, Merle, 28
Covell, Ill., 70
Crane, Jean, 50
Crane, Joe, See Chp. 2, 103, 127
Crane, Joyce, 38, 42
Crossett, Steve, 132
Crown Ring, 19
Cullom, Ill., 16, 25, 26, 27, 28, 29
Cullom Junior Fair, 26
Curtis Hall of Fame, 99
Curtis OX-5 Engine, 62, 67
Cut-away, 24, 58

D

"Daredevil Lindbergh", 56, 60
d'Arlandes, Marquis, 10
Dayton Herald, 124
Dayton, Ohio, See Chp. 6
DC-3, 89
Dean, Karen, 106
De Haviland DH-9, 66, 119
de Rozier, Pilatre, 10
Deveau, Ruby, 96, 97
de Vinci, Leonardo, 12
Dogneville Aerodrome, 79
Doylestown, Pa., 77
Drumheller, Ed, 132
Druskis, Linda, 26

E

Early Birds Club, 99
Ejecto Strap, 122
Ellington Field, Tx., 33
Ellis, Dave, 132
Emmons, Kim, 103
Emperor Shih Huang Ti, 12
Epinal Aero Club, 88
Evans, Hal, 148, 151
Evitt, Ardath, 108

F

FAA, 47
FAI, 41, 43, 46
Fairchild, Muir, 123
Falling Angels, 106, 107
Fangmeyer, Jim, 108, 131
"Father of American Parachuting", See Crane
Fayard, Paul, 132
Fechet, Maj. General James E., 45
Findleson Award, 134
Fitzwater, Jack, 106, 128
Fonck, Capt. Rene, 71
Fort Benning, Georgia, 100
Fortenberry, Richard, 103
Fox Movie Tone News, 39
Ft. Recovery, Ohio, 16

G

Gardner, Roger, 108
Garnerin, Andre-Jacques, 12, 93, 95
Garnerin, Elisa, 95
Garrison, A.R., 47
Gates Flying Circus, 140
Gebhardt, "Super Joe", 131
Geogel, Odette, 85
Gilding, 11
Giles, Skip, 110
Glassman, Don, 126
Glover, Ken, 130, 132
Godfrey, Alan, 132
Golden Knights, 108, 109
Goodwin, Jimmy, 78
Gordy, Al, 130
Grace Shannon Balloon Co., 96
Grant, Roy "Red", 76, 77, 78
Gray, Bobbie, 103
Greene County DZ, 126, 128, 129, 130, 131, 132, 133, 134
Gurney, Harlen "Bud", 55, 65

H

Habutai Silk, 116, 118
Halo Unit, 84
Hardin, Charles W., 56, 57, 59
Harrell, Anita, 26, 27, 29
Harris, Lt. Harold R., 123, 124
Hartman, Ralph, 131
Hartman-Nellen, Maxine, 104, 105, 106
Haslam, Scott, 108, 131
Hauppman, Bruno Richard, 72
Heaton, Norman, 99
Heinecke Parachute, 114
Heissman, Ken, 131
Hickey, Tom, 97
Hieatt, Bob, 132
Higgins, J.J., 115
High Altitude Parachuting, See Chp. 7
Hispano-Suizas engine, 67
Hoffman, Major E.L., 115, 116, 117, 118, 119, 120, 121
"Homecoming" Fair (Cullom), 26, 28
Horan, Michael, 3, 27
Houlton, Maine, 77
Houston, Texas, 105
Huddleston, Martha, 132
Hutton, Maurice, 124
Hymbaugh, Karen, 108
Hypoxia, 135, 144, 153

I

Indiana Banana, 27
Indianapolis, Indiana, 15, 16, 25
Inflation Trench, 17, 19
Inman, Gladys, 104
Irving Air Chute Co., 119, 120
Irvin, Leslie "Sky-Hi", 117, 118, 119, 120, 137
Istel, Jacques, 49, 148, 149

J

Joerns, Susan, 94, 104, 105
Johnson, Jimmie, 119
Jolly, Bill, 149
Jones, Genevieve (Crane), 38
JN-4D's (Jenny's), 62, 63, 66, 67
"Jumping Jack", (See Joe Crane)

K

Kelly Field, Tx., 33, 68
Kettering, Charles F., 115
Kharakhonoff, Major Boris, 143
Kiehfuss, Bob, 126, 127, 128, 129
King of the Caterpillars, 70, 71
Kittinger, Capt. Joseph W., 144, 145, 146, 148
Kitty Hawk, 76
Klink, Bob, 126
Klink, Jim, 126

Klink, Leon, 66
Kreig, Christy, 26
Kreig, Lisa, 26
Kreig, Peter, 25, 26, 27, 28, 29, 30
Kreig, Ruth, 26
Kuldoua, Dagmar, 103
Kurlin, Nancy, 106

L

Labroste, Jeanne-Genevieve, 95
Lakehurst, N.J., 102
Lakewood Parachute Center, New Jersey, 147
Lambert Field (St. Louis), 65
Latrobe, Pa., 37, 38
Le Bourget Airport (France), 72
Lenormand, Sebastien, 12
Leo Stevens Award, 46
Leonard, Chuck, 131
Letteman, Paul, 95
Lincoln, Nebraska, 54, 55, 96
Lincoln Standard Aircraft Corp., 55, 65
Lincoln Standard Biplane, 55
Lindbergh, Charles A., See Chp. 3, 40
Lindbergh, Charles, Sr., 61, 67
Lindbergh, Evangeline, 61
Little Falls, Minn., 61, 72
Lockheed Lodestar, 141
Lochridge, Kress 132
Loening Monoplane, 123
Lone Eagle, 71, 72, 73
Longacre Park (Indpls.), 16
"Loop King Brooks", 140
Los Angeles, Ca., 42
Loudakis, George, 130
Loudakis, Mike, 130
Lovelace, Col. W.R., 143
Lowell, Mass, 45
Lura, Phil, 131
Lynch, H.J. "Cupid", 59, 60

M

Mackersay, Ian, 126
Macungie, Pa., 16
Maison Blache, Algiers, 79, 80
"Making a Mayonnaise", 82
Manchester, Conn., 45
Manning, Spud, 41, 137
Marchant, Jayne, 108
Marion County Fair, 25
Martin, Glenn L., 98
Mason, Fred, 48
McAllister, Lt. C.D., 69
McCook, Anson, 115
McCook Field, 115, 116, 117, 118, 119, 120, 121, 122, 132

Medal of Honor, 72
Memphis, Tenn., 96
Meridian, Mississippi, 63
Metcalf, Doug, 132
Milliken, Chris, 108
Mineola, N.Y., 45, 72
Mitchell, General Billy, 114
Molitar, Don, 78
Monetti, Baby, 85
Montgolfier Brothers, 10, 12
Montpellier Observatory, 12
Mooresville, Ind., 108
Moran, Bill, 134
Muslin, "Black Rock", 18
Mumma, J.V., 114

N

NAA, 40, 42, 43, 46
NASA, 149
National Air Races, 33, 38, 39, 41, 42, 44, 127
National Balloon Races, 43
Nieland, James, 137
Noelcke, Carl, 128
Northrop, Marvin, 65, 66
NPJA, 41, 42, 43, 47, 50, 127
NPJR, 45, 46, 47, 48, 49

O

O'Conner, William, 125
Olsen, Andrew, 98
Olsen, Carolyn, 103
Orange, Mass., 49, 103
Orteig, Raymond (Prize), 71
OX-5 Club, 48, 99

P

Padded Sling, 21
Page, Ray, 55, 60
Pangborn, Clyde, 98, 99, 140
Parachute School, 34
Parachutes Incorp., 148
Parachutes String Out, 22
Parachutist Magazine, 50
Paulus, Katchen, 95
PCA, 49, 50
Pearson, James, 103
Perring, John, 26
Perry Victory Centennial, 98
Peru, Ind., 29
Philadelphia, Pa., 14
Piantanida, Janice, 149, 152
Piantanida, Nick, 146, 147, 148, 149, 150, 151, 152, 153, 154

Pierson, Terry, 134
Pioneer Parachute Company, 45, 120, 148, 149, 150
Piper Tripacer, 77
Pond, Nona, 103
Pontiac, Mi., 35
Port Huron, Mi., 36
Potter, Archie, 16
Professor Krug, 97
Project Excelsior, 144, 145, 146
Project Strato Jump, 148, 149, 150, 151, 152, 153, 154
Pugh, J.C., 130
Pumpville, Tx., 67
Pure Flight, 85

Q

"Queen of the Clouds", 96
Quincy, Ill., 25

R

Raven Industries, 148
Ravenswood Park (Indpls.), 16
Richmond, Ind., 16, 108, 111
Richenbacher Squardron, 33
Riggers Pledge, 101
Rites de Passage, 58
Riverside Park (Indpls.), 16
Roach, Karen, 132
Robertson Aircraft Corp., 69, 70
Robertson, Duane, 16
Roosevelt, F.D.R., 73
Roosevelt Field, N.Y., 39, 40, 72
Roquemore, Barbara, 106
Rose, Cliff, 78
Russell, J.M., 115, 121, 122
Russell Lobe Parachute, 121
Russell Parchute Co., 122
Ruth, Oscar E. "Mile High", 15, 16
Ryan Aeronautical Corp., 71
Ryle, Wilbur, 131

S

Sabe', Raoule, 80
Safe Aircraft Co., 121
Sanders, Jeff, 131
"Sang-Froid", 80
Santa Claus Jump, 36, 37
Saunders, Jeff, 108
Sauve, Dave, 132
Seaman, Harvey, 131
Schmiedeke, George, 127
Scrivin, Gen. George P., 98
SEAL Unit, 84
"Second Chance", 149, 152

Selfridge Field, Mi., 35
Shafer, Claude, 15, 16, 17, 18, 19, 20, 21, 22, 23, 24, 25, 26, 27, 28, 29, 30
Shakopee Airfield (Minn.), 64
Shearer, Jim, 129
Shearer, Suzanne, 106
Shroud Cloth, 18
Sikorsky, Igor, 71
Simbro, Muriel, 103, 104
Sisters of the Silk, 100
Skydiver Magazine, 78
Skydiving, 30, 49
Smith, Floyd, 112, 115, 116, 117, 118, 119, 120, 137
Smith, Glenn H., 45
Smithsonian Institute, 100
Snyder, Steve, 106
Sohn, Clem, 78, 79, 85, 86
Sopwith Camel, 113
Souther Field (Georgia), 62, 64
Southfield, Mi., 37
Speke Airport, England, 90
Spirit of St. Louis, 71, 72
Spurlock, Andy, 108
St. Clair, Milton, 124
St. Paul, Minn., 150
St. Yans, France, 48
Starnes, Art, 136, 139, 140, 141, 142, 143
Stearns, Cheryl, 109, 110, 111
"Swing of Death", 140
Switlik Parachute Co., 120

T

Taylor, Clyde, 108
Taylor, Thelma, 104
Terminal Velocity, 121
Thiel, Dave, 29
Thermometer (Balloon), 21
Thomas Morse MB-3, 123
Timm, Otto, 55
Timmerman, Verne, 124
Tivat, Yugoslavia, 31
Trapeze Bar, 21, 22
Triangle Parachute, 121, 127, 128
Triangle Parchute Co., 121
Trowbridge, J.T., 1
Turner, Roscoe, 140
Tyndall, Lt. Frank, 125

U

UDT Unit, 84
USAPT, 109
USPA, 43, 50, 105
U.S. Army, 100
U.S. Army Air Service, 33, 35

U.S. Paratroopers, 45, 46
Union City, New Jersey, 147

V

Valentin, Leo, 79, 80, 81, 82, 83, 84, 85, 86, 87, 88, 89, 90, 91, 92
Valley, Patt, 106, 107, 108, 131
Van Alstyne, Lewis ("Toby"), 26, 27
Vardell, 14
Vickers FB-5 Gunbus, 113
Villa Coublay Airport, 86
Von Derau, Bob, 111, 131, 132, 134
Vosges Air Club, 79

W

Wacker, Henry, 125
Waco Biplane, 127
Wagaman, Dick, 151
Walkerton, Ind., 16
Walko, Craig, 132
West, Jim, 128, 132
West, Lee, 132
Western Hills Airport, 127
Whitby, Harold L., 137, 138
Whitestown, Ind., 29

Williams, Al, 65
Wingfoot Express, 125
Wing Walking, 56
Wise, John, 14
Woodall, A.F. ("Woody"), 26, 27, 28, 29
Womens Army Corps., 100, 101
World Championships, 1951-48, 1954-48, 1956-49, 102, 1960-103, 1962-103, 1964-104, 1966-105
World Records, 35, 37
Worthington, Minn., 153
Wright Brothers, 76
Wright, Orville, 115

X

Xenia, Ohio, 106

Y

Yost, Ed, 149
Young, Raymond, 49
Young, Rusty, 131

Z

Zephyr Hills Parachute Meet, 99